KEY TO SYMBOLS

FLOWER FORM

Solitary or large and medium flowers

 Individual flowers with unfused petals (3 or less; 4; 5 or more)

 Individual flowers with fused petals (3 or less; 4; 5 or more)

 Tubular, funnel- or bell-shaped flowers

 Two-lipped flowers

 Pea-flowers

Small clustered flowers

 Tight rounded or semicircular heads

 Brush-like or button-like heads

 Dandelion-like heads (ray florets only)

 Daisy-like heads (ray and disk florets)

 Branched spikes or clusters

Solitary spikes, cones or catkins

Flat-topped or domed clusters

HABITAT

 Mountains (above tree-line), alpine meadows, rocks screes, cliffs

 Woodlands in lowlands and mountains

 Brushwood, thickets, maquis, heaths

 Grasslands (below tree-line)

 Stony and rocky ground, steppes, garigues, bare undisturbed ground

 Cultivated ground, disturbed ground, waste places, walls

 Marshes, swamps, bogs, water

 Coasts, rocks, sands, salt marshes, shingle

 Variety of lowland and hill habitats

DISTRIBUTION IN EUROPE

 North

 North and central

 Central

 West and south-west

 East and south-east

South and Mediterranean

South and central

Widespread and throughout

A Concise Guide to
the Flowers of
Britain and Europe

A Concise Guide to the Flowers of Britain and Europe

OLEG POLUNIN

assisted by
ROBIN S. WRIGHT

with 192 pages of photographs in
colour by the author and others

Oxford   New York
OXFORD UNIVERSITY PRESS
1988

Oxford University Press, Walton Street, Oxford OX2 6DP

Oxford New York Toronto
Delhi Bombay Calcutta Madras Karachi
Petaling Jaya Singapore Hong Kong Tokyo
Nairobi Dar es Salaam Cape Town
Melbourne Auckland
and associated companies in
Berlin Ibadan

Oxford is a trade mark of Oxford University Press

First published 1972 as an Oxford University Press paperback
Reprinted 1974, 1981, 1987 (twice)
First issued in flexible binding 1988

British Library Cataloguing in Publication Data
Polunin, Oleg
[The concise flowers of Europe]. A concise guide
to the flowers of Britain and Europe.
1. Europe. Flowering plants
I. [The concise flowers of Europe] II. Title.
III. Wright, Robin S. (Robin Southey)
582.13'094
ISBN 0–19–282561–5   100805592
ISBN 0–19–217630–7 (pbk)

Library of Congress Cataloging in Publication Data
Polunin, Oleg.
A concise guide to the flowers of Britain and Europe.
Rev. ed. of: Concise flowers of Europe, 1972.
Includes index.
1. Wild Flowers—Europe—Identification. 2. Wild
flowers—Great Britain—Identification. 3. Wild flowers—
Europe—Pictorial works. 4. Wild flowers—Great Britain—
Pictorial works. 5. Botany—Europe—Pictorial works.
6. Botany—Great Britain—Pictorial Works. I. Wright,
Robin S. H. Polunin, Oleg. Concise flowers of Europe.
III. Title
QK281.P6485 1987   582.13'094   86–28497
ISBN 0–19–282561–5
ISBN 0–19–217630–7 (pbk.)

Printed in Hong Kong

Contents

Acknowledgements

The generosity of British botanists is remarkable and a large number of people have offered the loan of photographs of European plants, taken in the field, for this volume. After looking through several thousand transparencies, I have selected the following and I must express my most sincere thanks to these expert photographers.

Mr. & Mrs. D. Parish: numbers 3, 156, 194, 220, 221, 254, (267), 331, 382, 398, 409, 434, 441, 448, 480, 635, 761, 782, 786, (883), 912, (912), 921, 925, 933, 941, 945, 946, 949, 953, (990), 1070, 1279, 1332, 1355, 1433, (1475), 1506, 1601, 1629, 1658, 1661, 1736, 1751, 1775, 1916, (1919), 1926. M. J. D'Oyly: numbers 34, 71, 104, (146), 197, 272, 337, 363, 372, 379, 397, 420, 473, 476, 483, 594, 622, 764, 831, 871, 917, 962, 975, 1003, 1091, 1094, 1118, 1127, 1132, 1164, 1166, 1174, 1215, 1223, 1269, 1281, 1287, 1309, 1362, 1443, 1479, 1570, 1636, 1671, 1835. B. E. Smythies: numbers 78, 157, 216, 217, 222, (378), (399), 514, (545), 796, 824, (945), (976), 1013, 1074, 1081, (1204), 1211, (1269), (1280), 1587, 1595, (1662), 1666, 1670, 1672, 1685, 1888, 1906. J. H. B. Birks: numbers 38, 85, 162, 169, (247), 333, 377, (427), 684, 698, 847, 911, (922), 923, (925), 935, 937, 965, 1032, (1220), 1280, 1307, (1923). L. E. Perrins: numbers 126, 142, (203), 223, 224, 300, 446, 457, 519, 530, 785, (967), 983, 999, 1064, 1277, (1315), 1497, 1913. A. J. Huxley: numbers 70, (309), 381, 435, 922, (956), 992, 1151, 1261, 1262, 1272, (1303), (1339), 1507, 1606, 1619, 1921. H. Crook: numbers 345, 386, 506, 754, (959), (992), (1332), 1350, (1352), 1626, 1664, (1664), (1685), 1892. Miss M. McCallum Webster: numbers 204, 267, 426, 641, 783, 892, 914, 1041, 1363, 1440, 1549. C. J. Dawkins: numbers 74, 201, 234, (309), (506), (944), 1254, 1714, 1737. Miss K. M. Firby: numbers 241, 520, 593, 1224, 1338, 1419, 1537, 1925. J. Crosland: numbers 400, (445), (919), 997, 1589, 1618. Dr. P. Smith: numbers 220, 1185, 1250. Miss B. S. Smither: numbers (1510), 1673, 1886. Miss B. A. Burrough: numbers 122, 565. H. Esslemont: numbers 248, 915. Miss M. J. Robinson: numbers 773, 777. Mrs. K. Hunt: number 1390.

To Robin S. Wright my thanks for help and advice at all stages in the preparation of this volume. Miss A. M. Adeley has prepared the index, and, once again, has been indispensable throughout.

Godalming, March 1972   Oleg Polunin

Preface

This book has been designed to make possible the easy identification of 1080 plants likely to be encountered on European travels. Nearly every plant described is illustrated in colour in the 192 pages of plates. It is based on *Flowers of Europe: a field guide*, whose text has been considerably shortened and simplified (with descriptions omitted of plants not illustrated) to create a book that will be widely welcomed by the layman and that will prove a useful field companion for the naturalist, horticulturist, conservationist, and botanist.

Great care has been taken in planning this book to enable the plant lover with no specialist knowledge to use it confidently and successfully. The text is arranged for easy reference by plant types and flower colours, and English common names have been used throughout – on the colour plates there are the scientific Latin names as well. Against the English name on the plates a page reference refers the reader to the appropriate description in this book, while the number against the Latin name refers to the fuller description in *Flowers of Europe*. The use of botanical terms has been kept to a minimum, but where their use was unavoidable a full explanation has been given in the illustrated Glossary (p. xiii). The months given at the end of each description are those during which the plant may normally be expected to flower. Many plants naturally will not be in these pages, but the user will find in almost every case he can discover a closely related species here and leave exact identification to the time when, with greater knowledge, he can find his way about more specialist publications.

To use this book

To identify a plant, one can start either from the colour plates or from the text.

The plates are arranged by flower families – all members of the daisy family from plate 141 to 160, all members of the orchid family from plate 187 to 192, and so on. If you have an idea to which family your flower belongs, look at the Family Index to Colour Plates (p. 92), then turn to the plates illustrating members of that family and work through them until you match your flower. Then check the text description to make sure the identification is correct. If you cannot assign your plant to a family, there is nothing for it but to work patiently through the colour plates.

Surprising identifications can be made directly from the plates. On the Yorkshire moors one summer a non-naturalist friend of mine was idly thumbing through *Flowers of Europe* when she announced, quite correctly, 'Well, we must be sitting among *Juncus effusus*' – not an easy plant to identify. One must bear in mind however that flowers have many subtle colour variations, only one of which can be illustrated in this book. In addition, certain colours, particularly violets and purples, are not easy to reproduce faithfully, and they tend to look redder on the page than they do in life. Care should also be taken to note the scale of the plates: $\times \frac{1}{2}$ means that the illustration is approximately half the size of the actual plant, $\times 2$ that the illustration is twice life size.

The text has been arranged in six chapters, with the plants grouped into broad categories which the beginner should have no difficulty in distinguishing: herbaceous plants, aquatic plants, shrubs, trees, woody climbers, and rushes, grasses, and sedges. Within these chapters are further divisions based mainly on flower colour, flower size, and plant size. The following categories are used:

Flower colour white; green; red, pink, pinkish-purple; blue, violet, bluish-purple; brown; yellow

Flower size

Large　over 3 cm across (over 1¼ in)

Medium 1½–3 cm (⅝–1¼ in)

Small　3 mm–1½ cm (⅛–⅝ in)

Minute　under 3 mm (under ⅛ in)

Plant size

Herbaceous Plants, ch. 1

Large　over 1½ m high (over 5 ft)

Medium 30 cm–1½ m (1–5 ft)

Small　under 30 cm (under 1 ft)

Shrubs, ch. 3

Tall　over 1 m high (over 3 ft)

Low　under 1 m high (under 3 ft)

The chapter on trees has been divided into *cone-bearing, catkin-bearing,* and *flowering* trees; and rushes, grasses, and sedges have their own categories based on the shape and number of spikes or spikelets (see pp. 86, 87, and 90).

These divisions must not be taken too literally; they cannot be exact. A characteristically tall plant may be dwarfed in certain conditions of soil and climate, or a normally small flower grow unusually big. Some plants, anemones for instance, may be found in a variety of colours – white, reds, and blues. These are described under their commonest colour and have a cross-reference from the appropriate place in the other colour sections.

Let us now take an example to identify. Imagine you have come across a tall plant, about 5 ft high, with pinkish, two-lipped flowers about an inch across, growing near water. You turn to chapter 1, Herbaceous Plants (since your plant falls into none of the other chapter categories), find the section dealing with red, pink, and pinkish-purple flowers (starting on p. 17). Your flower falls into the medium size-group (starting on p. 20), and your plant into the large size-group (also on p. 20). There are three plants here – Policeman's Helmet, Silkweed, and Great Marsh Thistle. Now the marginal symbols play their part. Looking down the extreme left-hand column you will see that only one of these three plants is two-lipped. A quick glance at the text and a check with the illustration on plate 70 will confirm that the rather sickly smelling plant you have found is indeed Policeman's Helmet (*Impatiens glandulifera*).

So it is quite simple to narrow down your field of possible plants using the categories into which the text has been divided. The marginal symbols (listed in full inside the covers) will then assist your final choice from this narrowed field. The first symbol shows the basic flower shape, and needs some explanation.

Everyone will recognize that the shape of a violet flower is different from that of a primrose, or that a daffodil has a different form to a dandelion. The left-hand set of symbols assigns all the plants to one of sixteen categories according to the form of their flower or the type of their inflorescence (flower cluster). Nine of the symbols refer to those plants whose relatively large, conspicuous individual flowers are not arranged into distinctive tight clusters; the remaining seven symbols refer to different shapes or types of distinctive clusters of many small flowers or florets. To take examples, the primrose has individual 5-petalled flowers; the dandelion head is made up of many small, tightly clustered, strap-like flowers (ray florets).

⅃ ⅂ ⅃ indicate individual flowers whose petals (or coloured sepals) are not fused (joined together) at their bases; with 3 or less, 4, or 5 or more petals or sepals. *Examples:* Christmas Rose (*pl. 19*) has 5 unfused sepals; Lady's Smock (*pl. 34*) has 4 unfused petals.

Ψ Ψ Ψ indicate individual flowers whose petals (or coloured sepals) are distinctly fused at their bases; again with 3 or less, 4, or 5 or more petals or sepals. *Examples:* Primrose (*pl. 90*) has 5 fused petals; Rock Speedwell (*pl. 154*) has 4 fused petals.

ℚ indicates flowers which are conspicuously tubular, funnel-shaped, or bell-shaped. (Corollas with narrow tubes and wide-spreading lobes, as in the forget-me-nots, *pl. 103*, fall under the preceding symbol. There are many gradations between this category and the preceding one.) *Examples:* Scopolia (*pl. 116*), tubular; Dwarf Convolvulus (*pl. 100*), funnel-shaped.

ℬ indicates flowers which are two-lipped, and covers a wide range of flowers from monkshoods (*pl. 19*) to dead-nettles (*pl. 111*) and orchids (*pls. 187–92*). Where the flower has a long tube but is also conspicuously two-lipped, as in the skullcaps (*pl. 108*), it has been included under this symbol.

ℛ indicates individual flowers with the quite distinctive pea-flower form. This shape, with its 5 unequal petals, is easily recognizable and is almost restricted to the pea family (*pls. 50–65*); see also the illustrated Glossary (p. xvi). In the case of clovers, where the tiny pea-like flowers are closely clustered into round heads, the next symbol has been used.

⚭ indicates tight rounded or hemispherical heads of small flowers. These flower heads are solitary. *Examples:* Common Globularia (*pl. 129*), round; Yellow Scabious (*pl. 137*), hemispherical.

⚘ indicates brush-like or button-like heads, where numerous florets are closely grouped together to form a 'brush' surrounded by a cup (involucre) of overlapping scales (bracts); characteristic of most thistles (*pl. 155*). The outer florets may be larger and spreading, as in Wig Knapweed (*pl. 156*), or the heads hard and button-like, as in Tansy (*pl. 147*).

indicates dandelion-like heads, where all the florets are similar and strap-shaped (ray florets) and radiate outwards. *Examples:* Rough Hawkbit (*pl. 158*); Dandelion (*pl. 159*).

indicates daisy-like heads, where the florets are of two types: tiny, densely packed central ones (disk florets) with minute bell-shaped corollas, and strap-shaped outer ones (ray florets) in one or two rows. *Examples:* Marguerite (*pl. 148*); Cone Flower (*pl. 146*).

indicates branched spikes or dense elongated irregularly branched clusters of small flowers, either branching from below or in a pyramid above. *Examples:* Fat Hen (*pl. 10*) and many grasses, such as Reed Sweet Grass (*pl. 180*), branching from below; Yorkshire Fog (*pl. 181*), in a pyramid.

indicates solitary spikes, where numerous small nearly stalkless flowers, or fertile parts, are closely arranged along an axis to form an elongated cluster. *Examples:* Hoary Plantain, Buck's-Horn Plantain (*pl. 133*); many sedges and grasses such as Timothy Grass (*pl. 181*). This symbol also covers cones and catkins.

indicates plants where numerous small flowers form flat-topped or slightly dome-shaped clusters. The best example of this type of flower head is the umbel of members of the umbellifer family (see illustrated Glossary, p. xix), for example, Sweet Cicely, Perfoliate Alexanders, Rock Samphire, and Hemlock Water Dropwort (*pl. 84*). Umbels may be simple, branched, or irregularly domed.

The second column of symbols shows the habitat in which the plants are most commonly found; and the third their general geographical distribution. This is of necessity only a rough indication: plants do not keep tidily to precise geographical areas. Explanations for all these symbols will be found in the key inside the covers of the book, but the following additional observations will be helpful:

may include Great Britain as well as Scandinavia and the low countries.

often covers the Pyrenees, Apennines, Carpathians, and Macedonian highlands as well as the Alps and the intervening highlands and lowlands.

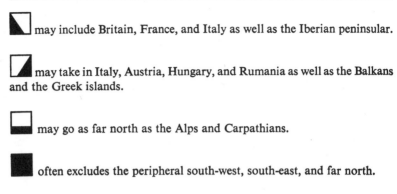

may include Britain, France, and Italy as well as the Iberian peninsular.

may take in Italy, Austria, Hungary, and Rumania as well as the Balkans and the Greek islands.

may go as far north as the Alps and Carpathians.

often excludes the peripheral south-west, south-east, and far north.

But it must be stressed again that categories cannot be applied too rigidly. Typically lowland plants may sometimes also be found in alpine regions (where they may perhaps grow smaller and flower later), a typically south-east European plant may become naturalized in central or northern Europe. The symbols establish helpful guidelines, not hard and fast rules.

Some of the most delightful and interesting European flowers are illustrated and described in this book. Many will already be familiar and others may be recognized as close relatives of well-known garden plants. But some are much less common and a great number of trips will have to be made before they can all be discovered in the wild. Yet some formerly almost inaccessible plants are now within easy reach of ever-growing tourist resorts and of new arterial roads. A serious outcome of this new accessibility is the near total extinction of some rare animal and plant species and the disappearance of hundreds of them from some of their age-old localities.

It is hoped that users of this book will do all they can to help conserve the environment – by joining local, national, or international bodies attempting to preserve wildlife for posterity, and by preventing further destruction by thoughtless collecting or disturbance. If you want to 'bring this plant home and try it in the garden', then by all means collect a few seeds, or take a small cutting with care (it is illegal to import live plants into Britain without a permit, though this does not apply to seeds). But do not dig up the plant; it will probably die in the end. One of the most harmless and perhaps the most rewarding forms of 'collecting' is to photograph your plant.

Finally, though the disappearance of a plant or animal species from an area is a serious loss, it is not the most serious. The greatest disaster comes from the total destruction of a whole community, with all the many hundreds of thousands of living organisms thriving in it and dependent on it. A careless match can do untold and sometimes irreparable harm. The delicate balance between the plants and animals in a forest may never be recreated after a fire – certainly not in our lifetime.

Glossary

adpressed Pressed flat to a surface; commonly used of flattened hairs (1).

alternate Leaves placed singly, at different heights on a stem (2).

annual A plant completing its life and seeding in one year or less.

anther The part of the stamen containing the pollen grains (3).

aquatic plants Submerged plants, floating plants, or plants with roots or rhizomes submerged.

awl-shaped Broad-based and tapering to a sharp point (4).

awn A long stiff bristle-like projection borne at the end or from the side of an organ (5).

axil, axillary The angle between the leaf and stem; hence axillary flower or bud (6).

bark The outer covering of a woody stem.

beak An elongated projection; usually referring to a slender extension of the fruit (7).

bearded A tuft or zone of hairs (29b).

berry A fleshy rounded fruit, usually with hard pips or seeds (8).

biennial A plant which feeds and grows in the first year, and fruits in the second year.

bifid, bilobed Cleft in two no further than to the middle (9).

blade The flattened part of an organ, such as a leaf or petal.

bract A little leaf or scale-like structure from the axil of which a flower often arises (12, 66a).

branched spike Flower cluster which is branched, with spikes (or clusters) of flowers borne on the branches.

bristle A stiff spine or fine projection; often referring to hairs.

brush-like Flower heads formed of many small florets and surrounded by an involucre of bracts, as found in members of the daisy family, especially in the thistles (36).

bulb (dim. **bulblet**) A swollen underground bud-like structure, remaining dormant below ground during unfavourable growth periods (13).

bulbil A small bulb or tuber arising from the axil of the leaf or among the flowers, and reproducing the plant (14a).

calyx, calices The sepals collectively; often joined together in a tube, the calyx tube (15a).

carpel A single unit or one of the units of the female part of the flower; either separate (23) or fused together into a fruit (17).

catkin A crowded spike of tiny flowers, usually hanging and tassel-like (18).

ciliate Fringed with hairs along the margin (10).

composite A member of the daisy family (19).

compound Two or more similar parts comprising one organ; hence a compound leaf has two or more separate leaflets (11, 51).

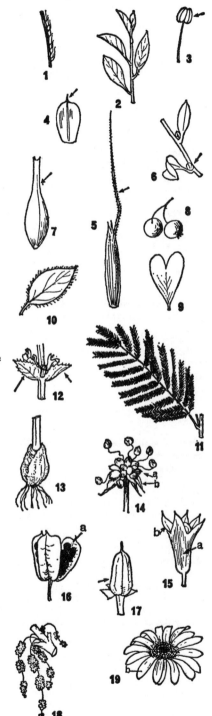

cone A distinct rounded or elongated structure composed of many overlapping scales which bear pollen or seeds when ripe (20).

coppiced Cut down periodically, esp. of hazel, Spanish chestnut, and hornbeam for use as stakes, fencing etc.

cordate Heart-shaped (21).

corolla The petals collectively; often joined together into a tube, the corolla tube (22, 74b).

daisy-like In the form of flower heads of the daisy family with both disk-florets and outer ray-florets (19, 25).

dandelion-like In the form of flower heads of the daisy family with only ray-florets present (54).

deciduous Falling off, as with leaves in the autumn.

decurrent When the blade or stalk of the leaf continues, as a rib or wing, down the side of the stem (24a).

deflexed Bent sharply downwards (56) = **reflexed**.

disk-florets The tube-like flowers at the centre of the flower heads of some members of the daisy family (25a).

dissected Cut or divided into parts, particularly of leaves (30, 61).

downy Covered with short, weak, soft hairs.

egg-shaped With an oval outline broader towards the base than the apex, and round-ended (26) = **ovate**.

elliptic Oval and narrowed to rounded ends in profile (27).

endemic Native of only one country or area.

entire Whole; without lobes or indentations.

epicalyx A calyx-like structure outside, but close to the true calyx (28).

evergreen Remaining green throughout the year.

falls In the iris family, the outer set of perianth segments which are usually turned down (29a), in contrast to the inner erect segments.

family A group of plants with many common characteristics; usually composed of many genera.

feathery Cut into many fine segments (30).

female flowers Flowers with a fertile ovary but without fertile stamens.

fetid Stinking, strong, and unpleasant-smelling.

flat-topped cluster A cluster of flowers in which all are at approximately the same height, either arising from the same point, as in an umbel (78), or arising from different levels.

floret A small flower usually one of a dense cluster, as in the daisy family (25a, 54).

flower The reproductive part of certain plants, usually comprising sepals, petals, stamens, and ovary.

flower head Term used where many small florets are closely clustered together, often surrounded by an involucre, as in the daisy family, scabious, plantain, eryngo etc. (19).

free Not joined to other similar or different organs.

fruit The ripened ovary bearing the seeds; other organs may be included (16, 23, 72, 82).

fused Petals (or other organs) joined edge to edge from their bases to form a tube or cup. Fusion may be slight or for most of the organ's length (15, 22, 48, 74).

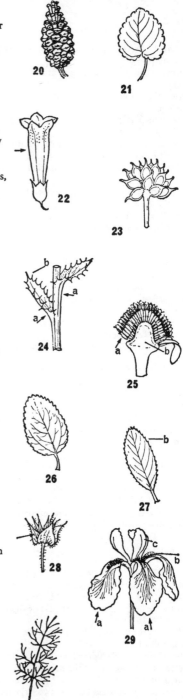

garigue, garrique Dry stony Mediterranean ground covered with low scattered bushes.

genus, genera A classificatory term for a group of closely related species; a number of genera forms a family. The generic name is the first part of the Latin binomial, as in *Ranunculus arvensis*, when *Ranunculus* is the generic name.

gland, glandular Organs of secretion usually on the tips of hairs; hence glandular-hairs (32).

glaucous Covered or whitened with a bloom which is often waxy, thus giving the organ a bluish or greyish colour.

glume A chaff-like bract surrounding the fertile organs of the florets of the grass family (31a).

grasses, grass-like See page 87.

hair A fine projection from a surface; one-celled or many-celled, simple or branched, straight or curved, etc. Special kinds of hair include glandular (32) and star-shaped (53) hairs. Long, soft hairs are described as woolly (33) and those pressed flat to a surface as adpressed (34).

head Of flowers or fruits which are crowded together at the end of a common stalk (35).

heart-shaped Oval-shaped with a blunt, rounded apex and rounded basal lobes projecting below the point of attachment, as, for example, the leaf-blade with the leaf-stalk (21)=**cordate**.

herb A plant which has no woody stem and is soft and leafy; also an aromatic plant used in seasoning or medicine.

herbaceous Non-woody, soft, and leafy. Of a plant organ, having the soft texture and green colour of leaves.

horn A tough narrow projection on an organ, e.g. on fruits.

hybrid A plant resulting from the cross-breeding of two different species, and possessing some of the characters of each parent. Hybrids are often infertile.

inflated Blown-up, bladdery; separated from the organ which it encircles.

inflorescence Flower branch, including the bracts, flower stalks, and flowers (66).

involucre, involucral A collection of bracts or leafy structures surrounding a flower head, groups of flowers, or a single flower; thus involucral bracts (36b).

keel A sharp central ridge on an organ resembling the keel of a boat. Also the lower petal of the flowers of the pea family (37a).

lance-shaped Shaped like a lance with the broadest part nearer the base, with an acute apex and regularly narrowed to the base (38)=**lanceolate**.

leaf A thin, expanded organ which is usually green and synthesizes food, arising from the node of a stem and commonly with a leaf-stalk and less commonly with basal stipules.

leaflet The individual part of a compound leaf which is usually leaf-like and possesses its own stalk (39a, 73b).

linear Of narrow leaves with parallel sides, as in grasses, irises, etc.

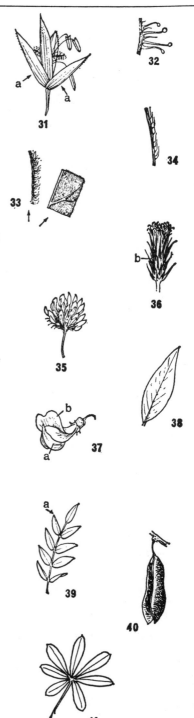

lobe A part or segment of an organ, deeply divided from the rest of the organ but not separated from it (15b, 42, 52).

male flower A flower containing fertile stamens but no fertile ovary.
maquis A thicket of tall shrubs and scattered trees characteristically developed in a Mediterranean climate.
midvein The central, more conspicuous middle-vein (of a leaf) (26, 27, 38, 42).

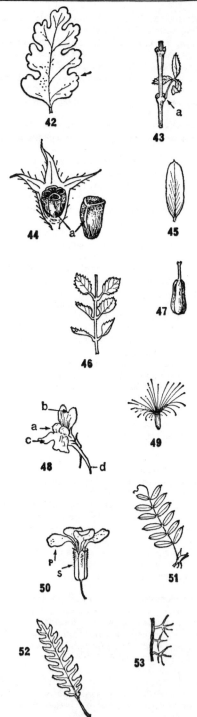

native A plant occurring naturally in an area and not introduced from elsewhere.
naturalized Thoroughly established in an area, but originally coming from another region.
nectary A gland which gives out a sugary liquid and serves to attract insects; variously situated in the flower.
needle-leaf A slender needle-like leaf, as found in pines.
node A point on the stem where one or more leaves arise (43a).
notch A V-shaped indentation in an organ, as in a petal apex (48b, 69c).
nut, nutlet A one-seeded fruit with a hard outer covering. Small nutlets are found in the mint family (44a).

oblong An elongated but relatively wide shape, as in a leaf with parallel sides (45).
opposite Of two organs; arising at the same level on opposite sides of the stem (46).
ovary The part of the flower containing the ovules and later the seeds, usually with one or more styles and stigmas (47).

palmate Lobed or divided in a palm-like or hand-like manner (41).
pappus Hairs or bristles on the fruits of some members of the daisy family which replace the calyx (49).
parasite An organism living and feeding on another living organism.
pea-like, pea flowers Typical flower structure of members of the pea family (37, 69).
perennial Living for more than two years and usually flowering each year.
petal An individual member of the inner set of sterile organs surrounding the sexual parts of the flower, usually brightly coloured (50p, 37a, b, 48c).
pinnate The regular arrangement of leaflets in two rows on either side of the stalk (51).
pinnately lobed A leaf with opposite pairs of deep lobes cut nearly to the midvein (52)=**pinnatifid**.
pod Usually a simple elongated fruit, containing seeds and splitting open when ripe (40).
pollard To lop off the top of a tree to produce a head of straight young twigs, for basket-making, etc.
procumbent Trailing or lying loosely along the surface of the ground.
prostrate Lying rather closely along the surface of the ground.

ray-florets The strap-shaped florets of many members of the daisy family (25b, 54, 19b).

recurved Bent backwards or downwards in a curve (55).

reflexed Bent abruptly backwards or downwards (56)=**deflexed**.

rhizome A creeping underground stem which sends up new leaves and stems each season (57).

rib Raised ridge on an organ.

root Underground organ which absorbs water and mineral salts; without buds or scales; cf. **rhizome**.

rootstock A short, erect, underground stem (58).

rosette The arrangement, usually of leaves, radiating outwards from the centre, overlapping and often spreading over the ground (59).

rush, rush-like See page 86.

saprophyte, saprophytic A plant which derives its food wholly or partially from dead organic matter.

scale Any thin dry flap of tissue; usually a modified or degenerate leaf (60a); also see **cone**.

sedge See page 90.

seed Contained within the ovary, produced as a result of fertilization. It consists of a coat, an embryo, and food reserves and is capable of germination.

segment One of the parts of a cut or divided leaf, calyx or corolla (15b, 48c, 61a).

sepal One of the outer set of floral segments, usually green and protecting in bud, less commonly coloured and petal-like (50s, 68b).

sheath A more or less tubular structure surrounding another; as in the lower part of the leaves of members of the grass family (62).

shrub A perennial with woody stems, usually branched, or with several branches arising from the base. Leaves deciduous or evergreen. See also **undershrub**.

shrublet A small woody-stemmed plant, usually less than 30 cm (1 ft) tall and often creeping over the ground.

silky Having a covering of soft fine hairs.

simple Of leaves: not divided up into segments (65); of stems or inflorescences: unbranched (66).

spadix A fleshy axis bearing clusters of stalkless flowers and often ending in a swollen club-like apex, as in the arum family (63).

spathe A large bract enclosing a flower head; it is sometimes conspicuous and coloured, as in the arum family (64), or papery as in onions (14b).

species A group of individuals having similar characteristics, and which interbreed. Species are grouped together into genera. The specific name is the second part of the Latin binomial. See also **genus**.

sphagnum Peat moss; a characteristic spongy moss growing in acid bogs and swamps.

spike A slender elongated cluster of more or less stalkless flowers, the youngest flowers at the apex, the oldest at the base (66).

spikelet In the grass family a group of one or more florets subtended by one or two sterile bracts or glumes (31, 67).

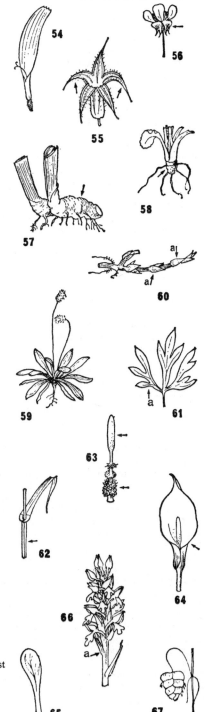

spine, spiny A sharp-pointed, narrow projection, often hard, woody, and piercing.

spur A hollow, more or less cylindrical projection from a petal or sepal; it usually contains nectar (48d, 68a).

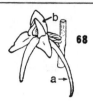

68

stamen One of the male reproductive organs of the flower, which bears the pollen (3).

standard The broad upper petal of the flower of the pea family (69a); also the inner erect petals of the flower of the iris (29c).

star-shaped Usually referring to branched hairs with several spreading branches (53).

stem The main axis of a plant, which is both leaf-bearing and flower-bearing.

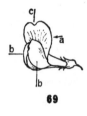

69

stigma The part of the female organ which receives the male pollen, it is normally situated at the top of the style. The stigma is sometimes lobed, hence *stigma-lobe* (70a); less commonly radiating, thus *stigma-ray* as in the poppy family.

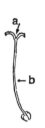

stipule, stipulate A scale-like or leaf-like appendage at the base of the leaf-stalk; usually paired (71).

stock See **rootstock**.

stolon, stoloniferous A stem that creeps above ground or underground and roots at the tip to give rise to a new plant.

70

subspecies, subsp. A group of individuals within a species which have some distinctive characteristics, and often a well-marked geographical range.

71

subtending Standing below and close to; as of a bract bearing a flower in its axil.

succulent Fleshy, juicy, and thick.

sucker A shoot originating and spreading below the ground and ultimately appearing above ground, often some distance from the main stem.

style A more or less elongated projection of the ovary which bears the stigma (70b, 72).

72

tendril A slender, clasping, twining organ, often formed from a leaf or part of a leaf (73a).

terminal At the tip; borne at the end of the stem.

throat The opening or orifice of a tubular or funnel-shaped corolla, or calyx (74a). Hence *throat-boss*, a swelling on the lower lip in the throat, as in toadflax (48a).

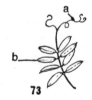

73

tight round heads Many small flowers clustered closely together (35), without a well-developed involucre and thus excluding members of the daisy family.

toothed, teeth With small triangular or rounded projections on a margin or rib (24b, 27b).

tree A long-lived woody plant with a single trunk branching only from above.

74

trifoliate, trefoil Having three leaflets, as in clover (75).

tube The fused part of the calyx (76) or corolla (74b).

tuber A swollen part of a stem or root, formed annually and usually underground (77).

75

tubular flower With petals fused into a tube or trumpet (22).

tufted With many stems arising thickly from the same point and forming a dense cluster of stems.

twig The youngest woody branches, usually of the present year's growth.

76

two-lipped Referring to the calyx or corolla, the mouth of which is partially cleft into upper and lower (often unequal) parts (48, 68, 74).

umbel A cluster of flowers whose spreading stalks arise from the apex of the stem, resembling the spokes of an umbrella (78).

umbellifer A member of the umbellifer family with flowers in umbels.

undershrub A woody perennial, rarely as much as 1 m. (3 ft) tall, generally less.

valve One of the parts into which a capsule splits (16a).

variety, var. A group of individual plants possessing one or more distinctive characteristics, e.g. a marked colour variation or an unusual leaf form.

vein A strand of strengthening and conducting tissue running through the leaf and other organs (79a).

viviparous With flowers sprouting into leafy shoots on the parent plant and not forming seeds (80).

whorl More than two organs of the same kind arising from the same level; thus whorled (81).

wing A dry thin expansion of an organ (82a). Also the lateral petals of the flowers of the pea family (69b).

woolly With long, soft, more or less tangled hairs (33).

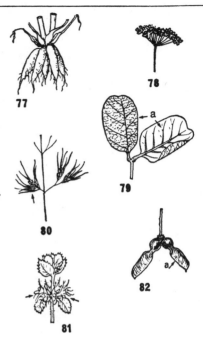

1 Herbaceous Plants

WHITE

Flowers large · Plant medium

Burning Bush *pl. 67.* Flowers either white with violet veins, or pink. The dark green leathery leaves have 5–9 oval leaflets. Whole plant aromatic and glandular, smelling strongly of lemon when crushed. May–June. *Rue family*

Thorn-Apple *pl. 118.* A very poisonous plant. The large trumpet-shaped white or rarely violet flowers (6–8 cm) are unmistakable, as are the fruits which are like horse-chestnuts, and split into 4 valves releasing many seeds. July–Oct. *Nightshade family*

Large-Flowered Thorn-Apple *pl. 118.* Like the commoner preceding plant but flowers much larger (15–20 cm) and often flushed pink. Also differs in being densely hairy with entire or shallowly lobed leaves. Native of India. July–Oct. *Nightshade family*

Bear's Breech *pl. 130.* A famous plant, the motif for the Corinthian capital. Flowers arise from spiny bracts; they have a three-lobed lower lip, often purple-flushed. The large, dark glossy green leaves are deeply lobed but not spiny. May–July. *Acanthus family*

Spiny Bear's Breech *pl. 130.* Like the previous plant but leaves stiff and thistle-like, with narrow spiny lobes. The bracts also have long spiny teeth. July–Aug. *Acanthus family*

Marguerite *pl. 148.* A common meadowland plant with large flower heads (2½–5 cm) with many spreading white rays. The lowest leaves are rounded, toothed, and long-stalked; the upper are oblong, toothed or deeply lobed, and half-clasp the stem. May–Sept. *Daisy family*

Asphodel *pl. 163.* A famous plant of dry, stony, over-grazed ground of the Mediterranean. Flowers white or pinkish (3–4 cm); petals with a darker midvein. Leaves coarse (2–4 cm broad) and V-shaped in section. Apr.–June. *Lily family*

St Bruno's Lily *pl. 163.* A slender delicate lily with slender grass-like leaves (1–4 mm wide), and trumpet flowers (4–5 cm). It is found in grassy meadows in the mountains of central Europe and Portugal. June–Aug. *Lily family*

St Bernard's Lily *pl. 164.* Not unlike the previous plant but flowers much smaller (2 cm long), and white petals spreading in a star. The petals are about twice as long as the stamens. Leaves (4–5 mm wide) are all basal. May–June. *Lily family*

Pheasant's-Eye Narcissus *pl. 173.* The solitary sweet-scented, slightly nodding flowers (4–6 cm) have a short trumpet. The narrow white pointed petals and yellow trumpet with a reddish fringe are characteristic. Grows abundantly in the wild in damp meadows. Apr.–May. *Daffodil family*

Sea Daffodil *pl. 174.* A very handsome, sweet-scented, pure white-flowered bulbous plant found in the dry hot sands of the Mediterranean shore (and Portugal). Leaves flat, broad and blue-green, like those of the daffodil. July–Sept. *Daffodil family*

See also: COLUMBINE *pl. 27*; OPIUM POPPY *pl. 28*; LARGE-FLOWERED MULLEIN *pl. 120*; SNAKE'S HEAD FRITILLARY *pl. 167*

Flowers large · Plant small

 Christmas Rose *pl. 19.* Flowering very early in mountain woods of central Europe. Flowers (3–10 cm) usually solitary, with varying amounts of pink flush; they are borne on leafless stems. The dark green leaves have 5–9 toothed leaflets. Jan.–Apr. *Buttercup family*

 Spring Anemone *pl. 22.* Very beautiful when first in flower as the snow recedes, the whole plant is densely covered with silky hairs. The young nodding flowers have silky petals flushed with violet, blue or pink. Stem leaves bract-like, deeply cut into slender segments. Apr.–June. *Buttercup family*

 White Alpine Poppy *pl. 29.* A rare white-flowered poppy of the Alps, with petals 1½–2 cm. The segments of the leaves are blunt. July–Aug. *Poppy family*

 False Daisy *pl. 142.* Very like the Common Daisy, but a larger plant with flower heads to 4 cm across. Also differing from the Daisy in having a fruit with a pappus of white hairs. Apr.–Sept. *Daisy family*

 Stemless Carline Thistle *pl. 151.* The very large flower head sits alone in the centre of a rosette of deeply lobed, spiny leaves; but it is sometimes shortly stalked. The shining papery bracts vary from silvery-white, pinkish to brownish; they take the place of the ray florets. May–Sept. *Daisy family*

See also: CROWN ANEMONE *pl. 21*; SCARLET ANEMONE *pl. 21*; SMALL PASQUE FLOWER *pl. 22*; ALPINE ANEMONE *pl. 23*; AUTUMN CROCUS, MEADOW SAFFRON *pl. 163*; DWARF IRIS *pl. 175*; ITALIAN ARUM *pl. 183*.

Flowers medium · Plant large

 Candelabra Thistle *pl. 153.* A tall graceful thistle covered with pale yellow spines and clusters of small whitish or pale yellow flower heads. A common wayside weed in Northern Macedonia. July–Aug. *Daisy family*

See also: SILKWEED *pl. 99*.

Flowers medium · Plant medium

 Greater Stitchwort *pl. 12.* A widespread plant with slender brittle stems, and narrow, pointed, very rough-margined leaves. Flowers with deeply cleft spreading petals (12–16 mm). Apr.–June. *Pink family*

 Nottingham Catchfly *pl. 15.* The slender, one-sided clusters of nodding white or pinkish flowers are characteristic, and as the flower matures the deeply notched petals roll back exposing the stamens even more. Upper parts of plant sticky. Leaves are paired and narrow. May–July. *Pink family*

 Bladder Campion *pl. 14.* Very variable; growing from the sea coast to the alpine regions in all countries of Europe. Distinguished by its bladdery calyx with 20 distinct veins interconnected by a network of smaller veins. Flowers 1½–2½ cm, petals deeply notched. Apr.–Aug. *Pink family*

 Garden Love-in-a-Mist *pl. 18.* This whitish-flowered love-in-a-mist is distinguished by the absence of the leafy collar round the flowers (found in *Nigella damascena*) and by fruits covered with small swellings. Sometimes grown for its edible seeds. June–July. *Buttercup family*

Narcissus-Flowered Anemone *pl. 22.* A handsome anemone with umbels of white or pinkish flowers (2–3 cm) and a frill of leafy bracts below. The leaves all basal and deeply cut into narrow lance-shaped segments, very hairy when young. June–July. *Buttercup family*

2

Salad Mustard *pl. 37.* A rough hairy plant of cultivated ground with pale yellow flowers (1½–2 cm) which turn whitish with violet veins. Leaves with 2–5 pairs of lateral lobes and a larger terminal lobe. Fruit with a sabre-shaped beak. Apr.–June. *Cress family*

 Rock Cinquefoil *pl. 46.* Flowers pure white (1–2 cm) in lax clusters. Note the extra row of smaller sepals (epicalyx). Upper leaves usually with 3 narrow leaflets, the lower with 2–4 widely separated pairs of broader leaflets. June–Aug. *Rose family*

 White Lupin *pl. 54.* A native of south-east Europe, often cultivated for fodder elsewhere. The white flowers tipped with blue (subsp. *graecus* of the Balkans has bright blue flowers) are arranged alternately. Pods with shaggy hairs and white seeds. May–June. *Pea family*

 Silver Sage *pl. 113.* A robust, sticky, and strong-smelling sage with a branched pyramidal cluster of pinkish-white flowers. Leaves silvery, covered with shaggy cobweb-like hairs. Apr.–June. *Mint family*

 Bladder Cherry *pl. 119.* Familiar as a garden plant with its reddish-orange 'Chinese lanterns' formed from the dry swollen calyx enclosing a red berry. Flowers dirty white (1½–2½ cm), funnel-shaped, drooping and inconspicuous amongst the oval, pointed leaves. May–Oct. *Nightshade family*

 Bean Broomrape *pl. 131.* Often found growing in abundance in bean fields and on other members of the pea family. Flowers (1½–3 cm) whitish and veined with blue-violet, tubular and somewhat two-lipped, the lower lip three-lobed. Stigma violet, rarely white. Apr.–June. *Broomrape family*

 Feverfew *pl. 148.* A strongly aromatic plant with rather yellowish-green, usually downy, lobed leaves. Flower heads (1–2½ cm) in a more or less flat-topped cluster. Ray florets rounded. A native of south-east Europe, now naturalized almost throughout. June–July. *Daisy family*

 Spiniest Thistle *pl. 154.* An extremely spiny thistle of damp pastures in the Alps. Flower heads (2–3 cm) densely clustered, encircled by much longer, pale, very spiny upper leaves. Lower leaves in a rosette and covered with numerous pale spines. July–Sept. *Daisy family*

 White Garlic *pl. 165.* The comparatively large pure white flowers (1–2 cm) and the triangular-sectioned stem distinguish this from similar garlics. Petals blunt, much longer than the stamens. Leaves 2–4 (1–1½ cm broad) arising near the base. Mar.–May. *Lily family*

 Triquetrous Garlic *pl. 165.* Distinguished from most other garlics by its drooping white, bell-shaped flowers borne in a one-sided cluster on a thick, sharply three-angled stem. Petals with a green midvein on the outside. Leaves broad (½–1 cm), strongly keeled below. Mar.–May. *Lily family*

 Summer Snowflake *pl. 172.* Distinguished by its 2–6 long-stalked, white flowers with green tips. Flower stalks unequal, the longer exceeding the green-tipped bract. Leaves strap-shaped, 1 cm broad. Apr.–June. *Daffodil family*

 Greater Butterfly Orchid *pl. 191.* Distinguished from the Lesser Butterfly Orchid (*pl. 191*) by the yellowish anthers which diverge widely below. Flowers white or greenish-white, lip 1–1½ cm, the spur down-curved and thickened towards the tip (2–3 cm). Two large basal leaves. May–July. *Orchid family*

  Long-Leaved Helleborine *pl. 191.* A slender orchid with narrow, grass-like upper leaves, and pure white flowers usually remaining half-opened and appearing rather tubular.

3

Lip short, half-concealed by the outer pointed petals, with a small orange spot in the throat. May–July. *Orchid family*

See also: RED GERMAN CATCHFLY *pl. 14*; BERRY CATCHFLY *pl. 15*; LARKSPUR *pl. 20*; DAME'S VIOLET *pl. 31*; STOCK *pl. 32*; NINE-LEAVED CORAL-WORT *pl. 33*; CORAL-WORT *pl. 34*; LADY'S SMOCK *pl. 34*; CHICKLING PEA *pl. 56*; PEA *pl. 56*; ALPINE SAINFOIN *pl. 61*; MOTH MULLEIN *pl. 120*; SEA ASTER *pl. 142*; GALACTITES *pl. 154*.

Flowers medium · Plant small

 Mountain Sandwort *pl. 12.* Sandworts (*Arenaria*) can be distinguished from chick-weeds (*Cerastium*) by their entire, not notched, petals. A small creeping plant of heaths and woods of Iberia and west France with relatively large flowers (2 cm) and greyish-green finely hairy leaves (1–2 cm). May–July. *Pink family*

 Alpine Mouse-Ear Chickweed *pl. 12.* A tiny plant of alpine screes or meadows, or of the Arctic. The small oval, grey-green leaves make a loose hairy mat. Flowers (to 2½ cm) solitary or in a cluster of 2–5. July–Aug. *Pink family*

 Wood Anemone *pl. 22.* A delightful early flowering plant of woodlands with solitary white or purple- or pink-flushed flowers (2–4 cm). The 3 leaves are three-lobed, and are borne two-thirds of the way up the stem. The fruits are nodding. Mar.–May. *Buttercup family*

 Glacier Crowfoot *pl. 26.* A beautiful white- or pinkish-flowered dwarf alpine of high mountains or of the Arctic. Flowers (1–3 cm) often turning pink or reddish as they age and remaining attached in fruit. Leaves rather fleshy. June–July. *Buttercup family*

 Oval-Leaved Crowfoot *pl. 25.* A small alpine plant of rocks and screes distinguished by its fleshy oval-heart-shaped lower leaves which are undivided; upper leaves smaller and narrower. Flowers white or reddish, 2–2½ cm across. June–Aug. *Buttercup family*

 Grass of Parnassus *pl. 42.* The large single flower (1½–2 cm) is carried on a slender stem with but a single oval to heart-shaped leaf. The petals are delicately veined; alternating with the 5 stamens are 5 fringed infertile stamens tipped with yellow glands. July–Sept. *Grass of Parnassus family*

 Cloudberry *pl. 44.* A creeping plant of northern bogs and woods with solitary black-berry-like flowers (2 cm) borne on slender leafless stems. Leaves shallowly five- to seven-lobed. Fruits at first red and then orange. June–Aug. *Rose family*

 Wood-Sorrel *pl. 62.* A pretty, frail plant of shady woods, with bright green trefoil leaves and delicate nodding white flowers faintly veined with lilac. The leaves and stems arise directly from a slender white scaly underground rhizome. Apr.–May. *Wood-Sorrel family*

 Dwarf Cornel *pl. 82.* A tiny creeping plant of mossy places and heaths in northern mountains. The white 'flower' consists of a tight head of 8–25 tiny blackish-purple flowers surrounded by 4 large white petal-like bracts. Fruit red (½ cm). July–Aug. *Dogwood family*

 One-Flowered Wintergreen *pl. 87.* A delicate creeping plant of damp mountain woodlands, with rounded, stalked leaves and nodding solitary flowers (1½–2½ cm). Style short, straight, longer than the petals. Anthers with long tubes. May–July. *Wintergreen family*

 Chickweed Wintergreen *pl. 93.* A slender plant of heaths and pine forests, with a characteristic rosette of stiff shining lance-shaped leaves borne near the top of the stem. Flowers (1½–2 cm), 1 or several, usually with 7 petals. May–Aug. *Primrose family*

4

Chamomile *pl. 147.* A spreading plant with finely cut leaves, and a pleasant aromatic smell when crushed. Flower heads (2–2½ cm), long-stalked; white rays usually present, but sometimes absent. Involucral bracts with broad papery white margins. June–Sept. *Daisy family*

Star-of-Bethlehem *pl. 170.* An attractive plant with a spreading flat-topped cluster of pure white, star-like flowers opening wide in the sun. Petals with a broad green band on the outside. Leaves narrow with a white band down the grooved centre. Apr.–June. *Lily family*

Spring Snowflake *pl. 172.* Usually only 1 drooping flower on each stem. Petals white with yellowish tips and the terminal papery bract longer than the flower stalk. Leaves 3–4, rather narrow. Feb.–Apr. *Daffodil family*

Three-Leaved Snowflake *pl. 172.* A beautiful little bulbous plant of open sandy woods and stony pastures in the Iberian peninsula. There are 1–5 white or often pink-tinged, drooping flowers (13 mm) and 3 thread-like leaves. Jan.–Apr. *Daffodil family*

Snowdrop *pl. 173.* This familiar spring-flowering plant of damp woods and meadows grows wild over most of Europe. The much shorter inner petals have green tips and are revealed only when the flower opens. Feb.–Mar. *Daffodil family*

White Hoop Petticoat Daffodil *pl. 173.* Distinguished from the common yellow-flowered plant of the Iberian peninsula by snowy-white flowers with a very conspicuous trumpet and narrow spreading petals. A rare plant of south-west Spain. Feb.–Apr. *Daffodil family*

Autumn Narcissus *pl. 173.* A slender, fragrant autumn-flowering daffodil with usually solitary white flowers (2–3 cm) with a very short golden trumpet and greenish tube. Leaves 1 or 2, slender and thread-like, often not produced at flowering. Sept.–Oct. *Daffodil family*

Purple Crocus *pl. 174.* A spring-flowering crocus of hill and mountain meadows of central Europe. Usually predominantly white with a violet tube, less commonly all violet. Stigmas orange and crisped at the apex. Feb.–May. *Iris family*

Lesser Butterfly Orchid *pl. 191.* A graceful orchid with a loose spike of sweet-scented, whitish flowers. Lip strap-shaped, spur slender horizontal, greenish (1½–2 cm). Distinguished by the pale yellowish anthers which lie parallel to each other. May–July. *Orchid family*

See also: PINK CLAYTONIA *pl. 11*; HEPATICA *pl. 20*; BLOODY CRANESBILL *pl. 63*; COMMON DOG VIOLET *pl. 76*; SWEET VIOLET *pl. 76*; PRIMROSE *pl. 90*; SOWBREAD *pl. 92*; EVAX *pl. 143*; EDELWEISS *pl. 144*; HYACINTH *pl. 171*; TOOTHED ORCHID *pl. 187*; SPOTTED ORCHID *pl. 189*.

Flowers small · Plant large

Japanese Knotweed *pl. 8.* A tall stout, cane-like plant (1–2 m) with many large oval leaves. It spreads rapidly by means of underground stems to form extensive thickets. Tassels of tiny white flowers are borne late in the summer. Aug.–Sept. *Dock family*

Hemlock *pl. 85.* A tall hairless plant, distinguished by its smooth furrowed stems conspicuously spotted with small purple dots. The whole plant smells of mice – and is intensely poisonous. Fruits rounded (3 mm) with wavy ribs. June–Aug. *Umbellifer family*

Giant Hogweed *pl. 86.* The giant among herbs, every part monstrously large; introduced to Europe from the Caucasus. The juice can cause severe skin irritation, and the plant is best not handled. Leaves (to 1 m) deeply divided and the enormous flower heads may be ½ m across. June–Sept. *Umbellifer family*

Flowers small · Plant medium

 Buckwheat   *pl. 9.* Often grown as a crop plant; though the flowers are whitish, they look pale pink in the mass. Flowers (3–4 mm) in dense somewhat flat-topped clusters. The edible seeds are brown, triangular and project beyond the withered petals. June–Aug. *Dock family*

 Lesser Stitchwort   *pl. 12.* A slender, delicate, hairless plant with opposite pairs of narrow, smooth-margined leaves, and square stems. The flowers (5–12 mm) have deeply cleft petals hardly longer than the pointed sepals. June–July. *Pink family*

 Common Mouse-Ear Chickweed   *pl. 12.* A common, insignificant, hairy annual with lax clusters of small flowers (5–7 mm). Petals notched, about as long as the papery-margined sepals. A very variable plant, not easily distinguished from other similar-looking chickweeds. Apr.–Sept. *Pink family*

 Water Chickweed   *pl. 12.* A weak-stemmed, scrambling chickweed of damp shady places and ditches. Flowers (12–15 mm) appear to have 10 petals but in reality there are 5 very deeply notched petals, longer than the sepals. Upper leaves stalkless, oval-heart-shaped, often wavy-margined. June–Aug. *Pink family*

 White Buttercup   *pl. 25.* An erect, widely branched, white-flowered buttercup of damp meadows and mountain woods. Flowers (1–2 cm); sepals reddish-brown soon falling after flowers open. Leaves cut into 3–5 nettle-like lobes. May–Aug. *Buttercup family*

 Climbing Corydalis   *pl. 30.* A delicate, slender herb, climbing by means of long branched tendrils at the ends of glaucous, lobed leaves. The cream-coloured flowers (5–6 mm) are tubular, two-lipped, with a short rounded spur. June–Sept. *Poppy family*

 Ramping Fumitory   *pl. 30.* A rather weak, climbing plant with dense, long-stalked clusters of predominantly cream-coloured flowers, varyingly dark reddish-purple at the tips. Flowers (1–1½ cm) tubular, two-lipped, flattened from side to side, with a short spur. Apr.–June. *Poppy family*

 Garlic Mustard, Hedge Garlic   *pl. 31.* Smells of garlic when bruised. Flowers (6 mm), at first in dense clusters, later in an elongated leafless spike of slender four-angled pods. Leaves wrinkled, glossy, hairless, and nettle-like. May–July. *Cress family*

 Large Bitter-Cress   *pl. 34.* A white- (or rarely purple-) flowered plant of damp places, with conspicuous violet anthers when young. Flowers (1 cm) with petals only twice as long as sepals. Leaves pale green, with 5–9 rounded leaflets, the terminal longest. Fruits explosive. Apr.–June. *Cress family*

 Sand Bitter-Cress   *pl. 35.* A hairy plant with flowers from white, purplish to lilac; white predominating in the north of its range. Lower leaves, often in a rosette, pinnately lobed. Pod, unlike the preceding species, not explosive. Apr.–July. *Cress family*

 Field Pennycress   *pl. 35.* Easily recognized by the flat and disk-like fruits, with a deep notch at the apex. Flowers (4–6 mm) white; petals twice as long as sepals. The pale green leaves clasp the stem and have an unpleasant smell when crushed. May–Sept. *Cress family*

 Hoary Pepperwort   *pl. 36.* Often growing as a wayside weed, with rather flattened clusters of tiny white flowers (5–6 mm). The grey-green leaves are irregularly toothed and the upper clasp the stem. Fruits heart-shaped (3–5 mm). Apr.–July. *Cress family*

 Seakale   *pl. 37.* A cabbagy plant growing on Atlantic seashores, with thick glaucous, lobed leaves. Flowers (8–16 mm) in a large, dense, much-branched cluster, usually white, sometimes reddish. The wild parent of the blanched vegetable. May–Aug. *Cress family*

6

Upright Mignonette   *pl. 38.* Has long slender spikes of white flowers (9 mm), with all petals cut into narrow lobes. Leaves deeply cut into narrow lobes with wavy margins. A plant of coasts in the south and waste places further north. May–Sept. *Mignonette family*

Rampion Mignonette   *pl. 38.* The rather lax spike of small whitish flowers (3–5 mm) is soon replaced by pendulous three-lobed fruits with enlarged green spreading sepals. Leaves narrow, pale green, downy, not usually lobed. June–Sept. *Mignonette family*

Orpine, Livelong   *pl. 40.* Flowers usually reddish-violet or lilac; less commonly, as in the subspecies photographed, greenish- or yellowish-white. A stout fleshy plant with oblong toothed, flattened, often glaucous leaves. June–Sept. *Stonecrop family*

Pyrenean Saxifrage   *pl. 41.* A most attractive saxifrage with a majestic rosette (6–18 cm) of narrow greyish lime-encrusted leaves, which produce a magnificent branched pyramid of white flowers. Grows on vertical, often inaccessible cliffs in the Pyrenees. July–Aug. *Saxifrage family*

Round-Leaved Saxifrage   *pl. 42.* A plant of damp shady places in the mountains with a rosette of rounded-toothed basal leaves with a narrow but distinctive horny border. Petals (6–11 mm) white, spotted with yellow or red. June–Aug. *Saxifrage family*

Meadow-Sweet   *pl. 44.* A rather robust plant of marshes and damp meadows with frothy bunches of cream-coloured flowers in multiple-branched clusters. Flowers with heavy penetrating fragrance; petals 2–5 mm. Leaves compound, paler grey-green beneath. June–Aug. *Rose family*

Dropwort   *pl. 44.* Like the preceding species but found in dry pastures, thickets, and clearings, with larger white flowers (petals 5–9 mm) flushed reddish-purple on the outside. Leaves differing having smaller, more numerous leaflets on the lowest leaves. Fruit hairless, straight (not twisted). May–July. *Rose family*

Milk-Vetch   *pl. 54.* A stoutish, straggling plant with 9–13 oval leaflets (1½–4 cm), and short-stalked dense clusters of creamy-white flowers, tinged greenish-grey. Flowers 1–1½ cm. The cylindrical pod is curved and pointed. May–Aug. *Pea family*

White Melilot   *pl. 57.* A slender, branched annual to 1 m or more, distinguished from other melilots by spikes of tiny white flowers. Flowers (4–5 mm) with upper petal (standard) longer than side wings. Leaves with 3 oblong leaflets. June–Aug. *Pea family*

Alsike Clover   *pl. 59.* An upright spreading plant with loosely packed white or pinkish globular clusters (1½–3 cm), becoming brownish. Flowers (6–7 mm long) on stalks longer than the pale calyx. Leaves not blotched; plant not creeping and rooting. May–Sept. *Pea family*

Mountain Clover   *pl. 59.* A mountain plant distinguished from the previous species in having the lower surface of the leaflets hairy, strongly veined and toothed at the margins. Flower heads very dense (1½ cm). May–July. *Pea family*

Hairy Dorycnium   *pl. 60.* A shrublet or herbaceous plant with rather short-stalked, globular heads of 4–10 tiny, whitish flowers (1–2 cm) flushed pink. Pods 6–12 mm. (This is *Dorycnium hirsutum* not, as on *pl. 60, D. rectum.*) Apr.–July. *Pea family*

Upright Dorycnium   *pl. 60.* Like previous species, but flowers smaller (3–7 mm) and more numerous (20–40) in each head. Pods longer (1–2 cm), twisted.   (This is *Dorycnium rectum* not, as on *pl. 60, D. hirsutum.*) May–Aug. *Pea family*

Enchanter's Nightshade   *pl. 80.* A slender plant of shady places with a terminal spike of tiny white or pinkish flowers and small burred fruits. Petals 2 (2–4 mm), deeply notched. Leaves opposite, oval with a heart-shaped base, pointed, and weakly toothed. June–Aug. *Willow-herb family*

Sweet Cicely *pl. 84.* A downy plant smelling strongly of aniseed when crushed. The long erect fruits (2–2½ cm) have sharp ridges and turn shining black when ripe. Flowers 2–4 mm. Leaves cut into fern-like segments. Apr.–Aug. *Umbellifer family*

 Ivory-Fruited Hartwort *pl. 86.* Quite unmistakable in fruit, with flattened rounded fruits with a thickened ivory-white border appearing crinkled on the inner margin. Flower umbels distinctive: the outer flowers with 1 much larger deeply divided petal. Apr.–June. *Umbellifer family*

 Common Vincetoxicum *pl. 99.* An upright, leafy, poisonous plant of woods, with clusters of whitish-green to yellowish flowers (¼ cm). Corolla shortly tubular, with 5 lobes and 5 scales in the throat. Leaves pale green, finely hairy. June–Sept. *Milkweed family*

 Marsh Bedstraw *pl. 99.* A delicate scrambling plant of wet places, distinguished by its blunt leaves in whorls of 4–6, and by the plant turning black when dried. Flowers (3–5 mm) in a loose pyramidal inflorescence. June–July. *Bedstraw family*

 Heliotrope *pl. 101.* An erect, softly hairy, greyish annual of cultivated ground. Flowers tiny (3–4 mm), white or pale lilac, numerous, on out-curved dichotomous branches. Calyx hairy, divided almost to the base, spreading in fruit. June–Oct. *Borage family*

 Eastern Comfrey *pl. 101.* A native of Turkey, sometimes naturalized elsewhere. Distinguished by softly hairy oblong leaves, abruptly narrowed to a distinct leaf stalk. The tubular white flowers (1½–2 cm) are two to three times longer than the blunt-lobed calyx. Apr.–May. *Borage family*

 Ground-Pine Germander *pl. 107.* A low shrubby-looking but not woody, plant, with hairy leaves cut into narrow, pointed segments with inrolled margins. Flowers white or pink (1–1½ cm), in whorls; upper lip of corolla very short, lower three-lobed. Apr.–Sept. *Mint family*

 White Horehound *pl. 109.* A greyish, downy, aromatic plant with wrinkled leaves and dense rounded axillary clusters of whitish flowers (1½ cm). Upper lip of flower flat, deeply notched; calyx with 10 out-curved teeth. May–Sept. *Mint family*

 Catmint *pl. 109.* Not the same as the plant (*Nepeta x faasenii*) with violet flowers grown in gardens. A greyish plant with a pungently minty smell and dense rounded clusters of white flowers (1–1½ cm) spotted with red. Leaves white-woolly beneath. June–Sept. *Mint family*

 Gipsy-Wort *pl. 116.* A mint-like plant of wet places with numerous stalkless whorls of whitish flowers spotted with purple in the axils of the upper pairs of leaves. Flowers tiny (3 mm) tubular; calyx with 13 veins and 5 spiny-pointed lobes. July–Sept. *Mint family*

 Danewort *pl. 133.* A bushy, strong-smelling perennial often growing in thickets to 1 m high, looking like elder but with non-woody stems. Flower clusters 7–10 cm across; flowers (¼ cm) white with dark purple anthers, sometimes reddish-tinged. Leaves with 7–13 lance-shaped toothed leaflets. June–Aug. *Honeysuckle family*

 Cut-Leaved Teasel *pl. 137.* A robust plant with narrow paired leaves fused round the stem to form a cup. Distinguished from Common Teasel (not illustrated) by deeply cut lower leaves with lobes further toothed or incised. Flower heads white or pale lilac, often with a topknot of spines. July–Aug. *Scabious family*

 Gallant Soldier *pl. 147.* An unattractive weed from South America, now widespread in Europe. Flower heads small (3–5 mm across), ray florets oval, three-toothed, few and widely spaced. May–Oct. *Daisy family*

8

White False Helleborine *pl. 162.* A robust poisonous plant of mountain pastures easily mistaken for the Great Yellow Gentian when not in flower, but leaves finely hairy beneath. Flowers (1½ cm) white within, greenish and hairy outside. July–Aug. *Lily family*

 Wild Leek *pl. 166.* The many smallish, long-stalked purple or whitish flowers are clustered into large globular heads (7–10 cm) on a thick cylindrical stem. Stamens longer than petals; bracts soon falling. Leaves flattened and keeled beneath. June–July. *Lily family*

 Sea Squill *pl. 169.* In autumn long quite leafless cylindrical spikes of white flowers push up from bare ground in Mediterranean coastlands. Later, broad strap-shaped glossy leaves appear and persist to the following autumn. Bulbs enormous (10–15 cm). Aug.–Oct. *Lily family*

 Solomon's Seal *pl. 171.* A graceful plant with neatly arranged, conspicuously veined leaves and hanging clusters of 3–5 white flowers with greenish tips. Corolla 1–2 cm long, somewhat pinched in the middle. Stems smooth. Apr.–June. *Lily family*

See also: SEA ROCKET *pl. 37*; GOAT'S RUE *pl. 53*; CROWN VETCH *pl. 62*; SOUTHERN MALLOW *pl. 73*; COMMON HEMP-NETTLE *pl. 111*; MOTHERWORT *pl. 112*; LESSER CALAMINT *pl. 114*; MARJORAM *pl. 115*; WATER MINT *pl. 116*.

Flowers small · Plant small

 Viviparous Bistort *pl. 9.* A creeping plant of alpine meadows, with narrow, lance-shaped leaves and slender spikes of white or pinkish flowers. Spikes distinctive, with tiny brownish-purple bulbils towards base. Stamens much longer than petals. June–Aug. *Dock family*

 Perfoliate Claytonia *pl. 11.* Immediately recognizable by the white flowers which arise from the centre of a saucer-shaped collar formed from the 2 uppermost leaves. Flowers 5–8 mm across; sepals 2. Lowest leaves oval, stalked, in a loose rosette. Native of North America. May–July *Purslane family*

 Illecebrum *pl. 13.* A creeping, rooting plant with tiny apple-green leaves and clusters of minute flowers with white, shining, rather thick and shaggy sepals, each with a fine bristle. Leaves oval, paired (2–6 mm). June–Sept. *Pink family*

 Small-Flowered Catchfly *pl. 16.* Flowers (1 cm) usually white or very pale pink, but in the variety photographed each petal has a dark red spot. The sticky calyx has 10 hairy veins and becomes much inflated in fruit. May–July. *Pink family*

 Creeping Gypsophila *pl. 16.* A creeping, mat-forming plant of mountain rock, screes and dry pastures in central Europe. Flowers white or pinkish (5–8 mm) in loose, flattish clusters; petals slightly notched. Leaves paired, narrow, curved, hairless. June–Sept. *Pink family*

 Cream Corydalis *pl. 30.* Native of the Balkans but sometimes introduced to rocks and walls elsewhere. Flowers creamy-white with pale yellow lips. Leaves glaucous on both sides, otherwise very similar to the Yellow Corydalis (*pl. 30*). May–July. *Poppy family*

 Alpine Rock-Cress *pl. 34.* A low mat-forming plant of hills and mountains with rosettes of greyish leaves covered with star-shaped hairs. Flowers pure white (petals 6–10 mm) in rather dense clusters at first. Fruits long and slender. Apr.–June. *Cress family*

 Sweet Alison *pl. 37.* The white or pink-flushed flowers (6 mm) are very sweet-scented. The leaves are numerous, narrow and usually covered with flattened silky hairs. A native of the littoral of the south, naturalized elsewhere. Dec.–Aug. *Cress family*

Hoary Whitlow-Grass *pl. 35.* A greyish-hairy annual rosette plant with a slender leafy stem bearing terminal clusters of small white flowers (3–5 mm). Petals slightly notched. Leaves lance-shaped, toothed. July–Aug. *Cress family*

 Danish Scurvy-Grass *pl. 36.* A small spreading annual with white or pale mauve flowers (½ cm) of rocks, salt marshes, and waste places inland. Leaves somewhat fleshy; lowest three- to seven-angled; middle triangular; the upper lance-shaped. Feb.–Mar. *Cress family*

 Annual Candytuft *pl. 36.* The flat-topped white or mauve clusters are easily distinguished by the unequal petals, the 2 outer being much larger. Leaves oblong, with widely spaced teeth or lobes. Fruit flattened, disk-like, notched, and in an elongate cluster. May–Oct. *Cress family*

 Great Sundew *pl. 38.* Sundews catch insects by sticky hairs, on the 'fly-paper' principle. The least common of the 3 species, distinguished by much larger leaf-blades (3 cm). Flowers white (¼ cm), stems much longer than the leaves. July–Aug. *Sundew family*

 Long-Leaved Sundew *pl. 39.* Like the previous plant, but all parts much smaller, and leaf blades to 7 mm. Flowers white on short stems about as long as the leaves and arising from the side of the rosette. July–Aug. *Sundew family*

 White Stonecrop *pl. 39.* Distinguished by its plump cylindrical leaves closely ranged up the stem, and often turning reddish. Flowers white or pinkish (6–9 mm), borne in rather flat-topped clusters. Petals 5; stamens 10. June–Aug. *Stonecrop family*

 Livelong Saxifrage *pl. 42.* Rosettes small to medium (1–5 cm), greyish, lime-edged, often forming mats on rocks in the mountains. Flower stem slender, bearing on its upper third a pyramidal cluster of small white, or cream-coloured, flowers (petals 4–6 mm), sometimes spotted with red. June–Aug. *Saxifrage family*

 Kidney Saxifrage *pl. 42.* One of several rather robust rosette-forming saxifrages of the west. Distinguished by its more or less cylindrical leaf stalk, two to four times as long as the rounded hairy blade. Flowers (petals 4 mm) white with a yellow basal blotch, sometimes reddish. May–July. *Saxifrage family*

 Starry Saxifrage *pl. 41.* A tiny rosette-forming saxifrage of mountains of central Europe or of the north. Leaves fleshy, shiny, spoon-shaped, sparsely toothed. Petals 3–7 mm, spreading, often turned down; anthers pink. June–Aug. *Saxifrage family*

 Androsace Saxifrage *pl. 41.* A tiny cushion-forming saxifrage of central Europe, looking like an androsace (*pls. 90, 91*), but distinguished by unfused petals, 10 stamens and 5-carpelled ovary. Petals (5–7 mm) sometimes notched. Leaves entire or three-lobed. May–July. *Saxifrage family*

 Rue-Leaved Saxifrage *pl. 41.* A puny annual with 3- to 5-lobed leaves and tiny flowers with notched petals (2–3 mm). The whole plant often reddish, glandular, sticky and rarely more than a few centimetres high. Apr.–June. *Saxifrage family*

 Fenugreek *pl. 58.* A leafy annual, native of Asia, sometimes grown as a fodder crop and naturalized. Flowers dull whitish, almost stalkless. Pods long, erect (7–10 cm), tapering to a slender beak. Leaves trifoliate. Apr.–May. *Pea family*

 Hare's-Foot Clover *pl. 60.* A small, greyish, hairy annual of sandy ground, easily recognized by its very downy cylindrical flower heads (1–2½ cm long). Individual flowers tiny (3–4 mm), white or pinkish, about half as long as the long-haired calyx teeth. May–Oct. *Pea family*

10

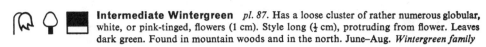

Intermediate Wintergreen   *pl. 87.* Has a loose cluster of rather numerous globular, white, or pink-tinged, flowers (1 cm). Style long ($\frac{1}{2}$ cm), protruding from flower. Leaves dark green. Found in mountain woods and in the north. June–Aug. *Wintergreen family*

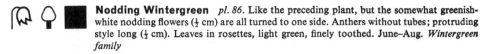

Nodding Wintergreen   *pl. 86.* Like the preceding plant, but the somewhat greenish-white nodding flowers ($\frac{1}{2}$ cm) are all turned to one side. Anthers without tubes; protruding style long ($\frac{1}{2}$ cm). Leaves in rosettes, light green, finely toothed. June–Aug. *Wintergreen family*

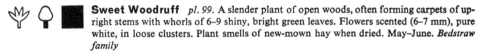

Sweet Woodruff   *pl. 99.* A slender plant of open woods, often forming carpets of upright stems with whorls of 6–9 shiny, bright green leaves. Flowers scented (6–7 mm), pure white, in loose clusters. Plant smells of new-mown hay when dried. May–June. *Bedstraw family*

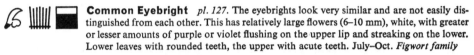

Common Eyebright   *pl. 127.* The eyebrights look very similar and are not easily distinguished from each other. This has relatively large flowers (6–10 mm), white, with greater or lesser amounts of purple or violet flushing on the upper lip and streaking on the lower. Lower leaves with rounded teeth, the upper with acute teeth. July–Oct. *Figwort family*

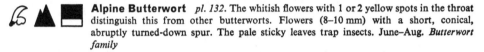

Alpine Butterwort   *pl. 132.* The whitish flowers with 1 or 2 yellow spots in the throat distinguish this from other butterworts. Flowers (8–10 mm) with a short, conical, abruptly turned-down spur. The pale sticky leaves trap insects. June–Aug. *Butterwort family*

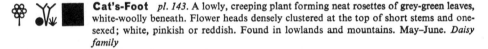

Cat's-Foot   *pl. 143.* A lowly, creeping plant forming neat rosettes of grey-green leaves, white-woolly beneath. Flower heads densely clustered at the top of short stems and one-sexed; white, pinkish or reddish. Found in lowlands and mountains. May–June. *Daisy family*

Dwarf Milfoil   *pl. 147.* A low, very aromatic alpine plant thickly covered with greyish woolly hairs. The lower leaves form almost white rosettes. Flower heads (1 cm) in a dense flat-topped cluster; the involucral bracts have dark brown margins. July–Aug. *Daisy family*

White Butterbur   *pl. 149.* Like the Common Butterbur (*pl. 149*) but flower heads whitish-yellow, and scales on flowering stem green (not purplish). The leaves also differ, being more conspicuously toothed and white-woolly beneath when mature. Mar.–May. *Daisy family*

Greek Lloydia   *pl. 164.* This is found in dry places in Greece and looks like a miniature lily only 5–15 cm tall. Flowers (1$\frac{1}{2}$ cm) white with purplish veins on the outside. Leaves slender, grass-like, shorter than the flowering stem. Mar.–June. *Lily family*

Lloydia   *pl. 164.* Similar to the preceding species, but a plant of rocks and dry pastures in mountains of central Europe. The solitary white flower is veined with purple outside. Basal leaves thread-like, very long. June–Aug. *Lily family*

Ramsons   *pl. 166.* One of many strong-smelling garlics, distinguished from most by the usually paired elliptic leaves. Often thickly covers large areas of woodland. Flowers 1 cm, with 6 narrow pointed petals, borne on a triangular or 2-angled stem. Apr.–June. *Lily family*

Sweet-Scented Solomon's Seal   *pl. 171.* The scented white flowers with green tips are solitary or paired, forming a one-sided arched cluster. The stem is angled, and the oval leaves are regularly placed up the stems. May–June. *Lily family*

Lily-of-the-Valley   *pl. 171.* This well-known plant with its paired glossy leaves and its short one-sided spike of supremely fragrant white bells grows in woods and thickets. The flowers (6–8 mm) are followed by scarlet berries which are poisonous. Apr.–June. *Lily family*

11

Autumn Lady's Tresses *pl. 192.* A small autumn-flowering orchid with a slender spike of tiny, sweet-smelling white flowers arranged in a spiral up the stem. Flowers (4–5 mm across) without a spur, and with a frilled green lip. Leaves in a basal rosette. Aug.–Oct. *Orchid family*

 Creeping Lady's Tresses *pl. 192.* A delicate orchid of shady mountain woods, distinguished from the previous plant by its stalked dark green leaves, often with lighter mottling, and conspicuously netted veins. Flowers creamy-white; lip with a cup-like base and narrow, furrowed, down-turned tip. July–Aug. *Orchid family*.

See also: ALPINE BASTARD TOADFLAX *pl. 6*; SEA SANDWORT *pl. 11*; PINK MEDITERRANEAN CATCHFLY *pl. 15*; MOSS CAMPION *pl. 16*; PURPLE CORYDALIS *pl. 30*; BURNT CANDYTUFT *pl. 36*; MUSKY SAXIFRAGE *pl. 42*; ALPINE MILK-VETCH *pl. 54*; KIDNEY-VETCH *pl. 61*; VARIABLE MILKWORT *pl. 68*; COMMON MILKWORT *pl. 68*; ALPINE ANDROSACE *pl. 91*; SOUTHERN RED BARTSIA *pl. 126*; DWARF EYEBRIGHT *pl. 127*.

Flowers minute · Plant large

 Goat's-Beard *pl. 44.* A tall handsome plant of shady woods in mountains with great branched plumes of tiny creamy flowers, thickly clustered along the branches. Leaves large, two to three times cut into large leaflets (to 14 cm). June–Aug. *Rose family*

Flowers minute · Plant medium

 Great Masterwort, Mountain Sanicle *pl. 83.* A tall upright plant of alpine meadows and woods with tiny white, pinkish or greenish closely clustered flowers, surrounded by numerous spreading coloured bracts (1½–5 cm). Leaves deeply divided into 3–7 coarsely toothed oval lobes. June–Sept. *Umbellifer family*

 Hemlock Water Dropwort *pl. 84.* A robust parsley-smelling plant of watersides, with hollow, ribbed stems and glossy, much-divided leaves. Very poisonous, particularly the large (sometimes exposed) tubers with yellow juice. Umbels (5–10 cm); flowers 2 mm. June–July. *Umbellifer family*

 Water Dropwort *pl. 84.* A greyish, hairless, little-branched plant with soft, hollow stems pinched in at the joints, and similar leaf stalks with a few narrow leaflets. Umbels dense flat-topped (1 cm); spherical in fruit. Fruit angular. June–Sept. *Umbellifer family*

 Fool's Watercress *pl. 85.* A weak, spreading plant of wet places with bright glossy leaves with 4–6 oval-lance-shaped leaflets, somewhat resembling watercress with which it often grows. The small almost stalkless umbels arise opposite the leaves; individual flowers minute (¼ mm). June–Sept. *Umbellifer family*

 Northern Lovage *pl. 85.* A shining, hairless, often tufted plant of sea cliffs in the north, with smooth-ribbed reddish stems. Leaves, smelling of celery when crushed, twice divided into 9 toothed segments. Umbels (4–6 cm) across, individual flowers (2 mm) greenish, white or pink-tinged. July. *Umbellifer family*

 Wild Carrot *pl. 87.* A stiff, usually erect, hairy plant, with the conspicuously divided papery-margined bracts, hanging down from the base of each umbel. Fruit oval (2–4 mm), with spiny ribs alternating with hairy ribs. Leaves much-divided, feathery. May–Oct. *Umbellifer family*

 Gromwell *pl. 105.* An undistinguished plant with erect leafy stems, branched above, bearing very small (3–4 mm), stalkless, cream-coloured tubular flowers. The fruits, though small, are shining white and conspicuous. May–July. *Borage family*

Flowers minute · Plant small

 Silvery Paronychia *pl. 13.* A flat, spreading plant of dry places, easily recognized by its silvery appearance. The dense flower clusters appear silvery-white because of conspicuous bracts, longer than the greenish flowers. The leaves have long silvery stipules. Apr.–June. *Pink family*

Small White Orchid   *pl. 192.* A small orchid of mountain pastures with a dense one-sided spike of half-drooping flowers (2–3 mm). Flowers bell-shaped, the three-lobed lip has a central turned-down lobe; spur not half as long as ovary. June–Aug. *Orchid family*

See also: LESSER SWINE-CRESS *pl. 36.*

GREEN

Flowers large · Plant medium

Greek Hellebore   *pl. 18.* Restricted to Greece and Macedonian Yugoslavia, distinguished by large open green flowers (5–6 cm). The leaves die each winter, new ones appear with the flowers and have 5–9 lance-shaped leaflets. Feb.–Mar. *Buttercup family*

Herb Paris   *pl. 170.* An unmistakable plant of shady woods with a single whorl of 4 large stalkless leaves. Flowers with 4 greenish sepals alternating with 4 narrower yellowish petals. Fruit a black berry, poisonous. May–July. *Lily family*

Snake's Head Iris, Widow Iris   *pl. 174.* A tuberous iris with rush-like, four-ribbed leaves. Flowers greenish or yellowish, with dark brownish or blackish-purple 'falls', borne singly from a large papery sheath. Fruit pods four-ribbed. Mar.–Apr. *Iris family*

Flowers medium · Plant large

Bitter Apple   *pl. 78.* A straggling plant with rough greyish leaves deeply cut into rounded lobes, and small greenish-yellow bell-shaped flowers. Fruits globular (3–8 cm), yellow and green, smooth; poisonous. May–Sept. *Gourd family*

White Bryony   *pl. 79.* A rough, brittle-stemmed herbaceous climber, with long spirally coiled tendrils. Flowers (10–18 mm) greenish-yellow, in clusters; male and female flowers occur on different plants. Leaves coarsely lobed. Berries (5–6 mm) bright, shining red, poisonous. May–Aug. *Gourd family*

Flowers medium · Plant medium

Berry Catchfly   *pl. 15.* A straggling plant with brittle stems and opposite oval leaves. Flowers nodding (1½–2 cm), with a wide calyx and 5 very ragged, greenish-white petals. A shining black berry protrudes from the persisting bell-shaped calyx. July–Aug. *Pink family*

Setterwort, Stinking Hellebore   *pl. 19.* Distinguished by clusters of many drooping, rather small (1–3 cm) greenish flowers with reddish-brown tips. In spring the paler inflorescence contrasts with the dark green over-wintering leaves. Jan.–Mar. *Buttercup family*

Small Tobacco   *pl. 119.* This tobacco is less commonly cultivated in southern Europe than the pink-flowered species. The tubular greenish-yellow flowers (2 cm) are borne in dense terminal clusters. Leaves hairy, shining, oval-heart-shaped. June–Aug. *Nightshade family*

Bath Asparagus   *pl. 169.* Recalling a slender leafless asparagus shoot before coming into flower. Flowers at first greenish-white, becoming yellowish as they dry. Leaves blue-green, narrow, withering before flowering. May–July. *Lily family*

Lizard Orchid   *pl. 190.* One of the strangest of all European orchids with a strong smell of billy-goats, a dull greenish-purple overall. The immensely long lower lip (3–12 cm) is unique; it is spirally coiled in bud and spotted; there are 2 narrow curled side-arms with greenish tips. May–July. *Orchid family.*

See also: DEADLY NIGHTSHADE *pl. 117;* GIANT ORCHID *pl. 190.*

Flowers small · Plant large

Hop *pl. 6.* A handsome rough, climbing plant with deeply lobed, vine-like leaves. Flower clusters green, inconspicuous; the plant often overlooked. Not so when the cone-like 'hops' (3–5 cm) appear, composed of pale green inflated glandular bracts, which give beer its flavouring. June–Sept. *Hemp family*

Hemp *pl. 6.* A tall, strong-smelling, dock-like plant, with neat fan-like leaves cut into 3–9 narrow pointed lobes. Flowers green, in irregular clusters. An important plant, cultivated in the south for its fibre, edible oil, and narcotic resin; often naturalized in waste places. June–Sept. *Hemp family*

Great Water Dock *pl. 9.* A tall, stately and robust dock with a narrow branched spike of greenish flowers, always found in damp places, often in water. The huge tapering leaves may be over 1 m long. Fruits triangular, with 3 large swellings. July–Aug. *Dock family*

Angelica *pl. 85.* A robust aromatic plant with stout stems and many large globular umbels of greenish flowers. Uppermost leaves reduced to large inflated sheaths from which the young umbels break out; lower leaves cut into large segments. July–Aug. *Umbellifer family*

See also: VIRGINIAN POKE *pl. 11.*

Flowers small · Plant medium

Water-Pepper *pl. 8.* A slender, insignificant plant of damp places. Flowers (3–5 mm), greenish or pinkish, covered with yellow glandular dots. The plant is bitter to the taste, hence its name. July–Oct. *Dock family*

Monk's Rhubarb *pl. 9.* Distinguished from other docks by its large leaves (15–40 cm), about as broad as long, with wavy margins. Flowering spike dense and narrow, at first greenish, then reddish-brown. Usually in alpine meadows near habitation. June–Aug. *Dock family*

Curled Dock *pl. 9.* Distinguished by its lower leaves, which are narrowly lance-shaped, with wavy, strongly crisped margins. Flower spike dense, little branched, of closely bunched whorls. Fruit usually with 3 unequal swellings. June–Aug. *Dock family*

Red-Veined Dock *pl. 9.* Despite its name, the commonest form does not have reddish leaf veins. The whorls of flowers are distantly spaced along the many branches, which are mostly leafless. Fruits usually with 1 swelling. June–Aug. *Dock family*

Beet *pl. 10.* A dock-like plant, the wild parent of vegetables such as the Sugar Beet, Beetroot, Mangold, Spinach Beet and Chard. The Sea Beet is a subspecies growing on the shore. It is erect or spreading, with thick shining leaves and long leafless spikes of tiny green flowers. June–Sept. *Goosefoot family*

Good King Henry *pl. 10.* An unattractive weed, with edible leaves, often greyish when young. Distinguished from other and non-edible goosefoots by the large (to 10 cm) triangular, untoothed leaves. Flowers numerous, small, green, in a dense, somewhat leafy spike. June–Sept. *Goosefoot family*

Strawberry Goosefoot *pl. 10.* A quite unmistakable weed with its strawberry-like clusters (1 cm) of fleshy fruits borne in the axils of the upper leaves. Usually a prostrate plant sprawling over the ground, with tiny green flowers. June–July. *Goosefoot family*

Pigweed *pl. 10.* An unattractive plant originally from America, now widely naturalized in Europe. Distinguished from similar docks and goosefoots by plume-like clusters of dry, rather papery flowers intermixed with spiny bracts. July–Sept. *Cockscomb family*

14

Spanish Catchfly   *pl. 15.* The branched leafless clusters of small (3–4 mm) greenish-yellow flowers distinguishes this from other catchflies. Flowers shortly stalked, in whorls forming long narrow spikes. Petals small and not notched. May–Aug. *Pink family*

 Sun Spurge   *pl. 67.* A common annual weed of disturbed ground with a characteristic flat-topped cluster of yellowish spurge flowers. Spurges have a ring of glistening, often moon-shaped glands surrounding several stamens, and a stalked, three-lobed fruit which hangs out. The inflorescence is composed of several branches which divide again, into a second, often three-flowered umbel. Apr.–Nov. *Spurge family*

 Caper Spurge   *pl. 67.* A tall handsome spurge with 4 very regular neat ranks of paired, bluish-green leaves with prominent pale veins. Fruits large (8–20 mm), but unlike true capers are *not* edible. Bracts lance-shaped. May–July. *Spurge family*

 Wood Spurge   *pl. 66.* A stoutish plant of woodlands, recognized by the rosette-like cluster of rather dark green leaves a third of the way up the stem, contrasting with the pale green upper leaves. Bracts 2, fused to one third, forming a cup. Apr.–June. *Spurge family*

 Large Mediterranean Spurge   *pl. 66.* The largest and most spectacular of all European spurges, often forming great clumps. Stems stout, leafy, bearing rounded mop-head clusters of yellowish-green flowers. Bracts fused into a cup. Glands dark reddish-brown or yellowish, with rounded or long horns. Apr.–July. *Spurge family*

 Sea Spurge   *pl. 66.* A distinctive spurge of sandy shores and dunes, with stiff, stout stems and numerous fleshy, pointed leaves. Bracts round flowers fleshy; glands with short horns. May–Sept. *Spurge family*

 Wild Madder   *pl. 98.* A straggling, climbing plant with recurved prickles on 4-angled stems and along margins of the shining leathery leaves. Flowers greenish-yellow or cream-coloured with 5 spreading pointed lobes. Fruit black, fleshy. May–July. *Bedstraw family*

 Cocklebur   *pl. 146.* An unattractive grey-green leafy weed, probably from America. Fruit with very spiny burs (12–15 mm), with numerous hooked spines and 2 horn-like spines at the apex, readily catching in clothing. July–Oct. *Daisy family*

 Spiny Cocklebur   *pl. 146.* Another weed from America with similar burs to those of the preceding plant. However, this is a bushy plant with fearsome, three-pronged, yellow spines. Leaves dark green, white-veined above, white-felted beneath. July–Sept. *Daisy family*

See also: <small>PALE PERSICARIA</small> *pl. 8*; <small>WHITE FALSE HELLEBORINE</small> *pl. 162.*

Flowers small · Plant small

 Alpine Bastard Toadflax   *pl. 6.* A small spreading plant of mountain pastures, with a loose, leafy, one-sided cluster of tiny greenish-yellow flowers. Flowers arising from axils of 3 linear leafy bracts. Leaves narrow, leathery, often yellowish-green. June–Aug. *Sandalwood family*

 Sea Sandwort, Sea Purslane   *pl. 11.* A creeping, mat-forming plant of the seashore, with very fleshy oval, closely overlapping leaves. Flowers (6–10 mm) greenish-white with small widely separated petals. May–Aug. *Pink family*

 Annual Knawel   *pl. 13.* Usually a densely branched, erect or spreading annual of disturbed ground. Flowers green, and petals absent. Leaves (½–1½ cm) awl-shaped. May–Oct. *Pink family*

 Mouse-Tail   *pl. 26.* A little tufted annual with slightly fleshy, grass-like leaves. Flowering stems bear solitary greenish flowers with tube-like petals (3–4 mm). Fruiting heads soon enormously elongated (2½–7 cm), hence its popular name. Mar.–May. *Buttercup family*

Wall Pennywort, Navelwort *pl. 39.* The circular fleshy lower leaves (1½–7 cm), depressed in the centre, give it its popular names. Flowers (7–10 mm) numerous, closely packed in a long spike, greenish-white to pinkish, tubular and drooping. May–July. *Stonecrop family*

Musky Saxifrage *pl. 42.* Flowers usually greenish-yellow, but sometimes red or whitish. Petals widely separated (3–4 mm), with the shorter sepals showing between. A very delicate, tufted plant forming low cushions. July–Aug. *Saxifrage family*

Dogs Mercury *pl. 65.* Common in shady woods where the young shoots appear very early. Plants one-sexed: males more conspicuous, with several erect greenish spikes; females (4–5 mm) at the end of a short branch. Mar.–June. *Spurge family*

Moschatel, Town Hall Clock *pl. 137.* A delicate plant of shady woods, unlike any other, and placed in a family of its own. Flowers in a tight head of 4–6, each flower facing a different direction. Two leaves, deeply lobed. Mar.–May. *Moschatel family*

Pineapple Weed, Rayless Mayweed *pl. 148.* Probably a native of Asia, now found as a weed in most regions of Europe. A quite hairless, apple-scented annual, with distinctive conical heads of greenish-yellow florets, and ray florets absent. May–Nov. *Daisy family*

Musk Orchid *pl. 190.* One of the smallest of the European orchids. The greenish-yellow flowers (4 mm) have a conspicuous three-lobed lip, about as long as the petals. Leaves usually 2, oval, at the base of the flowering stem. May–July. *Orchid family*

Coral-Root Orchid *pl. 192.* A slender, leafless orchid found on rotting vegetation in mountain forests. Flowers greenish-yellow, distinctive because the outer sepals curve downwards close to the whitish, crimson-marked, 3-lobed lip. June–Aug. *Orchid family*

Flowers minute · Plant medium

Large-Leaved Nettle *pl. 6.* Very like other stinging nettles, but upper flowers (male flowers) borne on the upper side of a long, rather broad, swollen branch. Feb.–July. *Nettle family*

Roman Nettle *pl. 6.* A stout, very painfully stinging nettle, more hurtful than the common nettle. Easily identified by its rounded fruiting balls (1 cm), borne on long stalks from the upper leaves. Male flower clusters branched. Apr.–Oct. *Nettle family*

Erect Pellitory-of-the-Wall *pl. 7.* An undistinguished hairy plant of walls or rocks, usually with greenish clusters of tiny axillary flowers, but sometimes appearing reddish. Flower clusters often bunched and forming a continuous leafy spike. June–Oct. *Nettle family*

Fat Hen *pl. 10.* An upright greyish-green mealy weed with often reddish-streaked stems and lance-shaped or diamond-shaped toothed leaves. Flower spike, of numerous tiny green flowers, either broad and branched or narrow and slender. Seeds black. June–Oct. *Goosefoot family*

Field Eryngo *pl. 83.* Usually a pale green, domed, stiff, densely branched, spiny plant. Flower heads greenish, small (1–1½ cm), surrounded by 3–6 narrow spine-tipped bracts two to three times as long; individual flowers whitish-green or pale blue. Lowest leaves with narrow, spiny-toothed segments. June–Sept. *Umbellifer family*

See also: GREAT MASTERWORT, MOUNTAIN SANICLE *pl. 83.*

Flowers minute · Plant small

Procumbent Pearlwort *pl. 13.* A tiny, flat, matted plant with insignificant green flowers, sometimes with yellowish petals. Sepals 4. Fruit splitting into 4 spreading segments. May–Sept. *Pink family*

Lesser Swine-Cress *pl. 36.* A small, spreading, weedy and peppery-smelling plant, introduced from South America. The elongated clusters of unwrinkled fruits distinguishes it from the common Swine-Cress (not illustrated). Petals, if present, white. Jan.–Sept. *Cress family*

 Alpine Asphodel *pl. 162.* A tiny alpine plant of damp pastures and rocks. Flowers minute, greenish, rarely reddish, in elongated clusters (2–8 cm). Leaves grass-like, several, tufted. June–Sept. *Lily family*

RED, PINK, PINKISH-PURPLE

Flowers large · Plant large

 Tree Mallow *pl. 72.* A robust annual or perennial to 3 m, with a thick, woody stem. Flowers 3–4 cm across; epicalyx much longer than calyx. Leaves large (20 cm), rounded, shallowly lobed, often folded fanwise, and wrinkled and downy. Apr.–Sept. *Mallow family*

 Marsh Mallow *pl. 72.* A stout erect plant covered in soft velvety hairs and distinctly greyish in appearance. Flowers pale pink, usually relatively small (2½–5 cm). The plant produces a gum which was used in medicine and confectionery. June–Sept. *Mallow family*

 Eastern Hollyhock *pl. 72.* Like the garden hollyhock, with a tall slender wand-like spikes of pink flowers. Flowers (6–9 cm) often with a yellowish centre. Leaves greyish, woolly-haired, rounded in outline and bluntly lobed. Apr.–July. *Mallow family*

Flowers large · Plant medium

 Ragged Robin *pl. 15.* A plant of wet places, unmistakable with its deeply and raggedly cut narrow pink petals. Leaves narrow and opposite. The whole plant often becomes flushed with reddish-purple. May–June. *Pink family*

 Corn Cockle *pl. 16.* A handsome cornfield weed, recently fast decreasing through modern methods of cultivation. Characteristic are the long, pointed sepals which spread well beyond the reddish-purple petals. Apr.–June. *Pink family*

 Superb Pink *pl. 17.* One of the most striking of the pinks with its deeply cut, feathery petals. There are green spots on the uncut parts of the petals. The flowers are scented. June–Aug. *Pink family*

 Peony *pl. 27.* Magnificent when in flower and later when the coral pink fruits split to reveal shiny blue-black seeds. Distinguished by its leaves which are twice-cut into many lance-shaped and toothed lobes. May–June. *Peony family*

 Biternate Peony *pl. 27.* Very like the preceding species, but leaves differing in being twice-cut into fewer (9–16) oval divisions. which are usually hairless below. Flowers (8–14 cm) usually deep red, very occasionally whitish or yellowish. May–June. *Peony family*

 Corn Poppy *pl. 29.* With modern agricultural methods scarlet fields of poppies are becoming rare, but not so in peasant smallholdings. Distinguished by its rounded flat-topped fruits, and by its spreading bristly hairs on the stems. Petals often black-blotched, deeper red in the south. May–July. *Poppy family*

 Red Horned-Poppy *pl. 29.* Recalling the more widespread Yellow Horned-Poppy (*pl. 29*) of coasts, but flowers scarlet to orange. Both species have glaucous leaves and very long pods (10–20 cm). The pods of this plant are bristly-haired. May–June. *Poppy family*

 Large-Flowered Mallow *pl. 72.* A handsome, upright plant with large flowers (5–7 cm) crowded together at the tip of the leafy stem. Minute star-shaped hairs cover stem and calyx, but the finely ribbed fruit is hairless. Leaves variable, rounded in outline, shallowly or deeply lobed. June–Sept. *Mallow family*

 Annual Mallow *pl. 72.* A tall annual to 1 m with large bright pink flowers (5–7 cm). Leaves rounded, shallow-lobed. Nutlets of fruit covered by a distinctive disk-like cap, unlike other species. Apr.–July. *Mallow family*

 Mallow-Leaved Bindweed *pl. 100.* Often climbing up through scrub but as often found sprawling over the ground. The attractive funnel-shaped flowers (3–4½ cm) are long-stalked and solitary. Lower leaves heart-shaped; uppermost deeply cut into unequal narrow lobes, softly silky-haired. Apr.–Aug. *Convolvulus family*

 Elegant Bindweed *pl. 100.* Very like the preceding species but restricted to the Balkans. The leaves and stems are covered in dense shiny silvery hairs giving the plant a whitish appearance. Most leaves deeply divided into narrow segments. Apr.–July. *Convolvulus family*

 Sea Bindweed *pl. 100.* An unexpected plant to find pushing up through loose sand on the strand above high water mark. It has creeping underground stems and rounded fleshy leaves. May–Oct. *Convolvulus family*

 Pink Everlasting *pl. 151.* A distinctive slender, greyish annual of the south, with bright shining pink flower heads. The florets are yellowish and the pink colour is due to the inner, longer, spreading involucral bracts. Outer bracts, silvery-brown, papery, 'everlasting'. June–July. *Daisy family*

 Musk Thistle *pl. 152.* A stout, spiny thistle with very large nodding, reddish-purple fragrant flower heads. Involucral bracts with sharp, stout spiny tips. Stem directly below flower heads unwinged and spine-free but winged and spiny lower down. June–Sept. *Daisy family*

 Woolly Thistle *pl. 154.* A magnificent, robust thistle, distinguished by the woolly cobweb-like hairs covering the involucral bracts. Leaves fearsomely spiny, with 2 rows of spiny lobes, one pointing upwards and one downwards. July–Aug. *Daisy family*

 Milk-Thistle, Holy Thistle *pl. 155.* The large rosettes of broad shining green, spiny-lobed leaves, marbled with white veins, are distinctive before flowering. Flower heads reddish-purple (4–8 cm), extremely spiny, with outcurved, needle-shaped spiny involucral bracts. June–Aug. *Daisy family*

 Scotch Thistle, Cotton Thistle *pl. 155.* A striking, tall, branched, white-felted thistle with conspicuously winged upper stems and branches. Flower heads rather small (3–5 cm), pale purple. Involucral bracts woolly-haired. Over-wintering rosettes large, handsome, white-felted. June–Sept. *Daisy family*

 Southern Scotch Thistle *pl. 155.* A very stout, very spiny, white-felted plant like the preceding species, but involucral bracts with abruptly down-curved, purple, spiny tips. The spiny wings of the stems are much narrower. July–Aug. *Daisy family*

 Wig Knapweed *pl. 156.* An attractive knapweed with several flower heads with spreading marginal florets and distinctive involucral bracts. Involucre oval (1½–2 cm long); bracts with long slender recurved apices with numerous brown comb-like bristles. Middle and upper leaves with heart-shaped or rounded base. July–Aug. *Daisy family*

 Giant Knapweed *pl. 156.* The huge solitary reddish-purple flower head (5–11 cm) borne on stout almost leafless stems is unmistakable. Involucre with conspicuous jagged papery-margined rusty-brown bracts. Leaves very large, oval, white-woolly beneath. July–Aug. *Daisy family*

Martagon Lily   *pl. 167.* A very beautiful lily with pink, or pale purple, thick, curved-back petals with dark purple swellings on the underside. Leaves mostly in whorls of 4–10, the uppermost may be alternate. June–July. *Lily family*

 Red Lily   *pl. 166.* A rare Turk's cap lily of rocky hills on the French and Italian Rivieras which must on no account be disturbed if found. It is a very strong-smelling plant. May–June. *Lily family*

 Snake's Head, Fritillary   *pl. 167.* Quite unmistakable with its beautiful nodding chequered flowers (rarely white) with a tear-drop gland at the base of each petal within. This plant should never be picked or damaged. Apr.–May. *Lily family*

 Eyed Tulip   *pl. 168.* This scarlet tulip, with its characteristic black blotch surrounded by a yellow band at the base of each petal, is a native of Turkey. Occasionally naturalized in fields in the south where the bulb lies below the furrow of the plough. Apr. *Lily family*

 Field Gladiolus   *pl. 176.* Often occurring in abundance in spring cornfields in the south and making a splash of pink in the young corn. Distinguished by the uppermost petal which is twice as broad as, and separated from, the shorter side petals. Apr.–June. *Iris family*

 Eastern Gladiolus   *pl. 176.* Very like the previous species but flowers darker purple, and the 3 upper petals all much the same size and close-pressed to each other. Seeds flattened, winged. Apr.–May. *Iris family*

See also: COLUMBINE *pl. 27*; BURNING BUSH *pl. 67*; LARGE SNAPDRAGON *pl. 121*; ASPHODEL *pl. 163*

Flowers large. Plant small

 Red Hottentot Fig   *pl. 11.* A striking South African plant, now well established on the Mediterranean seashore. It forms extensive mats of triangular-sectioned fleshy leaves, covered for many weeks by the brilliant flowers (12 cm). Apr.–July. *Mesembryanthemum family*

 Crown Anemone   *pl. 21.* One of the harbingers of spring in the Eastern Mediterranean. The flowers occur in many colour forms locally, from red, blue, pink to white. Distinguished by the much-cut, leaf-like bracts below the flowers. Feb.–Apr. *Buttercup family*

 Scarlet Anemone   *pl. 21.* Like the previous species occurring in many colour forms, but distinguished by the 3 lance-shaped bracts below the flower which are entire or three-lobed. Petals 8–9, often paler at the base. Feb.–Apr. *Buttercup family*

 Broad-Leaved Anemone   *pl. 21.* Very like the preceding species, with similar bracts below the flowers, but petals more numerous (12–19), distinctly narrower and separating from each other in full flower. Feb.– Apr. *Buttercup family*

 Small Pasque Flower   *(not illustrated)* Flowers drooping and never properly opening, varying regionally from purple, reddish-violet, greenish-yellow to white. Fruits with long conspicuous feathery styles. Leaves densely silky when young. May. *Buttercup family*

 Stemless Thistle   *pl. 154.* Distinguished by its stalkless flower heads arising from the centre of a rosette of thistle leaves; sometimes short-stalked. Flower heads (2–5 cm) with purplish hairless, spine-tipped bracts. July–Sept. *Daisy family*

 Plume Knapweed   *pl. 156.* A plant of alpine pastures with russet-coloured involucral bracts with a long slender arched apex with comb-like bristles along its length. Flower heads usually solitary (4–6 cm) with wide-spreading marginal florets. Upper leaves strongly toothed. July–Aug. *Daisy family*

Cone Knapweed *pl. 157.* Distinguished by its conspicuous shining brown, papery involucre, recalling a pine-cone. Flower heads solitary. Leaves green, white-felted beneath, usually pinnately cut into narrow lobes. May–Aug. *Daisy family*

 Merendera *pl. 163.* An autumn-flowering plant of mountain pastures similar to an autumn crocus, but distinguished by the petals, which are not fused together at their base, only closely pressed together. Leaves narrow, grooved, usually not seen till spring. Aug.–Sept. *Lily family*

 Autumn Crocus, Meadow Saffron *pl. 163.* Often flowers in great numbers in damp meadows in autumn. Distinguished from a true crocus by the 6 stamens. Leaves 3, only appearing in spring, shining, elliptic, often with a fruit at their centre. Aug.–Sept. *Lily family*

 Bulbocodium *pl. 163.* Very like the previous species but flowering in spring in mountain pastures as the young leaves appear. Petals at first hooked together at the base, soon becoming free and spreading in a star. Leaves 3, grooved. Feb.–May. *Lily family*

See also: DWARF IRIS *pl. 175*; PYGMY IRIS *pl. 176*.

Flowers medium · Plant large

 Policeman's Helmet *pl. 70.* A striking fetid plant, with thick almost translucent stems, and pink two-lipped flowers with a stout sac-like spur narrowed to a slender tucked-under tip. Fruits explosive. A native of the Himalaya now spreading rapidly. June–Sept. *Balsam family*

 Silkweed *pl. 99.* A robust plant from North America with milky juice, grown as an ornamental and sometimes self-seeding. Flowers sweet-scented, dull purple or white. From each flower project 5 hood-like lobes with an incurved horn. June–Aug. *Milkweed family*

 Great Marsh Thistle *pl. 153.* A mildly spiny thistle of mountain woods and damp pastures, with dense clusters of several purple flower heads. Bracts of involucre not spiny, often curved and black-tipped. Leaf blades decurrent, bristly. July–Aug. *Daisy family*

Flowers medium · Plant medium

 Flower of Jove *pl. 14.* This cheerfully named campion is a shaggy-haired greyish-white plant which sends up flat-topped clusters of purplish, scarlet or rarely white flowers. Petals deeply notched, sometimes further divided; calyx shaggy-haired. June–Aug. *Pink family*

 Red German Catchfly *pl. 14.* Unlike any other plant in having brownish sticky stems below each pair of upper leaves. Flowers (2 cm) varying from reddish-purple to white, arising in whorls from the upper leaves and forming a lax cluster. The pale scales on the petals are often conspicuous. May–June. *Pink family*

 Red Campion *pl. 15.* Sometimes a clearing in a wood can be brilliant with these flowers. A handsome, upright, rather hairy plant with oval leaves, and often reddish stems. Flowers one-sexed (1½–2 cm), rose-pink or sometimes white. Petals deeply notched. May–Sept. *Pink family*

 Soapwort *pl. 16.* The handsome terminal clusters of pink or flesh-coloured flowers (2½–3 cm) are pleasantly scented. Conspicuous calyx often pinkish. Leaves oval-elliptic. Still used to cleanse delicate coloured fabrics. June–Sept. *Pink family*

 Carthusian Pink *pl. 17.* Distinguished by dense clusters of many or few bright pink purple or rarely white flowers; usually without green bracts surrounding the flower cluster. Leaves linear, joined together in a long sheath, often tufted. June–Oct. *Pink family*

Fringed Pink   *pl. 17.* Petals cut to about half their length into a fringe of narrow teeth, leaving a more or less oval uncut central blade. Flowers fragrant, pink or rarely white, often marked with brown-purple. Epicalyx long-pointed. May–Aug. *Pink family*

 Wood Pink   *pl. 17.* A densely tufted, rather variable pink usually with scentless flowers and toothed or entire hairless petals. Calyx smooth, rather long (1¼–3 cm); epicalyx scales oval, blunt, leathery, a quarter as long as calyx. June–Aug. *Pink family*

 Pheasant's Eye   *pl. 24.* The shining scarlet flowers opening wide in the sun are unmistakable; petals usually black-blotched. Leaves finely cut into narrow lobes, bright green and feathery. Fruits in a tight cylindrical head. May–Aug. *Buttercup family*

 Stock   *pl. 32.* A handsome plant of sea cliffs and walls etc. inland, the parent of several strains of garden stocks. Flowers very sweet-scented, bright reddish-purple or white. Leaves narrow, usually grey-haired; stem stout. Mar.–June. *Cress family*

 Sea Stock   *pl. 33.* A bushy, grey, woolly-haired plant found by the sea, with conspicuous pale purple flowers (2–2½ cm). Upper leaves entire with crinkly margins, lower often deeply cut. Pods long, narrow, without conspicuous horns at the tip. May–Sept. *Cress family*

 Coral-Wort   *pl. 34.* Easily distinguished by the tiny purplish bulbils in the axils of the upper leaves. Flowers pale lilac to white (12–18 mm). Lower leaves deeply cut into lance-shaped lobes. Pale underground stem covered with fleshy scales. Apr.–June. *Cress family*

 Five-Leaved Coral-Wort   *pl. 34.* Distinguished by the leaves, which are cut into 3–5 lance-shaped leaflets which fan out like the fingers of a hand. Flowers violet or pink, in rather dense clusters. Apr.–June. *Cress family*

 Lady's Smock   *pl. 34.* A very variable plant of damp meadows with pale pink, violet or white flowers (1½–2 cm). Leaves with several pairs of leaflets, those of the basal leaves oval or rounded, those of the upper leaves narrow lance-shaped. Apr.–June. *Cress family*

 Honesty   *pl. 35.* Its seed pod is unlike any other – rounded in outline and wafer-thin when dry, like a monocle. The closely related Perennial Honesty (not illustrated) differs in its elliptic fruits, and stalked upper leaves; it is more commonly found. Apr.–June. *Cress family*

 Water Avens   *pl. 45.* The nodding flowers with rather orange-pink petals, scarcely longer than the reddish-purple sepals, are quite distinctive. Fruits soon conspicuous, with long crooked styles. Lower leaves have 3–6 pairs of oval leaflets. May–July. *Rose family*

 Marsh Cinquefoil   *pl. 46.* An unusual-looking plant of marshes and bogs, with dull reddish-purple flowers (2–3 cm), the coloured sepals much longer than the petals. Leaves carried above the water, divided into 5–7 oblong coarsely toothed leaflets. June–Aug. *Rose family*

 Earth-Nut Pea   *pl. 56.* A hairless, climbing pea which has swollen edible root tubers. Flowers (1½–2 cm) crimson, sweet-scented, 2–7, in a stalked cluster much longer than the leaves. Leaves with 2 fine-pointed leaflets and a simple or branched tendril. June–Aug. *Pea family*

 Everlasting Pea   *pl. 56.* The clusters of reddish-carmine or pink flowers are very conspicuous and contrast with the greyish-green foliage. The stems and leaf stalks have wide wings. Leaves with a single pair of leaflets and a branched tendril. June–Aug. *Pea family*

Crimson Pea   *pl. 56.* A slender scrambler; upper leaves have 2–4 pairs of narrow leaflets and a branched tendril; lowest leaves undivided. Flowers (1½–2 cm) with bright reddish-purple standards and often paler bluish-purple wings and keel. Apr.–June. *Pea family*

Spring Pea   *pl. 56.* A hairless, non-climber of woods and thickets. Flowers (1½–2 cm) at first purple, then blue and finally brownish-purple. Leaves with 2–4 pairs of large broadly oval, long-pointed shining leaflets. Apr.–June. *Pea family*

 Sea Pea   *pl. 56.* A hairless, creeping, bluish-green pea of the littoral, with angled stems. Flower clusters conspicuous, borne on stalks shorter than the leaves. Flowers 1½–2 cm. Leaflets oval, 2–5 pairs; tendrils simple or branched. July–Aug. *Pea family*

 Pea   *pl. 56.* Probably the wild parent of the Garden Pea. Distinguished by large stipules, even larger than the leaflets. Flowers variable, often pink or violet, with white, or black-purple wings. Apr.–June. *Pea family*

 Round-Leaved Restharrow   *pl. 57.* A beautiful plant with relatively large (1½–2 cm) pink or rarely whitish flowers in a dense cluster, and distinctive trifoliate leaves. Leaflets almost circular, conspicuously toothed, sticky and hairy. May–Aug. *Pea family*

 Italian Sainfoin   *pl. 62.* An attractive plant, particularly when grown in fields as a fodder crop (in Sicily, for example). Flowers large (2 cm), in long-stalked oval heads. Pods distinctive, with 2–4 rounded joints covered with rough projections. Apr.–July. *Pea family*

 Alpine Sainfoin   *pl. 61.* A plant of alpine meadows and rocks with flowers from red-dish-purple, violet, to whitish-yellow, borne in an elongated, one-sided cluster. Leaves with 5–10 pairs of leaflets, and a terminal one. Pod with 2–5 winged constrictions. July–Aug. *Pea family*

 Mountain Sainfoin   *pl. 59.* Flowers rather large (to 1½ cm), pink with purple veins, or crimson, in a dense cluster. Keel of flowers longer than the standard. Leaves with 3–8 pairs of narrow leaflets. Pod roundish, with a network of pits on the sides. July–Aug. *Pea family*

 Mountain Cranesbill   *pl. 63.* A leafy, downy plant with numerous rosy-purple paired flowers (1½ cm) in a loose branched cluster. Petals deeply notched. Leaves with rounded blades, cut to two-thirds into 5–9 lobes, uppermost leaves often three-lobed. June–Oct. *Geranium family*

 Rock Cranesbill   *pl. 64.* A handsome cranesbill with blood-red or carmine flowers (2½ cm) opening flat, conspicuously revealing the projecting stamens and style. Sepals red-flushed, inflated, long-pointed. Leaves pale green, neatly divided in broadly oval, toothed lobes. July–Aug. *Geranium family*

 Pink Evening Primrose   *pl. 81.* A shrubby native of America, sometimes naturalized. The small pink flowers (1½ cm) are solitary, and the fruits club-shaped, eight-angled. June–July. *Willow-Herb family*

 Rosebay Willow-Herb, Fireweed   *pl. 80.* A handsome plant often abundant in clearings in woods, making a brilliant sheet of colour. Flowers (2–3 cm) with 4 petals, protruding stamens and a down-curved 4-pronged style. Fruits slender, bursting to produce rows of silky plumed seeds. June–Sept. *Willow-Herb family*

 Great Hairy Willow-Herb   *pl. 81.* Another handsome willow-herb with large, deep rosy-purple flowers (½–2½ cm) and robust leafy stems, growing by watersides. Leaves lance-shaped (to 12 cm), usually opposite and half-clasping the stem. Seeds plumed. July–Aug. *Willow-Herb family*

 Bastard Balm   *pl. 109.* A hairy, strong-smelling plant with large (3½–4½ cm) handsome, pink, funnel-shaped flowers with two lips. Flowers sometimes white, spotted with pink. Calyx two-lipped, with a broad upper lip and three-lobed lower lip. May–July. *Mint family*

22

Tuberous Jerusalem Sage *pl. 110.* A robust plant with numerous tight whorls of pink flowers crowded towards the top, but widely separated lower down. Calyx teeth bristly. Lower leaves triangular-heart-shaped, coarsely toothed, stalked and nearly hairless. June–July. *Mint family*

 Spotted Dead-Nettle *pl. 111.* Flowers rather large (2½–3 cm), pinkish-purple, with a curved tube longer than the calyx and with a ring of hairs within; upper lip hairy round margin. Leaves often blotched with white. Apr.–Oct. *Mint family*

 Large Red Dead-Nettle *pl. 111.* The dull purple or pink flowers are comparatively large (2½–3 cm); distinguished from similar species by the hairless anthers. The arched upper lip has a conspicuous margin of hairs. Stem and leaves nearly hairless. May–June. *Mint family*

 Downy Woundwort *pl. 112.* So thickly covered with silky hairs that it often appears whitish. Flowers in dense whorls, pale rose-purple, the upper lip densely woolly-haired. Calyx woolly-haired, with triangular, bristle-tipped teeth. June–Sept. *Mint family*

 Large-Flowered Calamint *pl. 114.* The largest-flowered of the calamints, with few-flowered axillary clusters of reddish-purple, tubular, two-lipped flowers (2½–4 cm). Calyx tubular, up-curved, about half as long as the corolla tube. Leaves coarsely toothed, sparsely hairy, aromatic. June-Sept. *Mint family*

 Wild Basil *pl. 115.* Distinguished from similar species by globular terminal whorls of flowers (1½–2 cm) with few widely separated lower whorls. Calyx tube curved, woolly-haired, not swollen at the base, with few or no hairs within and 13-veined without. An unbranched, softly hairy plant. July–Sept. *Mint family*

 Scopolia *pl. 116.* Like the Deadly Nightshade, but less robust with brownish-purple or yellow tubular flowers, olive-green within. And the fruits are quite different; they are dry, globular capsules, surrounded by the much-enlarged calyx. Apr.–June. *Nightshade family*

 Large Tobacco *pl. 119.* Widely cultivated as a field crop in southern Europe, readily distinguished by its large green leaves which are harvested and dried for tobacco. Native of South America. The large handsome pink or purple tubular flowers are in dense terminal clusters. July–Aug. *Nightshade family*

 Weasel's Snout *pl. 122.* A slender hairy annual with a leafy cluster of stalkless small pinkish-purple, yellow-throated snapdragon flowers (1–1½ cm) with narrow calyx lobes as long as or longer than the corolla. June–Sept. *Figwort family*

 Foxglove *pl. 125.* The most beautiful of all European foxgloves. The densely hairy thimble-shaped flowers are conspicuously spotted within. Leaves forming an over-wintering rosette of silvery-green, softly hairy leaves. Poisonous; still widely used as a source of a drug, digitalin. May–Sept. *Figwort family*

 Field Cow-Wheat *pl. 128.* A very striking semi-parasite with a dense terminal head of coloured fringed bracts and 2 ranks of tubular, two-lipped, pinkish-purple flowers (2–2½ cm) with orange throats. Lower leaves narrow lance-shaped, entire, the upper toothed and gradually changing to the fringed bracts. May–Aug. *Figwort family*

 Woolly Burdock *pl. 152.* Easily distinguished from the other burdocks by the cobweb-like hairs stretching between the hooked bracts of the involucre. A robust almost shrubby plant with large broad leaves which are white-cottony beneath. June–Sept. *Daisy family*

 Syrian Thistle *pl. 153.* Distinguished by the circlet of extremely spiny, purple-flushed leaves which surround the purple flower heads. A stiff erect annual with broadly lobed, spiny-toothed, white-veined leaves. Apr.–July. *Daisy family*

Grey Thistle *pl. 153*. A whitish, densely woolly-haired annual with winged upper stems, and dense clusters of 1–4 purple flower heads encircled by much longer, very spiny leaves. Leaves narrow, with long yellow spines and shorter bristles. June–Aug. *Daisy family*

 Tuberous Thistle *pl. 153*. Distinguished by its solitary dark reddish-purple heads, borne on long, grooved, cottony stems, leafless above the middle. Leaves green, with bristly margins (not spiny), the lower long-stalked and deeply double-lobed. June–Aug. *Daisy family*

 Saw-Wort *pl. 155*. Flower heads reddish-purple in a branched, often dense, flat-topped cluster. Involucre narrow, ovoid (1½–2 cm long); bracts purplish with downy margins; florets all similar. Leaves entire or pinnately cut into narrow lobes. July–Oct. *Daisy family*

 Hollow-Stemmed Asphodel *pl. 163*. A distinctive, rush-like plant, with slender branched stems and pale pink starry flowers ranged along the branches. Flowers (2 cm) with a darker pink midvein. Stems hollow; leaves long, narrow. Apr.–May. *Lily family*

 Wavy-Leaved Monkey Orchid *pl. 187*. A handsome orchid with a basal rosette of long narrow, pale wavy-edged leaves, and a compact conical head of pink, spotted flowers. The helmet of narrow pointed petals is conspicuously veined with darker purple. The lip is man-like with 'arms' and 'legs'. Mar.–May. *Orchid family*

 Lady Orchid *pl. 187*. Has very dark blackish-purple buds and a reddish-purple helmet to the flowers. Lower lip with raised purple swellings, and 2 linear basal lobes and 2 broader, finely toothed, apical lobes with a tooth between; spur short, half as long as ovary. Apr.–June. *Orchid family*

 Jersey Orchid *pl. 187*. An orchid of marshy meadows, with dark pinkish-purple unspotted flowers, the lip with 2 lateral lobes folded downwards against each other revealing the pale centre. Spur horizontal or upward-pointing, swollen and notched at tip. Bracts reddish-purple. Mar.–June. *Orchid family*

 Broad-Leaved Marsh Orchid *pl. 187*. Flowers reddish- to lilac-purple in a dense oval cluster. The lip is shallowly 3-lobed with a wavy margin, strongly marked with dark dots and lines. Spur stout, downward-pointing. A plant of damp places. May–July. *Orchid family*

 Giant Orchid *pl. 190*. A massive orchid with very dense cylindrical clusters of reddish-violet to dull greenish-purple flowers and similar-coloured large leafy bracts. The large lip has 2 sickle-shaped side lobes and a deeply divided middle lobe with a toothed or fringed margin. Feb.–Apr. *Orchid family*

 Marsh Helleborine *pl. 191*. A rather wiry-stemmed orchid, hairy above and with a somewhat one-sided loose spike of reddish-purple flowers. Petals greenish outside, brownish within, streaked with purple. Lip broad, hinged, pale, with a yellow spot and reddish veins. June–Aug. *Orchid family*

 Red Helleborine *pl. 191*. The bright pink petals remain closely pressed together. The short lip is inconspicuous, outlined with red-violet and bearing crested yellow ridges. Leaves lance-shaped, pointed; stem glandular-hairy above. May–July. *Orchid family*

See also: NOTTINGHAM CATCHFLY *pl. 15*; LARKSPUR *pl. 20*; NARCISSUS-FLOWERED ANEMONE *pl. 22*; ORANGE BALSAM *pl. 70*; PURPLE VIPERS BUGLOSS *pl. 106*; SILVER SAGE *pl. 113*; GRATIOLE *pl. 124*; RUSTY FOXGLOVE *pl. 125*; SPANISH RUSTY FOXGLOVE *pl. 125*; CLOVE-SCENTED BROOMRAPE *pl. 131*; GREATER BROOMRAPE *pl. 131*.

Flowers medium · Plant small

 Pink Claytonia *pl. 11*. A North American plant, sometimes naturalized in north-west Europe. Quite hairless, with rather fleshy paired upper leaves, and bearing a lax cluster of pink or white flowers with deeply notched petals. Sepals 2. Apr.–July. *Purslane family*

 Sad Stock *pl. 33*. The flowers may be dingy rust-coloured or dull violet. The rosy-purple form with grey-green leaves which grows on cliffs is attractive. Fruit long and slender, with or without terminal horns. Mar.–May. *Cress family*

 Pink Cinquefoil *pl. 46*. A lovely dwarf, tufted, woody-based alpine, with silvery-haired trifoliate leaves and solitary pink flowers. The only pink-flowered European member of this genus, though white and pale pink forms are not uncommon, particularly on lime-free soils. July–Aug. *Rose family*

 Asparagus Pea *pl. 61*. Usually spreading, with trifoliate leaves and solitary, comparatively large dark red-purple flowers, often with a blackish keel. Pods unmistakable: cylindrical with 4 broad wavy wings often as broad as the pod itself. Cultivated forms have edible pods. Mar.–May. *Pea family*

 Small Italian Sainfoin *pl. 62*. A spreading annual with pinnate leaves and long stalked globular clusters of pinkish-purple pea-like flowers (1½–2 cm). Calyx usually less than a third the length of petals. Leaflets 4–8 pairs, oblong-wedge-shaped, often with dense adpressed hairs beneath. Apr.–July. *Pea family*

 Bloody Cranesbill *pl. 63*. Has large solitary bright crimson-purple flowers (2½–3 cm) with slightly notched petals (rarely pink or white). Leaves small (5 cm), with rounded blades deeply cut to the base into 5–7 narrow lobes, which are often further cut. June–Sept. *Geranium family*

 Least Primrose *pl. 91*. One of the most charming of all European primulas with solitary, almost stalkless flowers arising from a much smaller rosette of tiny toothed, shining, wedge-shaped leaves. Flowers (1½–3 cm); petals deeply notched, throat yellowish. June–July. *Primrose family*

 Red Alpine Primrose *pl. 91*. Like the following plant, but flowers bright purple with a white 'eye' in clusters of 1–3 on short stems. Leaves rounded, toothed and very sticky on both sides. Alps and Pyrenees. Apr.–July. *Primrose family*

 Entire-Leaved Alpine Primrose *pl. 91*. A delicate alpine plant of rocks and pastures with 1–3 flowers borne on a short, often reddish stem. Flowers (about 2 cm) bright pink to lilac. Leaves bright green, oval, untoothed with hairy margins, in a rosette. May–Aug. *Primrose family*

 Alpine Bells *pl. 91*. A delicate alpine plant with a terminal cluster of drooping primula-like flowers. Leaves forming a basal cluster, long-stalked, rounded, with 5–7 shallow rounded and toothed lobes. June–July. *Primrose family*

 Sowbread *pl. 92*. Scentless, pale pink or almost white flowers appear in autumn before the leaves, unlike any other species of cyclamen. The flap-like projections of the 5-sided throat are distinctive. Silvery-mottled leaves persist throughout the summer. Aug.–Nov. *Primrose family*

 Common Cyclamen *pl. 92*. The commonest summer-flowering species. Flowers very sweet-scented, appearing with the leaves and with a rounded, not angular, throat. Leaves reddish-purple beneath, usually entire, and often silver-blotched. June–Oct. *Primrose family*

 Greek Cyclamen *pl. 92*. A very handsome autumn-flowering species with reddish-pink flowers with a plum-coloured basal blotch and conspicuous ear-like flaps. Leaves beautifully marbled with pale grey; margins horny-toothed. Oct.–Nov. *Primrose family*

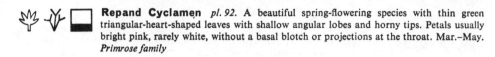

Repand Cyclamen *pl. 92.* A beautiful spring-flowering species with thin green triangular-heart-shaped leaves with shallow angular lobes and horny tips. Petals usually bright pink, rarely white, without a basal blotch or projections at the throat. Mar.–May. *Primrose family*

Purple Gentian *pl. 97.* A rather uncommon gentian of alpine meadows with stout erect stems and a cluster of barrel-shaped, purplish-red flowers. The flowers are yellowish at the base, striped and spotted with green within, or rarely yellowish throughout. They rarely open widely. July–Aug. *Gentian family*

German Gentian *pl. 96.* Gentianellas are distinguished from gentians by a fringe of long hairs in the throat or on the petal margins. Distinguished from the Field Gentian by its larger flowers, twice as long as the calyx, and 5 (not 4) petals. May–Oct. *Gentian family*

Bellardia *pl. 126.* The 2-lipped flowers are borne in a dense 4-sided pyramidal spike among broad overlapping bracts. Flowers pink with varying amounts of yellow; sometimes yellow throughout. Calyx inflated, bell-shaped, deeply 2-lobed. Apr.–July. *Figwort family*

Toothwort *pl. 130.* An unusual pale, almost colourless parasite found growing on roots of trees or hazel. Flowers drooping (1½–2 cm), often tinged dull purple. Green leaves absent; only scales present on arched then erect stem. Mar.–May. *Broomrape family*

Toothed Orchid *pl. 187.* Its fragrant flowers, from pink to white and conspicuously spotted, are tightly packed in a rounded head. Its lip, which is 4-lobed, has 2 broad side lobes and a deeply cleft wedge-shaped central lobe, often with a tooth between. Mar.–May. *Orchid family*

Soldier or **Military Orchid** *pl. 189.* Flowers man-like with darker 'arms' and 'legs' and a paler whitish and spotted 'body'. Helmet an unusual grey-ashy colour, flushed rose or violet. Leaves flat, not wavy-edged. Apr.–June. *Orchid family*

Spotted Orchid *pl. 189.* The commonest orchid in north and central Europe. Lip conspicuously three-lobed, the lobes all more or less similar in size, boldly marked with curved reddish lines. Spur thick. Basal leaves broad, blunt, usually spotted. May–July. *Orchid family*

Southern Serapias *pl. 189.* Restricted in its distribution to France, Italy, Yugoslavia. Distinguished by its pale lip, which is broadly heart-shaped at the base where it is attached to the 2 darker lateral lobes. Helmet reddish-violet. Mar.–Apr. *Orchid family*

Long-Lipped Serapias *pl. 189.* The tongue-like flowers, hanging between long narrow bracts flushed with reddish-brown, are quite unmistakable. Upper petals merging into a helmet; lip with 2 dark, nearly parallel humps in its throat. Apr.–June. *Orchid family*

See also: YELLOW CYTINUS *pl. 8*; HEPATICA *pl. 20*; OVAL-LEAVED CROWFOOT *pl. 25*; GLACIER CROWFOOT *pl 26*; VIRGINIA STOCK *pl. 32*; HARE'S-FOOT CLOVER *pl. 60*; PRIMROSE *pl. 90*; HYACINTH *pl. 171*; ELDER-FLOWERED ORCHID *pl. 189.*

Flowers small · Plant large

Virginian Poke, Pokeweed *pl. 11.* A coarse plant (1–3 m) with reddish stems and large leaves. Flowers pinkish or greenish in dense cylindrical spikes in angles of the branches. Fruit a cluster of fleshy berries, first red then purple; used for colouring and dyeing. June–Oct. *Pokeweed family*

Purple Loosestrife *pl. 79.* A handsome plant of wet places with long slender spikes of bright rosy-purple flowers. Flowers 1–1½ cm, petals 6, stamens 12. Leaves paired or in whorls of 3, lance-shaped, half-clasping the stem. June–Sept. *Loosestrife family*

26

Flowers small · Plant medium

Pale Persicaria *pl. 8.* A weed of disturbed ground or damp places with pale pink or greenish-white flowers in dense cylindrical spikes. Distinguished from other species by scattered yellow glands on the flower stalks and petals. Leaves often black-blotched. July–Sept. *Dock family*

Amphibious Bistort *pl. 8.* The plant illustrated is the aquatic form, with floating, stalked and hairless leaves. Terrestrial forms of damp places have erect stems with broad, lance-shaped, stalkless, roughly hairy leaves. July–Aug. *Dock family*

Deptford Pink *pl. 17.* The small rose-red flowers (8 mm) are borne in dense clusters of 2–10 and are surrounded by narrow leaf-like bracts. Petals white-spotted, toothed. Calyx and whole plant hairy, which is unusual in the pink family. June–Aug. *Pink family*

Sea Rocket *pl. 37.* A fleshy plant of coasts, often found growing in sand as near to the high tide mark as any. Flowers variable, from violet, to pink, or white, sweet-scented. Fruit of 2 sections, the upper mitre-shaped June–Sept. *Cress family*

Shaggy Vetch *pl. 55.* Distinguished from the Bush Vetch (not illustrated) by the calyx which has a small rounded swelling at the base. Also the claw (the basal stalk-like part) of the standard is twice as long as the blade of the standard. Very variable, with violet, purple or blue flowers (12–16 mm). June–Aug. *Pea family*

Reddish Tufted Vetch *pl. 55.* Recalling the Bush Vetch (not illustrated), but distinguished by larger reddish flowers (1–1½ cm), with blackish-purple tips. Flower clusters short-stalked, the whole shorter than the leaves. Fruit hairy. Mar.–June. *Pea family*

Common Vetch *pl. 55.* A variable trailing or climbing plant, often grown as a forage crop. It has almost stalkless purple, violet or bi-coloured flowers in ones or twos in the axils of the upper leaves. Leaves with 4–7 pairs of leaflets and a branched tendril. Apr.–Sept. *Pea family*

Grass Vetchling *pl. 55.* Difficult to spot amongst the grass, until it comes into flower. Flowers small (1½ cm), crimson. Leaves narrow lance-shaped, grass-like, without leaflets or tendrils. May–July. *Pea family*

Black Pea *pl. 56.* An erect, non-climbing plant without tendrils. The violet or purple flowers (1–1½ cm) are borne in stalked clusters of 2–10 from each upper leaf. Pod black when ripe. The whole plant blackens on drying. May–July. *Pea family*

Crimson Clover *pl. 59.* This striking clover is an erect downy plant with conical or cylindrical densely packed heads of flowers. Calyx with long, ribbed, bristly-haired teeth, very conspicuous in fruit. Leaflets heart-shaped. Flowers rarely pink or white. May–July. *Pea family*

Wood Purple Clover *pl. 59.* The conspicuous cylindrical heads of reddish-purple flowers are up to 6 cm long. Calyx with very long, bristly-haired teeth, the lowest teeth several times longer than the upper. Leaflets rather thick and leathery, with prominent veins and finely toothed margins. June–Aug. *Pea family*

Zigzag Clover *pl. 59.* Not unlike the common Red Clover (not illustrated), but reddish-purple flowers in a somewhat flattened globular head (2–4 cm). Petals 2–3 times as long as the calyx. Stipules with the free part awl-shaped (triangular in Red Clover). May–July. *Pea family*

Crown Vetch *pl. 62.* Has globular heads of pink, lilac or white flowers, and compound leaves without tendrils. Flowers (1 cm) usually with whitish wings and pink- or purple-tipped keel. Leaves with 7–12 pairs of leaflets. Pods slender-pointed. May–Aug. *Pea family*

Slender Loosestrife *pl. 80.* A much more slender, hairless plant than the similar Purple Loosestrife. Leaves narrow, opposite, tapering towards the base. Flowers rosy-purple, few in each whorl, about 1¼ cm across. June–Aug. *Loosestrife family*

 Broad-Leaved Willow-Herb *pl. 81.* A slender, sparsely hairy plant with small pale rose flowers (6–9 mm) in a leafy cluster. Differs from similar species in the leaves, which are shortly stalked (to 6 mm), broadly lance-shaped, with a rounded base. Flower buds drooping. June–Aug. *Willow-Herb family*

 Hound's-Tongue *pl. 102.* A softly hairy, grey-green plant, smelling strongly of mice. Flower clusters branched, unfolding in a coil; flowers dark reddish-purple, or rarely white, with a short tube. Nutlets 4, lozenge-shaped, covered with spines. May–July. *Borage family*

 Pale Bugloss *pl. 105.* An extremely rough, bristly plant with long pyramidal spikes of very pale pink or bluish flowers with long projecting, coloured stamens. Leaves narrow, bristly haired, many in a rosette below. Whole plant grey or whitish. Apr.–Aug. *Borage family*

 Common Hemp-Nettle *pl. 111.* A variable plant but generally rather stiff, erect and simply branched, with whorls of pink or white flowers, and a bristly-toothed calyx. Flowers 1–2 cm, corolla tube usually about as long as calyx teeth. Stems swollen, bristly-haired at the nodes. July–Oct. *Mint family*

 Motherwort *pl. 112.* A distinctive, unbranched aromatic plant with a congested spike of very numerous whorls of pinkish, or whitish densely hairy flowers. Leaves progressively smaller and less divided from below upwards, paler beneath. June–Sept. *Mint family*

 Black Horehound *pl. 112.* A straggling, bushy nettle-like plant, strongly fetid when crushed. Flowers small (1¼ cm), two-lipped, reddish-purple, borne in dense clusters in the axils of the opposite, stalked leaves. Calyx funnel-shaped with 5 spreading or recurved teeth when in fruit. May–Sept. *Mint family*

 Marsh Woundwort *pl. 122.* A hairy, almost bristly, scentless plant, with long spikes of closely grouped whorls of dull pinkish flowers. Corolla hairy on the outside; calyx hairy, about half as long as the narrow corolla tube. June–Sept. *Mint family*

 Lesser Calamint *pl. 114.* A strongly aromatic plant with loose multiple clusters of small pale lilac or whitish flowers (about 1 cm). Upper clusters longer than leaves, which are grey-haired, oval, and almost entire. July–Oct. *Mint family*

 Marjoram *pl. 115.* A very sweetly aromatic plant with rounded clusters of rosy-purple or whitish flowers. Flower buds dark purple due to the dark purple bracteoles; white-flowered plants have green bracteoles. Often used as a pot herb. July–Sept. *Mint family*

 Truncate Lousewort *pl. 128.* Distinguished by its short compact head of brownish-purple flowers with their upper lips cut-off (not long-beaked). Calyx hairless with pointed unequal lobes. Leaves arranged alternately, fern-like in their lobing. July–Aug. *Figwort family*

 Common Lousewort *pl. 128.* A widespread lowland plant of damp ground, low-spreading and partially parasitic, with few-flowered clusters of pink flowers. The calyx has 4 small leaf-like toothed lobes and is usually hairless. Apr.–July. *Figwort family*

 Valerian *pl. 136.* A rather stout erect plant of damp places with dense branched, flat-topped clusters of small pale pink tubular flowers (¼ cm long). Leaves variable, with few broad or narrow, entire or toothed leaflets. Fruit with a pappus of hairs. May–July. *Valerian family*

28

Three-Leaved Valerian *pl. 136.* A smaller plant than the previous species, of shady places in mountains. Leaves of flowering stems deeply three-lobed, grey-green and nearly stalkless. On non-flowering shoots they are long-stalked, oval-heart-shaped and coarsely toothed. June–Aug. *Valerian family*

 Mountain Valerian *pl. 136.* Distinguished from the similar preceding plant by its bright green shining unlobed leaves. Flowering stem leaves oval-lance-shaped, stalkless; leaves on non-flowering stems oval and narrowed to a short stalk. Apr.–July. *Valerian family*

 Red Valerian *pl. 136.* A tufted plant of rocks and walls with branched pyramidal clusters of deep pink flowers and glaucous stems and leaves. Flowers with long slender tubes with minute spurs at the end and a single projecting stamen, very sweet-scented; sometimes white. May–Sept. *Valerian family*

 Narrow-Leaved Red Valerian *pl. 137.* Like the preceding species but flower clusters dense, rounded, flat-topped. Flowers with a tiny spur about as long as the ovary. Leaves much narrower, mostly linear (2–14 mm broad); plant glaucous. May–July. *Valerian family*

 Wood Scabious *pl. 138.* Distinguished from the Field Scabious by the broadly lance-shaped, long-pointed stem leaves, usually toothed but not lobed. Flower head lilac or purplish; involucral bracts about as long as the flowers. A plant of shady places and meadows in the mountains. June–Sept. *Scabious family*

 Mournful Widow, Sweet Scabious *pl. 138.* Flower heads variable, dark reddish-purple, red-violet to lilac; outermost florets longer and spreading. The fruiting head becomes cylindrical; the individual fruits are eight-ribbed, with a papery cup-like crown and 5 blackish or russet-coloured bristles at the centre. June–Oct. *Scabious family*

 Hemp Agrimony *pl. 141.* A stout, leafy, downy plant of wet places, with flat-topped clusters of numerous reddish-purple (rarely whitish) flower heads. Each flower head is 1 cm long with 5–6 florets surrounded by purple-tipped involucral bracts. July–Aug. *Daisy family*

 Common Adenostyles *pl. 150.* A stout plant of mountain woods and watersides, with flat-topped clusters of numerous, tiny reddish-purple flower heads, not unlike the previous plant. Leaves large, broad (to ½ m across), undivided, mostly basal, often conspicuously white- or grey-cottony beneath. Some stem leaves clasping. July–Aug. *Daisy family*

 Star Thistle *pl. 156.* A branched, bushy, thistle-like plant with small reddish-purple flower heads (1–1½ cm), and stiff, yellow, spreading spines with small stout spines at their bases. Leaves rough, deeply cut into narrow segments and with few bristle-pointed teeth. Aug.–Sept. *Daisy family*

 Chives *pl. 165.* The hollow, rush-like leaves which grow in clumps smell pleasantly and mildly of onions; they are used for flavouring. Flower heads globular (2½–3½ cm), pale pink or violet-pink with 1–3 short papery bracts. June–July. *Lily family*

 Round-Headed Leek *pl. 165.* A typical leek with a tall leafless stem and a globular cluster (2–2½ cm) of dark reddish-purple flowers. Flowers bell-shaped, stamens projecting. Leaves almost cylindrical, hollow and grooved; few at the base of the stem. June–July. *Lily family*

 Keeled Garlic *pl. 165.* Distinguished by thin flat leaves with rough margins, arising half-way up the stems, and by flower heads with bulbils and long bracts. Fertile flowers long-stalked, usually with conspicuously protruding stamens when open. June–Aug. *Lily family*

Rose Garlic *pl. 166.* A most attractive garlic, with handsome rose-pink, or violet bell-shaped flowers, and a very pungent garlic smell. Stem cylindrical, not angled; leaves grass-like, flat; keeled below. Apr.–June. *Lily family*

Pyramidal Orchid *pl. 190.* Tight conical heads of numerous small rosy-purple flowers are characteristic. 2 small swellings are present at the base of the lip. Flowers smell of foxes; spur thread-like, downward-pointing. May–July. *Orchid family*

Fragrant Orchid *pl. 190.* Very fragrant with a slender cylindrical spike of rose-violet flowers quite like the previous species. The lip differs, being shallowly three-lobed and there are no basal swellings. Spur slender (11–13 mm), nearly twice as long as the ovary. May–July. *Orchid family*

See also: WATER-PEPPER *pl. 8*; BUCKWHEAT *pl. 9*; RAMPING FUMITORY *pl. 30*; SEAKALE *pl. 37*; ORPINE, LIVELONG *pl. 40*; ALSIKE CLOVER *pl. 59*; NARROW-LEAVED LUNGWORT *pl. 104*; GROUND-PINE GERMANDER *pl. 107*; CATMINT *pl. 109*; PENNY-ROYAL *pl. 116*; WILD LEEK *pl. 166.*

Flowers small · Plant small

Cliff Spurrey *pl. 13.* A plant of sea cliffs, with clusters of deep pink flowers (8–20 mm) on sticky glandular branches. Leaves fleshy, pointed, in bundles, with small silvery scales (stipules) at their base. June–Aug. *Pink family*

Sand Spurrey *pl. 13.* A low spreading, often matted plant of open ground with inconspicuous pink flowers (3–5 mm). Papery-margined sepals usually longer than petals. Leaves greyish-green, narrow, tapering to a bristle-like tip; silvery scales conspicuous. May–Sept. *Pink family*

Red Alpine Catchfly *pl. 14.* A tufted mountain plant with a basal rosette of narrow leaves and erect stems with dense terminal heads of rosy-purple flowers. Flowers (to 1 cm) with spreading, deeply notched petals; rarely white. June–Aug. *Pink family*

Moss Campion *pl. 16.* Usually forming dense, compact, bright green cushions of tiny pointed leaves (6–12 mm), amongst rocks in high mountains. Flowers solitary (9–12 mm), from rose-pink to whitish, short-stalked, carried just above the leaf rosettes. June–Aug. *Pink family*

Pink Mediterranean Catchfly *pl. 15.* A rather slender plant often an abundant weed of vineyards and olive groves. The petals deeply two-lobed, pink or white with a frill of scales at the throat. Calyx (11–13 mm) densely hairy, at first cylindrical, later club-shaped. Apr.–May. *Pink family*

Rock Soapwort *pl. 16.* An attractive plant forming loose spreading mats of sticky, hair-fringed leaves. The neat pink flowers have a brightly coloured, rather inflated cylindrical calyx. Lower leaves oval; upper narrower, acute. May–July. *Pink family*

Purple Corydalis *pl. 30.* A small delicate plant of shady places, with a dense spike of long-spurred, two-lipped, purple or whitish flowers (1½–2½ cm). Differs from most other species in the deeply lobed leafy bracts of the lower flowers. Mar.–May. *Poppy family*

Round-Leaved Pennycress *pl. 36.* A tiny plant of screes found in the Alps and Apennines. Flowers (6–8 mm), sweet-scented, in dense clusters. Lower leaves rounded, in a rosette; the upper clasping the stem. June–Aug. *Cress family*

Burnt Candytuft *pl. 36.* A glaucous, leafy, often woody-based plant with leathery leaves and rounded clusters of small rose-pink, violet or white flowers. The fruits are flattened, broadly winged and notched at the apex. Apr.–Aug. *Cress family*

Cobweb Houseleek *pl. 39.* The globular leaf rosettes, covered with a network of white cobweb-hairs, are unmistakable. Flowering stems stout, with reddish scale-like leaves and a compact head of starry, rose-carmine flowers. July–Sept. *Stonecrop family*

Mountain Houseleek *pl. 39.* The rosetttes of leaves (1–5 cm) are distinguished by their dull green colour and sticky surface, with their margins fringed with hairs. Flowers usually reddish-purple, sometimes yellowish, borne on a short stout stem covered with fleshy leaves. July–Aug. *Stonecrop family*

Hairy Stonecrop *pl. 40.* A weak hairy plant of marshes and bogs with plump sticky, downy leaves. Flowers pink or lilac; petals with a darker midvein, usually 5, spreading in a star. June–Aug. *Stonecrop family*

Purple Saxifrage *pl. 41.* An attractive low spreading, mat-forming mountain plant with tiny overlapping leaves in 4 rows, with thickened tips and lime glands. Flowers solitary, purple or pink (1 cm), almost stalkless. May–Aug. *Saxifrage family*

Arctic Bramble *pl. 43.* Probably the smallest bramble, growing only to 15 cm, and with underground creeping stems. Flowers (1½ cm) solitary, bright pink. Leaves with 3 leaflets. Fruit bright red, with few berries. June–July. *Rose family*

Star Clover *pl. 60.* An insignificant, woolly-haired clover with small globular heads of pale pink flowers, but with striking fruiting heads. Calyx teeth enlarging and often turning a deep pink or dull crimson, and spreading in a star; consequently the fruiting heads are conspicuous in the surrounding vegetation. Apr.–June. *Pea family*

Alpine Clover *pl. 60.* A creeping mountain plant, identified by lax heads of few, comparatively large (2 cm) rosy-purple (or rarely white) scented flowers. Leaves all basal, trifoliate, with narrow lance-shaped, finely toothed leaflets. June–Aug. *Pea family*

Mountain Kidney-Vetch *pl. 61.* A mat-forming plant of rocks in the mountains with hairy leaves with 8–15 pairs of leaflets (5–10 mm). Dense purple or pink flower heads are surrounded by 2 deeply-cut leafy bracts and arise on leafless stems direct from the woody base. June–July. *Pea family*

Shining Cranesbill *pl. 63.* An almost hairless, brittle plant, with shining, rounded, deeply lobed leaves which often turn reddish. The pink flowers have an enlarged, hairless, five-angled calyx, with transverse ridges between the angles. Apr.–Aug. *Geranium family*

Variable Milkwort *pl. 68.* Flowers comparatively large (8–10 mm), pink, blue or white. The colour mostly comes from 2 large oval sepals (wings), longer than the petals and conspicuously netted with veins. Lower leaves oval, the upper narrower. Apr.–July. *Milkwort family*

Small Wintergreen *pl. 86.* The globular, pale pinkish flowers are borne on a leafless stem arising from a loose rosette of pale green, oval leaves (2½–4 cm). The style of this species is shorter than the stamens and straight. May–July. *Wintergreen family*

Bird's-Eye Primrose *pl. 91.* A delicate primula of peaty places in mountains, with a white or yellow mealy dust covering the stem, undersides of the leaves and calyx. Flowers (1 cm) rose-lilac with a yellow throat; petals deeply notched. June–July. *Primrose family*

Alpine Androsace *pl. 91.* A delicate, flattened, cushion-forming plant of screes, with rosettes of pointed leaves covered with minute star-shaped hairs. Flowers (½ cm) solitary, short-stalked, pink or white with a yellow throat. Calyx covered with star-shaped hairs. July–Aug. *Primrose family*

Flesh-Coloured Androsace *pl. 90.* Cushion-forming, but leaves linear acute and nearly hairless. Flowers (½–1 cm) borne in short-stemmed clusters of 2–10, pink with a yellow eye. Damp places in alpine regions. July–Aug. *Primrose family*

 Sea Milkwort *pl. 92.* A small creeping and rooting plant of salt marshes and sea shores, with 4 ranks of numerous narrow, fleshy leaves. Flowers (½ cm) small, axillary, bell-shaped. Calyx pink, five-lobed, petals absent. May–Sept. *Primrose family*

 Thrift, Sea Pink *pl. 94.* A coastal plant forming dense springy cushions of narrow, bright green, soft, somewhat fleshy leaves. Flower heads globular (1½–2½ cm), pinkish, sometimes white, with brownish papery sheaths below the heads. May–Aug. *Sea Lavender family*

 Spiny Thrift *pl. 94.* Stiff, spiny-tipped, glaucous leaves distinguish it from most other thrifts. The plant forms dense spiny cushions, the new leaves mixed with numerous old, tough, curved leaves. Flower heads pale pink (1½–3 cm), with a rusty-brown sheath below. May–June. *Sea Lavender family*

 Common Centaury *pl. 95.* A small, regularly branched, hairless plant forming a loose cluster of bright pink flowers (5–6 mm) with spreading petals. There is a neat basal rosette of narrow pale green oval leaves and scattered stem leaves. June–Sept. *Gentian family*

 Wall Germander *pl. 107.* This spreading, shrubby, tufted plant bears whorls of pinkish-purple flowers in short, rather one-sided leafy spikes. Upper lip of flowers absent. Leaves small, shiny, leathery and conspicuously toothed. May–Sept. *Mint family*

 Henbit *pl. 111.* A slender plant recognized from other dead-nettles by the cup-shaped leafy bracts encircling the upper whorls of flowers. Two-lipped flowers with long tubes three times as long as calyx. Sometimes smaller unopened flowers are formed. Mar.–Oct. *Mint family*

 Red-Topped Sage *pl. 115.* Usually obvious by its bright violet or pink tufted top-knot of leafy bracts above the long spike of flowers (but sometimes absent). Flowers (1–2 cm) violet, purple or pink, in whorls, subtended by heart-shaped, often coloured bracts. Apr.–June. *Mint family*

 Alpine Calamint *pl. 114.* A prostrate spreading plant with bright violet, rarely pink or white, inconspicuously 2-lipped flowers with a pale throat and a long corolla tube (12–20 mm). Calyx two-lipped, the upper lip with 3 nearly equal narrow lobes. June–Sept. *Mint family*

 Alpine Erinus *pl. 127.* A low, hairy, tufted rosette plant (sometimes found on lowland walls), with crowded clusters of pink or purple flowers. Flowers with a narrow tube and 5 spreading notched petals. Calyx hairy, deeply divided into 5 narrow lobes. May–Oct. *Figwort family*

 Southern Red Bartsia *pl. 126.* A small unbranched, often reddish, glandular-sticky annual with a dense cluster of reddish-purple flowers, between large, lobed, sticky bracts. Flowers (1 cm), variable in colour, often reddish with a white tube; sometimes all yellow or white. Mar.–June. *Figwort family*

 Red Bartsia *pl. 126.* A low bushy, usually reddish, semi-parasitic annual with a leafy one-sided spike of reddish-purple two-lipped flowers. Flowers (8 mm), covered with flattened hairs. Leaves lance-shaped, stalkless, strongly toothed. May–Oct. *Figwort family*

 Rhaetian Lousewort *pl. 128.* A small rosette-forming plant of damp alpine pastures of France and Switzerland. Its pink flowers have a long slender beak to the upper lip and its finely hairy calyx has leafy, toothed lobes. June–Aug. *Figwort family*

Fedia _pl. 137._ A low, rather fleshy, hairless annual with hollow forked stems and dense terminal clusters of small, long-tubed pink flowers, two-lipped and with tiny pouches at their bases. Leaves oval, shallowly toothed, in opposite pairs. Mar.–June. _Valerian family_

  Shining Scabious _pl. 138._ A mountain plant of the Pyrenees, Alps and Carpathians, with broad, oval, usually glossy, basal leaves, contrasting with the upper deeply divided stem leaves. Flower heads (1–2 cm), varying from rose-lilac, violet to deep mauve. Calyx bristles black in fruit, three to five times longer than the pappus cup. June–Sept. _Scabious family_

  Devil's Claw _pl. 140._ An unusual plant of crevices in limestone and dolomitic mountains in Italy and Austria. Flowers from pale pink to violet-red; the fused tip is violet. Leaves glossy, with conspicuous pointed teeth. July–Aug. _Bellflower family_

 Butterbur _pl. 149._ The pale reddish or violet cylindrical inflorescences often appear before the leaves. Flower heads one-sexed, the male (7–12 mm) and the female (3–6 mm) on different plants. Leaves coarse, very large, long-stalked with rounded blades, often occurring in large patches. Mar.–May. _Daisy family_

 Alpine Coltsfoot _pl. 150._ A delicate plant of alpine pastures with solitary, reddish-violet flower heads borne on slender unbranched, almost leafless stems. Basal leaves with circular, shallowly toothed, shiny blades (2–4 cm), dark green above, purplish and hairy beneath. June–Sept. _Daisy family_

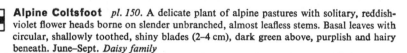 **Dog's Tooth Violet** _pl. 168._ Quite unlike any other plant, with beautiful bright pink flowers with recurved petals, exposing bluish anthers and three-lobed stigma. Leaves usually curiously and attractively mottled with brown. Mar.–May. _Lily family_

 Pink Butterfly Orchid _pl. 187._ A very beautiful orchid with conspicuously veined rosy-pink flowers and a broadly fan-shaped lip with a toothed margin. Spur short, conical, down-curved. Bracts conspicuous, flushed rosy-purple. Mar.–May. _Orchid family_

 Bug Orchid _pl. 187._ For experienced noses an easy plant to identify for it smells of bed-bugs, (var. _fragrans_, with darker red flowers, smells of vanilla). Flowers variable, often brownish-purple, variously tinged with greater or lesser amounts of green. The narrow pointed 'helmet', the three-lobed lip with larger pointed middle lobe and the short, conical and downward-pointing spur are distinctive. Apr.–June. _Orchid family_

 Dark-Winged Orchid, Burnt Orchid _pl. 187._ The dark maroon colour of the unopened buds gives it a 'singed' appearance. Lower lip 'man-like' with 2 'arms' and 2 'legs', often with a tooth between the latter. Helmet dark, becoming paler as the flower matures. Apr.–July. _Orchid family_

 Four-Spotted Orchid _pl. 189._ A graceful orchid of the eastern Mediterranean with pale pink or violet flowers with a whitish centre, with 2 or 4 conspicuous purple spots; flowers sometimes white. Spur long, slender, downward-pointing. Lip with 3 more or less equal lobes. Leaves unspotted. Apr.–May. _Orchid family_

 Black Vanilla Orchid _pl. 189._ No other orchid has this dark blackish-purple colour; the small flowers are always borne in tight conical clusters. A plant of alpine pastures, smelling of vanilla. Lip triangular, directed upward, spur sac-like. June–Aug. _Orchid family_

 Lesser Twayblade _pl. 192._ An insignificant orchid of mountain woods and peaty moors. At the base of the flowering stem are 2 rounded heart-shaped leaves (to 2½ cm). Flowers (3–4 mm) with a reddish man-like lip with 'arms' and 'legs'. July–Sept. _Orchid family_

See also: VIVIPAROUS BISTORT *pl. 9*; CREEPING GYPSOPHILA *pl. 16*; SMALL-FLOWERED CATCH-FLY *pl. 16*; ANNUAL CANDYTUFT *pl. 36*; WALL PENNYWORT *pl. 39*; WHITE STONECROP *pl. 39*; MUSKY SAXIFRAGE *pl. 42*; KIDNEY-VETCH *pl. 61*; COMMON MILKWORT *pl. 68*; CAT'S-FOOT *pl. 143*.

Flowers minute · Plant medium

Great Burnet *pl. 45.* Its completely globular, dark red heads (1–2 cm) are borne on slender, unbranched, nearly leafless stems. Petals absent but there are 4 red sepals to each miniature flower. Leaves compound with 7–15 oval, toothed leaflets which are glaucous beneath. June–Sept. *Rose family*

See also: ERECT PELLITORY-OF-THE-WALL *pl. 7*; GREAT MASTERWORT *pl. 83.*

Flowers minute · Plant small

Common Dodder *pl. 101.* A parasitic plant, feeding on a variety of host plants by means of suckers. Green chlorophyll is lacking and the whole plant is reddish or pink. Flowers tiny, bell-shaped, in globular heads (½–1 cm). June–Oct. *Convolvulus family*

BLUE, VIOLET, BLUISH-PURPLE

Flowers large · Plant large

Ivy-Leaved Morning Glory *pl. 100.* An ornamental climber with large blue or purple trumpet flowers, distinguished by its shallowly and widely 3-lobed leaves. Calyx hairy, with 5 pointed lobes. A native of tropical America. July–Sept. *Convolvulus family*

Globe Artichoke *pl. 154.* The enormous flower heads (15 cm across) have leathery involucral bracts, the fleshy bases of which are eaten as a vegetable. A robust plant with large, silvery-grey, deeply cut leaves. Widely cultivated in southern Europe; unknown in the wild. July–Aug. *Daisy family*

Flowers large · Plant medium

Common Monkshood *pl. 19.* A beautiful but very poisonous plant. Distinguished by the hood of the flowers, which is broader than long. Leaves rounded in outline, deeply cut into narrow lobes (1–8 mm wide). June–Sept. *Buttercup family*

Alpine Larkspur *pl. 20.* A parent of the garden delphiniums. The long spur (1½–3 cm) and central dark brown hairy petals, contrasting with the outer blue petals, are characteristic. Leaves cut into many lance-shaped lobes. June–Aug. *Buttercup family*

Blue Clematis *pl. 24.* One of the 2 clematis species of Europe which are not woody, and one of 3 with purple flowers. The solitary, drooping, bell-shaped flowers, coupled with the oval, entire leaves, are unique. June–Aug. *Buttercup family*

Columbine *pl. 27.* A well-known, widespread plant, with 5 long, backward-pointing spurs. There are as many as 27 different species, mostly very local. This species has sharply curved spurs (15–22 mm long) with a knob at the tip. The flower colours vary from violet, pink to white. May–July. *Buttercup family*

Alpine Columbine *pl. 27.* A delicate plant with drooping flowers (3–4½ cm) and 5 straight or slightly curved spurs. Leaves rather small, nearly hairless, twice cut into 3 rounded, toothed lobes. July–Aug. *Buttercup family*

Opium Poppy *pl. 28.* An erect annual with greyish, waxy, bloomed stems and leaves. Flowers very large (to 18 cm), with 4–6 purple, lilac to white petals, often dark-blotched at the base. Leaves broadly lobed, clasping the stem. An important medicinal plant. June–July. *Poppy family*

Violet Horned-Poppy *pl. 28.* A typical poppy, with floppy petals which soon fall, but unusual in its deep violet-blue colour. Distinguished after flowering by very long (5–10 cm) horn-like fruits. Leaves finely divided, segments with minute terminal bristles. May–June. *Poppy family*

Willow Gentian *pl. 97.* A leafy plant, the lance-shaped leaves (3–8 cm) usually in 4 ranks, though sometimes 2-ranked on arched stems. Flowers large (3½–5½ cm) spotted violet within, with paler stripes outside, arising stalkless from the axils of upper leaves. Aug.–Sept. *Gentian family*

Apple of Peru *pl. 119.* A leafy, hairless, strong-smelling plant with large solitary blue or violet, pale-centred, funnel-shaped, short-lived flowers. The calyx enlarges, becoming a papery and bladder-like bag enclosing the brown berry. Very poisonous; sometimes grown as an ornamental and naturalized. June–Oct. *Nightshade family*

Narrow-Leaved Bellflower *pl. 139.* Readily distinguished from other bellflowers by its narrow-lance-shaped shining leaves, and its broad funnel-shaped flowers (3–4 cm) with shallow, rounded lobes. May–Aug. *Bellflower family*

Bats-in-the-Belfry *pl. 139.* A roughly hairy bellflower with sharply angled stems and long leafy spike-like clusters of blue flowers. Corolla lobes fringed with hairs, one-third as long as corolla tube. Lower leaves large, nettle-shaped, long-stalked; upper narrower, shortly stalked. June–Sept. *Bellflower family*

European Michaelmas Daisy *pl. 142.* An attractive plant, usually with a loose cluster of flower heads, with bluish-lilac (not pinkish) rays, much longer than the width of the yellow disk. Lower leaves oval, stalked; upper narrower, stalkless. Aug.–Sept. *Daisy family*

Globe-Thistle *pl. 152.* The quite spherical spiny blue flower heads are unmistakable. The stems and undersides of the leaves white-felted, upper side of leaves hairless, shiny green. All leaves thistle-like and extremely spiny. July–Sept. *Daisy family*

Chicory *pl. 158.* A stiff plant with grooved stems and stalkless blue dandelion-like flower heads ranged along the stems. Leaves lance-shaped with backward-pointed lobes. A bitter flavoured salad plant. June–Sept. *Daisy family*

Salsify *pl. 158.* Similar to the Goat's-Beard (not illustrated) with flower heads which open for a very short time, but flowers bluish-purple, usually fringed by the longer, pointed involucral bracts. Leaves grass-like, half-clasping. Fruit forms magnificent globular heads of large brown 'parachutes' with delicate radiating feathery hairs. Apr.–June. *Daisy family*

Blue Lettuce *pl. 160.* A hairless plant with milky juice and blue-green leaves with narrow lobes. The flower heads are blue and violet (not pink) and are borne in branched leafless clusters. Fruit black; pappus hairs white. May–Aug. *Daisy family*

Spanish Iris *pl. 175.* A commonly grown garden plant, with large, solitary violet-purple flowers at the ends of stout stems ensheathed by large swollen bracts. 'Falls' with large yellow patch on the blades, which are shorter than the purple 'shafts'. Leaves very slender, grooved. May–Aug. *Iris family*

Pyrenean Iris *pl. 175.* A beautiful plant, sometimes cultivated as the English Iris. Flowers bright blue with an orange patch on each 'fall'. Differs from the preceding species in its larger flowers, with 'falls' with a notched blade and much longer than the petal-like stigmas; leaves also broader. July–Aug. *Iris family*

Grass-Leaved Iris *pl. 175.* A beautiful little iris with short-lived sweet-scented flowers appearing amongst the grassy leaves. The 'falls' have small, purple-veined blades, much shorter than the 'shaft'. Flowering stems flattened and two-edged. May–June. *Iris family*

Common Iris *pl. 175.* The most widely grown ornamental iris, native of the south, but often naturalized further north. The shortly branched stems with brown papery sheaths below the flowers are characteristic. The 'falls' are very broad, very dark purple, with a yellow beard at their base. Leaves glaucous, 2–5 cm wide. Apr.–June. *Iris family*

 Limodore *pl. 191.* A very unusual saprophytic orchid, like a purple shoot of asparagus before flowering. Flowers violet to yellowish-violet, in a lax spike on a long slender stem with no true leaves, only dark purplish bracts. May–July. *Orchid family*

See also: SUPERB PINK *pl. 17*; THORN-APPLE *pl. 118.*

Flowers large · Plant small

 Pasque Flower *pl. 22.* A very attractive plant with large, solitary, erect violet-purple flowers opening wide in the sun and revealing the golden-yellow stamens. Bracts below each flower cut into narrow segments; the whole plant is very hairy. Mar.–May. *Buttercup family*

 Long-Spurred Pansy *pl. 76.* Differs from other pansies (in particular Mountain Pansy) in larger, broader flowers (3 cm), with longer, slender spurs (8–15 mm). Flowers violet or yellow. Leaves oval-oblong, mostly in a rosette; stipules oblong, entire or toothed. June–July. *Violet family*

 Trumpet Gentian *pl. 96.* The most wonderful of all gentians with large, brilliant dark blue trumpets (5–6 cm), spotted with green inside. Flowers solitary, shortly stalked, arising from a loose rosette of leaves 5–15 cm across. Likes acid soils. July–Aug. *Gentian family*

 Stemless Trumpet Gentian *pl. 96.* Very similar to the preceding plant and just as beautiful but flowers bright blue within and usually without green spots. Leaves leathery, much longer than broad, pointed. Likes limestone soils. July–Aug. *Gentian family*

 Marsh Gentian *pl. 96.* An attractive gentian of wet heaths, with clusters of 1–7 large blue trumpet-shaped flowers (2½–4 cm), streaked with greenish-yellow on the outside. Leaves narrow, pointed, borne in pairs on slender, rather weak stems. July–Oct. *Gentian family*

 Dwarf Convolvulus *pl. 100.* Unmistakable with its funnel-shaped, three-coloured flowers, predominantly blue but with zones of orange and white in the throat. A hairy non-climbing annual of the south, sometimes grown for ornament. Apr.–June. *Convolvulus family*

 Alpine Aster *pl. 142.* A lowly plant of dry pastures and rocks, with blue-lilac or violet flower heads (3½–5 cm) with a yellow centre, on short stems. Leaves mostly basal, spoon-shaped, three-veined, the upper narrower. July–Sept. *Daisy family*

 Purple Autumnal Crocus *pl. 174.* The leafless flowers push up through the grass in autumn, often in large numbers. Distinguished from the Autumn Crocus by having 3 (not 6) pale yellow stamens. The leaves which appear in spring also differ; they are narrow, with a central white line. Sept.–Nov. *Iris family*

 Pygmy Iris *pl. 176.* The commonest colour of this iris is violet-purple, but it varies from brownish-purple to yellowish-white. Solitary flowers are borne on stems shorter than the out-curved, sickle-shaped glaucous leaves (7–17 mm wide). The 'falls' have a conspicuous central tuft of hairs. Mar.–May. *Iris family*

 Dwarf Iris *pl. 175.* The flowers vary from blue, purple, yellow to white. 'Falls' tinged or veined with brown, with a bright orange-yellow beard. Distinguished from other dwarf irises by the 1–2 flowers carried on short stalks above the leaves at flowering time. Mar.–Apr. *Iris family*

See also: CROWN ANEMONE *pl. 21*; SCARLET ANEMONE *pl. 21*; SMALL PASQUE FLOWER *pl. 22.*

Flowers medium · Plant large

 Blue Sow-Thistle *pl. 159.* A robust plant with a partly reddish-haired furrowed stem and dandelion-like, blue-violet flower heads. Leaves somewhat blue-green, large, with triangular non-spiny lobes. July–Sept. *Daisy family*

Flowers medium · Plant medium

 Field Love-in-a-Mist *pl. 18.* Blue flowers, conspicuous fruit with carpels fused half way, and pointed stamens, distinguishes this from the common garden plant. This Greek form has frilly leaves under the flowers, most have none. June–July. *Buttercup family*

 Scaly-Seeded Larkspur *pl. 20.* The commonest of the slender annual delphiniums, very like a true larkspur, but distinguished by the 3 (not 1) carpels, and 4 inner unfused petals. Flowers blue-violet usually in a long compact leafless spike; spurs straight, up-pointing. May–June. *Buttercup family*

 Larkspur *pl. 20.* The flowers are usually blue, but they may be pink or white. Spur almost straight (13–18 mm). Leaves are much-divided, feathery in appearance. The most commonly grown garden larkspur. June–July. *Buttercup family*

 Field Larkspur *pl. 20.* Differs from the previous species in the usually longer spur (1½–2½ cm) and the quite hairless fruits. Flowers often in loose much-branched clusters, but they may occur in dense spikes. Bracts all undivided. June–July. *Buttercup family*

 Dame's Violet *pl. 31.* A tall, handsome, much-branched plant with rather dense clusters of purple-lilac or white flowers (2–2½ cm), with the delicious sweet fragrance of stocks. Usually found by watersides or damp ditches. May–Sept. *Cress family*

 Violet Cabbage *pl. 37.* A Mediterranean plant with grey-green, somewhat fleshy cabbage-like leaves clasping the stem above, and terminal clusters of violet-purple flowers (2½ cm). Pods long, slender (to 8 cm), four-angled. Apr.–May. *Cress family*

 Chickling Pea *pl. 56.* Widely cultivated as a forage crop in central and south-eastern Europe, but country of origin unknown. Distinguished by solitary lilac, blue or whitish flowers (1½ cm) on a jointed stalk, and by the pod which has 2 leafy wings. Mar.–July. *Pea family*

 Broad-Leaved Cranesbill *pl. 63.* Its leaves are cut to three-quarters the width of the blade into 3–5 rather broad, toothed lobes. Flowers lilac (2–2½ cm), with darker veins. Stems swollen at the joints. July–Aug. *Geranium family*

 Wood Cranesbill *pl. 63.* An erect, mountain meadow plant, with loose clusters of purple or violet flowers (1½–2½ cm), often with paler centres. Flower stalks remain erect after flowering. Leaves deeply divided, usually into 7 toothed lobes, further cut into shallow lobes. June–Aug. *Geranium family*

 Dusky Cranesbill, Mourning Widow *pl. 64.* Unmistakable with dark blackish-purple flowers, the petals turned backwards and with conspicuous projecting stamens and style. Petals crinkly-edged and pointed. Leaves often blotched brown. June–Aug. *Geranium family*

 Long-Beaked Storksbill *pl. 64.* Distinguished by very long fruits (8–11 cm), amongst the longest of any European species. Flowers (2 cm); petals falling very easily and often missing. Ripe fruits split into sections, each of which twists like a corkscrew but does not catapult out the seed. Apr.–May. *Geranium family*

 Perennial Flax *pl. 65.* This slender, branched plant bears loose clusters of clear blue flowers on wiry stems. Petals soon falling; sepals oval, the inner with broad papery margins. Leaves stiff, narrow, usually one-veined. May–Aug. *Flax family*

Shrubby Pimpernel *pl. 93.* A very striking brilliant blue pimpernel of southern Iberia, the largest-flowered (1–2 cm) of any European species. A spreading woody-based perennial with narrow alternate leaves. Feb.–Nov. *Primrose family*

 Cross Gentian *pl. 96.* One of the less attractive of the gentians, with dull blue flowers in terminal leafy clusters. Flowers barrel-shaped (2–2½ cm long). Leaves oval to lance-shaped, opposite, the upper sheathing the stem. June–Sept. *Gentian family*

 Marsh Felwort *pl. 95.* An unusual-looking plant of mountain bogs and marshes, with pale green leaves and dark, rather dull-coloured, violet-purple flowers. Flowers 2½–3½ cm, the petals opening widely in a star revealing 2 dark violet glands at their base. July–Sept. *Gentian family*

 Jacob's Ladder *pl. 100.* This attractive plant has a crowded spike of wide-opening bright blue, rarely white, flowers, with long projecting stamens. Leaves neatly cut into 6–12 pairs of narrow oval, pointed leaflets and a terminal leaflet. May–Aug. *Phlox family*

 Borage *pl. 103.* A rather coarse, bristly, branched annual with bright blue flowers (2–2½ cm). The fine-pointed widely spreading petals reveal a central cone of blackish-purple anthers. Calyx bristly, enlarging in fruit. Apr.–Sept. *Borage family*

 Eastern Borage *pl. 103.* A rare plant of shady woods of Bulgaria and eastern Greece. Flowers borne in almost leafless branched clusters, bluish-violet; petals narrow and curled backwards, the stamens projecting conspicuously forwards. Apr.–May. *Borage family*

 Large Blue Alkanet *pl. 102.* A bristly plant with stalkless, rough, thick, lance-shaped upper leaves. Flowers (1½–2½ cm) with a narrow tube and a brush-like tuft of white hairs in the throat, and spreading bright blue petal-lobes. Calyx five-lobed, enlarging in fruit. May–Aug. *Borage family*

 Blue Gromwell *pl. 104.* Flowers rather few, first reddish-purple, soon bright blue. Corolla funnel-shaped (1½–2 cm), hairy outside. A slender plant often producing many non-flowering leafy shoots from an underground creeping stem. Apr.–June. *Borage family*

 Vipers Bugloss *pl. 104.* A stiff erect, bristly plant with bright blue flowers (1½–2 cm), pink in bud, (rarely white). Stamens purple, with 4 projecting beyond the oblique mouth of the corolla, the fifth much shorter. Basal leaves in a rosette, narrow lance-shaped. May–Aug. *Borage family*

 Purple Viper's Bugloss *pl. 106.* An erect, bristly-leaved plant with rather large tubular flowers with an oblique mouth and only 2 projecting stamens. Corolla (2½–3 cm) first reddish-purple, later bluish-purple. Basal leaves in a rosette, oval with prominent mid-veins and side veins. Apr.–July. *Borage family*

 Ground Ivy *pl. 109.* A softly hairy creeping plant of shady places, which roots at the nodes. Flowers (1½–2 cm), usually violet, purple-spotted on the lower lip, borne in whorls on erect shoots in the axils of the upper pairs of leaves. Mar.–May. *Mint family*

 Clary *pl. 113.* A robust, glandular, aromatic plant with loose spikes of pale violet-flushed flowers, and conspicuously coloured broad papery bracts flushed violet or pink. Flowers (2½–3 cm), lower lip often yellowish. Leaves large, greyish, wrinkled, conspicuously lobed or toothed, clasping the stem. May–Sept. *Mint family*

 Meadow Clary *pl. 114.* A handsome plant with long sticky spikes of bright blue, violet (or rarely white or pink) flowers, 1½–2½ cm long. The projecting style and unusual pair of hinged stamens are distinctive. Leaves oval-heart-shaped, wrinkled, mostly basal. May–July. *Mint family*

Deadly Nightshade   *pl. 117.* Better known by name than appearance, a very poisonous stout bushy, leafy perennial of shady places. Flowers (2½–3 cm long) solitary, drooping, brown-purple or greenish. The shining globular black berries (1½–2 cm) can cause death. Still used as a medicinal plant. June–Sept. *Nightshade family*

Purple Mullein   *pl. 121.* One of the few purple-flowered mulleins, with a long, wand-like, usually unbranched, glandular-hairy spike of flowers. Flowers (2½ cm) long-stalked, solitary in the axils of narrow bracts. Stamens all equal, with violet hairs. Leaves green, irregularly and coarsely toothed. June–July. *Figwort family*

Great Purple Toadflax   *pl. 122.* A handsome plant with narrow, glaucous, whorled leaves and possibly the largest flowers (2½–4 cm) of any purple-flowered toadflax. Flowers striped violet-purple, with a yellow throat-boss, and a long straight, very pointed spur. June–July. *Figwort family*

Spiked Bellflower   *pl. 138.* The numerous funnel-shaped flowers (1½–2 cm) are densely clustered, at the start of flowering, later occupying about two-thirds of the stout unbranched stem. Leaves rough, hairy, strap-shaped, mostly basal. July–Aug. *Bellflower family*

Clustered Bellflower   *pl. 138.* Distinguished by its dense globular cluster of rather large, funnel-shaped flowers, closely surrounded by the uppermost leaves. Possible to mistake for a gentian, but this is a downy plant with 3–5 stigmas (not 1 or 2). Uppermost leaves clasping, the basal leaves long-stalked. June–Aug. *Bellflower family*

Creeping Bellflower   *pl. 140.* Has a one-sided leafless spike-like cluster of flowers (2–3 cm). Petal lobes about as long as the tube, with spreading hairs; calyx reflexed after flowering, hairy. Upper leaves narrow lance-shaped; lower oval-heart-shaped. July–Aug. *Bellflower family*

Pale Bellflower   *pl. 140.* Has pale blue-lilac, rather small, spreading-bell-shaped flowers (1–2 cm) in a dense spike-like pyramidal cluster. Corolla lobes hairless; calyx lobes slender, spreading in fruit. Leaves densely white-woolly beneath. June–Aug. *Bellflower family*

Diamond-Leaved Bellflower   *pl. 140.* Differs from the Creeping Bellflower in its stalkless, oval-lance-shaped upper leaves with broadly rounded bases, only two to three times as long as broad. Flowers hairless, few, in a one-sided spike; petal lobes blunt. Stems angled. June–Aug. *Bellflower family*

Sea Aster   *pl. 142.* A robust, fleshy, hairless plant with Michaelmas Daisy-like flower heads. Ray florets from bluish-purple to whitish (occasionally absent). Fleshy leaves oblong to lance-shaped, usually not toothed. July–Oct. *Daisy family*

Alpine Saussurea   *pl. 152.* A short, unbranched, woolly-stemmed plant of rock crevices and exposed ridges, with bluish-lilac flower heads in a dense terminal cluster. Flower heads (1½–2 cm) without ray florets. Leaves densely white-haired beneath, hairless above. Aug.–Sept. *Daisy family*

Galactites   *pl. 154.* A delicate erect thistle. Stems and undersides of leaves white cottony. Flower heads few, rose-purple or lilac, in lax clusters. Outer florets large, spreading corolla, lobes linear. Involucral bracts with cobweb-hairs, and with grooved spiny tips. Apr.–July. *Daisy family*

Cornflower   *pl. 156.* An annual with flower heads with bright blue spreading outer florets and central red-purple florets. Bracts of involucre with pale or brownish fringe of teeth. Upper leaves narrow lance-shaped, greyish. May–Aug. *Daisy family*

Cupidone *pl. 157.* A very attractive, slender, greyish little-branched 'everlasting' plant. The silver-papery bracts of involucre and the blue flower heads with numerous ray florets are unlike any other. Leaves narrow, with few lobes. June–Aug. *Daisy family*

 Prenanthe *pl. 160.* An erect hairless, glaucous perennial of shady places in the mountains. Flower heads violet-purple, rarely white (2 cm) with only 2–5 florets. Leaves narrowed in the middle, violin-shaped, clasping the stem. July–Sept. *Daisy family*

 Spanish Bluebell *pl. 169.* Very like the common bluebell but flowers in a conical cluster, each one opening into a wide bell. Anthers blue, not yellow. Leaves broad (1½–2½ cm). The most commonly cultivated bluebell. Mar.–June. *Lily family*

See also: CORAL-WORT *pl. 34*; FIVE-LEAVED CORAL-WORT *pl. 34*; LADY'S SMOCK *pl. 34*; WHITE LUPIN *pl. 54*; SEA PEA *pl. 56*; SPRING PEA *pl. 56*; PEA *pl. 56*; ALPINE SAINFOIN *pl. 61*; BASTARD BALM *pl. 109*; SCOPOLIA *pl. 116*; BEAN BROOMRAPE *pl. 131*; BROAD-LEAVED MARSH ORCHID *pl. 187*.

Flowers medium · Plant small

 Blue Wood Anemone *pl. 22.* Very like the Wood Anemone but flowers blue, and narrow petals more numerous (8–14). Petals hairy beneath; sometimes white. Fruiting head held erect. South-east Europe but not occurring south of Macedonia. Mar.–May. *Buttercup family*

 Eastern Blue Wood Anemone *pl. 21.* Almost indistinguishable from the previous species but restricted to the southern part of the Balkan Peninsula, Crete, and the Aegean Islands. Flowers blue, pink or white, petals hairless. Fruiting heads drooping. Mar.–June. *Buttercup family*

 Hepatica *pl. 20.* The blue anemone-like flowers and unusual shallowly 3-lobed leaves are unmistakable. Flowers often pink or white, on slender stems arising directly from the stock; there are 3 green, oval sepal-like bracts below each flower. Leaves usually purplish beneath. Mar.–May. *Buttercup family*

 Virginia Stock *pl. 32.* A slender, little-branched, slightly downy annual with a loose cluster of violet, pink (rarely white) flowers, with paler centres. Leaves oblong, somewhat fleshy. Pod long, slender. Native of Greece, naturalized elsewhere. May–July. *Cress family*

 Wild Pansy *pl. 75.* A charming little pansy with variable but conspicuous bright yellow or violet flowers, often streaked and with white or yellow. Spur usually short. Leaves often cut fanwise into oblong segments, the middle one longest. Mar.–Sept. *Violet family*

 Sweet Violet *pl. 76.* This well-known violet can be distinguished by its delicious sweet scent. Flowers usually deep violet or white, rarely purple or pink; sepals blunt. The plant forms long runners rooting at the tips. Mar.–May. *Violet family*

 Common Dog Violet *pl. 76.* Like the previous plant, but quite unscented. Flowers usually blue-violet, with a stout and paler spur which is often upcurved, and furrowed or notched; sepals acute. Runners are not formed in this species. Apr.–May. *Violet family*

 Sticky Alpine Primrose *pl. 89.* A low sticky-hairy plant of the high Alps and Pyrenees, with a pale green rosette of coarsely toothed oval leaves. The violet-purple flowers (1½ cm) are fragrant and carried in short heads of 3–20. June–July. *Primrose family*

 Spring Gentian *pl. 96.* The bluest gentian of all European species. Flowers (1½–3 cm across) always solitary, arising on short stems from a loose cushion of rosettes with oval-lance-shaped leaves. Mar.–Aug. *Gentian family*

Herbaceous Periwinkle   *pl. 97.* Like the widespread Lesser Periwinkle, but trailing stems soft and herbaceous (not woody), not rooting at the nodes. Flowers (2½–3 cm) violet-blue, with blunt-tipped petals. Leaves soft, margins finely hairy. Feb.–May. *Dogbane family*

 Alpine Skullcap   *pl. 108.* A low spreading plant of rocks and screes, with dense quadrangular clusters of blue-violet flowers, 2–2½ cm (rarely purple or white), arising from the axils of purple-flushed, papery bracts. Leaves oval, toothed, in opposite pairs. June–Aug. *Mint family*

 Large Self-Heal   *pl. 110.* A creeping perennial with erect stems bearing dense rounded terminal heads of bright blue-violet flowers. Heads borne on short stems above the uppermost pairs of leaves. (Leaves *immediately* below head in Common Self-Heal (not illustrated).) Flowers 2–2½ cm; bracts often purple-flushed. June–Oct. *Mint family*

 Mandrake   *pl. 118.* Forms large rosettes of flattened wrinkled leaves arising from a stout, forked root. Fruits orange or yellow, like miniature tomatoes. There are 2 closely related species: one with greenish-yellow flowers appearing in the spring; the other with violet flowers found in the spring or autumn. *Nightshade family*

 Alpine Toadflax   *pl. 122.* A delicate spreading toadflax of rocks and screes, with whorls of slightly fleshy glaucous leaves and deep violet flowers, usually with an orange throat-boss (sometimes white). Flowers 2 cm long, spur almost straight. June–Sept. *Figwort family*

 Ramonda   *pl. 131.* A very distinctive rock-crevice plant of the Pyrenees with handsome flattened rosettes of broad greyish wrinkled leaves. Flowers saucer-shaped, varying in colour from blue to violet, with a cone of yellow stamens in the centre. June–Aug. *Gloxinia family*

 Purple Toothwort   *pl. 130.* An unusual parasitic plant with a dense cluster of stout, bright purple flowers pushing up from the roots of the tree on which it lives. Green leaves absent; only scale-like bracts borne on the rhizome below ground. Apr.–May. *Broomrape family*

 Common Butterwort   *pl. 132.* A charming plant with a flat rosette of pale yellowish-green, sticky leaves to which insects are attracted. Flowers violet-like, from violet to lilac, with a horizontal spur. Distinguished by the lobes of the lower lip, which are longer than broad. May–July. *Butterwort family*

 Large-Flowered Butterwort   *pl. 132.* Like the preceding species, but larger. Lower lip of flower with 3 overlapping lobes, broader than long; spur more than half as long as the petals. An insectivorous plant of bogs and wet rocks in the Pyrenees, Western Alps and Ireland. May–June. *Butterwort family*

 Bearded Bellflower   *pl. 139.* The delicate, pale milky-blue, drooping bell-shaped flowers with many long white hairs in the throat are quite distinctive. Flower clusters one-sided. The basal leaves are in a rosette. June–Aug. *Bellflower family*

 Scheuchzer's Bellflower   *pl. 140.* A mountain plant of central and south-east Europe usually with solitary flowers (2–3 cm), nodding in bud. Stem leaves all narrow lance-shaped, with spreading hairs on the margin, basal leaves rounded. July–Aug. *Bellflower family*

 Fairy's Thimble   *pl. 140.* A small cushion plant of the mountains with rounded rosette leaves. Flower stems slender, with one or a few blue, violet or rarely white flowers (1–2 cm). Upper stem leaves lance-shaped, quite different from lower leaves. June–Aug. *Bellflower family*

Venus' Looking-Glass *pl. 141*. A slender, little-branched annual, with bright, dark blue-violet flowers with a central white eye, opening wide in the sun. Leaves oblong, with wavy margins, rough to the touch. Fruits cylindrical (1½–3 cm). May–July. *Bellflower family*

 Blue Fleabane *pl. 143*. A slender, softly hairy annual with small flower heads (1–1½ cm) of numerous pale purple, narrow ray florets and yellow disk florets. Leaves not toothed, lower broadly lance-shaped, stalked, upper narrower, stalkless. June–Sept. *Daisy family*

 Blue Grass-Lily *pl. 162*. Like a tuft of rush stems until it bursts into flower. Each leafless stem bears at its tip an oval cluster of russet bracts, from which arise the starry blue flowers, one by one. Flowers (2½ cm) with darker midveins (rarely all white). Leaves reduced to sheaths; stems glaucous, ribbed. Apr.–July. *Lily family*

 Alpine Squill *pl. 170*. Distinguished by its paired, shiny, grooved, outward-curving leaves which appear to arise halfway up the flowering stem. The bright blue flowers are conspicuous, and borne in a branched leafless cluster (rarely white or pink). A bulbous plant of shady places in the lowlands and mountains. Mar.–Aug. *Lily family*

 Bluebell *pl. 170*. A beautiful woodland plant of western Europe. The nodding clusters of scented, narrow bell-shaped flowers (1½–2 cm) are distinctive. Petals neatly curved backwards at their tips but remaining pressed together in a tube at the base. Leaves shiny, strap-shaped, all basal. Apr.–May. *Lily family*

 Hyacinth *pl. 171*. Probably only native in Yugoslavia, but widely cultivated, sometimes naturalized (in blue, white or pink forms). The scented flowers have narrow curved petals, fused into a tube below and borne on leafless stems. Leaves shining, strap-shaped (1–2 cm wide). Mar.–May. *Lily family*

 Barbary Nut *pl. 175*. The smallest European iris with variable-sized blue flowers (1–3 cm) with a contrasting white centre. The flowers emerge about noon from swollen papery brownish bracts. Leaves rush-like, grooved. Apr.–May. *Iris family*.

See also: MOUNTAIN PANSY *pl. 76*; ALPINE BELLS *pl. 91*; PURPLE CROCUS *pl. 174*.

Flowers small · Plant medium

 Goat's Rue *pl. 53*. Grows in erect leafy clumps, with stalked clusters of numerous pale lilac or white flowers (each 8–15 mm) longer than the leaves. Calyx hairless, swollen at the base, and with 5 bristle-like teeth. Leaves pinnate with 9–17 pairs of oblong leaflets. June–Aug. *Pea family*

 Narrow-Leaved Lupin *pl. 54*. Very like a small garden lupin but with narrow lance-shaped leaflets spreading fanwise and hairy only below. Flowers (1 cm) arranged alternately (not whorled) in a long dense spike (10–20 cm long). Apr.–June. *Pea family*

 Pitch Trefoil *pl. 54*. The crushed leaves smell strongly of tar or bitumen. The dense rounded heads of blue-violet, clover-like flowers are unmistakable. Leaves trifoliate, leaflets almost rounded on lower leaves. Apr.–July. *Pea family*

 Tufted Vetch *pl. 55*. Common and often draping hedges or scrambling through other plants. Flowers (1 cm) blue-violet, drooping in dense, long-stalked, one-sided clusters. Leaves pinnate with 6–20 pairs of oblong leaflets. June–Aug. *Pea family*

 Blue Fenugreek *pl. 57*. A fodder crop unknown in the wild, but often naturalized; also used for flavouring cheese. Flowers blue-lilac, small (5–7 mm), closely clustered in a dense rounded head. Leaves with 3 oval, toothed leaflets. June–July. *Pea family*

Lucerne, Alfalfa *pl. 58.* Widely grown as a forage crop, particularly in dry regions. Unknown in the wild, but introduced throughout Europe. Flowers (8 mm) purple or blue in a rather dense head. Leaflets 3. Pod distinctive, forming an open spiral of 2–4 turns. June–Sept. *Pea family*

 Soft Storksbill *pl. 64.* A common annual of the Mediterranean, with soft rather distinctive oval-heart-shaped, shallowly lobed or toothed leaves. Flowers lilac, small (1–1½ cm), on a long glandular-hairy stalk longer than the leaves. Beak of fruit quite short (2–4 cm). Feb.–June. *Geranium family*

 Southern Mallow *pl. 73.* One of several small-flowered mallows with bunched clusters of pale lilac, or whitish flowers (1–1½ cm) in the axils of the upper leaves. They can be distinguished by their fruits; this plant has usually hairless, strongly netted nutlets. May–July. *Mallow family*

 Sea Holly *pl. 83.* An exceedingly spiny, stiff, bluish-green plant with holly-like leaves growing in sands and shingles by the sea. Flower heads globular, bluish, also spiny. The fruits are covered with hooks. June–Sept. *Umbellifer family*

 Winged Sea Lavender *pl. 94.* An 'everlasting' plant. The bright bluish-mauve colour (not, as in the plate, pinkish-mauve) is due to the calyx, which is dry and papery. Flowers tiny, yellowish. The stems are conspicuously winged and the flat rosette has wavy-edged leaves. Apr.–Sept. *Sea Lavender family*

 Field Madder *pl. 99.* A small spreading annual of cultivated ground, with square stems, and whorls of 5–6 leaves. Small clusters of pale lilac flowers (½ cm long) are encircled by longer leafy bracts. Leaf margins and midribs beneath covered with tiny prickles and very rough to the touch. Mar.–Sept. *Bedstraw family*

 Blue Hound's-Tongue *pl. 101.* The pale blue (not as in the plate, purple) flowers veined with violet are distinctive. Leaves soft and silvery-grey. Nutlets rounded and covered with short spines and swellings. Apr.–July. *Borage family*

 Blue Comfrey *pl. 102.* The tubular drooping flowers (1½–2 cm) are blue or purplish, rarely pinkish. A plant of hybrid origin with rough stems and leaves which run only a short way down the stems. Grown for fodder, widely naturalized. May–July. *Borage family*

 True Alkanet *pl. 103.* There are several similar-looking species, but this plant is distinguished by the deeply cleft calyx with acute teeth, and leaves which have flat, not undulate or crisped margins. Flowers (1 cm) purple (not, as in the plate, pink), with a long funnel-shaped throat closed by velvet-haired scales. June–Aug. *Borage family*

 Alkanet *pl. 102.* Bright blue forget-me-not flowers with white centres, and oval, pointed, bristly-haired leaves distinguish this rather robust plant. Flowers (1 cm) borne in dense, branched leafy clusters. Upper leaves stalkless, the lower stalked. Apr.–July. *Borage family*

 Northern Shorewort, Oyster Plant *pl. 103.* A beautiful, fleshy, spreading shore plant, covered by a purple bloom, with pink tubular flowers (6 mm across) which turn bluish-purple. Leaves oval in 2 rows, upper sides dotted with glands and said to taste of oysters. June–Aug. *Borage family*

 Water Forget-me-Not *pl. 103.* Usually found in damp places but not growing in water. Flowers (½–1 cm) bright blue with yellow eye (rarely pink or white). A rather weak-stemmed plant with pale, nearly hairless lance-shaped leaves. May–Sept. *Borage family*

 Narrow-Leaved Lungwort *pl. 104.* A downy plant with large lance-shaped, white-spotted, stalked basal leaves, and narrow, half-clasping upper leaves. Flowers (½ cm across)

at first pink then blue. Stamens project from corolla, alternating with tufts of hairs within. Apr.–May. *Borage family*

 Blue Bugle   *pl. 105*. Flowers much brighter and truer blue than those of the widespread Common Bugle and unlike it in having no creeping, rooting overground stolons. Bracts becoming bluish. Stems hairy all round (not on 2 opposite sides only). May–Aug. *Mint family*

 Skullcap   *pl. 108*. A downy, creeping plant of damp places, with erect stems bearing a loose, leafy, one-sided spike of paired blue-lilac flowers. Flowers (1½–2 cm) tubular, two-lipped, slightly curved; calyx two-lipped, with a transverse flap on the back. June–Sept. *Mint family*

 Penny-Royal   *pl. 116*. A sprawling, often downy plant smelling of mint, with numerous globular, widely spaced whorls of lilac or pink flowers. Stamens protruding; inflorescence with a topknot of leaves. Leaves (1–2 cm), the upper shorter than the upper flower whorls. July–Oct. *Mint family*

 Water Mint   *pl. 116*. An erect mint of damp places with terminal globular lilac or white flower clusters which are not topped by a cluster of leaves. Lower whorls of flowers few, often separated. Smells strongly of peppermint when crushed. July–Sept. *Mint family*

 Horsemint   *pl. 116*. An erect, rather coarse, strong-smelling greyish mint with long slender, densely cylindrical spikes of numerous whorls, with only the lowest separated. Flowers usually lilac but may be pinkish; very variable. July–Sept. *Mint family*

 Bittersweet, Woody Nightshade   *pl. 119*. A scrambling, woody-based plant with inconspicuous deep purple flowers (1–2 cm) with a central yellow cone of stamens. Fruit a shining, pea-sized berry, at first green, then yellow and finally red. Leaves oval, the lower usually deeply lobed. June–Sept. *Nightshade family*

 Pale Toadflax   *pl. 122*. Has long slender, lax spikes of numerous small (7–14 mm) pale lilac or whitish-striped, two-lipped flowers. Spur stout, straight; the throat-boss yellow. Leaves numerous, very narrow and glaucous, whorled below, alternate above. June–Sept. *Figwort family*

 Blue Snapdragon   *pl. 123*. Slender flowering spikes arise from a rosette of narrow leaves. Flowers cylindrical (3–5 mm long), somewhat two-lipped, with a short spur curved under the corolla. Stem leaves deeply cut fanwise and differing from the toothed rosette leaves. Mar.–Aug. *Figwort family*

 Brooklime   *pl. 124*. A plant of damp ditches and streams with somewhat fleshy, rounded, shining leaves and weak, hollow, often reddish stems. Petals bright blue, with a white centre, and 2 white stamens. May–Sept. *Figwort family*

 Field Scabious   *pl. 138*. A tall, slender plant with hemispherical heads (3–4 cm) of bluish-lilac flowers, the outer florets distinctly longer than the inner. Flower heads on long, nearly leafless stems. Lower leaves deeply cut into oblong lobes, basal leaves usually entire. Fruit with 8 bristle-like teeth. May–Oct. *Scabious family*

 Blue-Spiked Rampion   *pl. 141*. Rampions have dense heads of small flowers, with narrow petals joined together at the tips, though separated at the base. Flower spike blue or lilac, oval to cylindrical. Stem leaves all linear. June–Aug. *Bellflower family*

 Round-Headed Rampion   *pl. 141*. Has globular flower heads (1½–2½ cm), surrounded by broadly lance-shaped bracts about as long as, or shorter than, the head. Basal leaves in a rosette, long-stalked, heart-shaped to triangular. May–Oct. *Bellflower family*

Peruvian Squill *pl. 168.* The hemispherical domes of small blue-violet flowers are unmistakable; flower clusters usually short-stalked and carried a short distance above the leaves by a stout stem. Leaves broad (4–6 cm) shining and strap-shaped, spreading outwards over the ground. Mar.–May. *Lily family*

Tassel Hyacinth *pl. 169.* A striking, unusual-looking plant with a topknot of erect, long-stalked, brightly coloured, sterile flowers, contrasting with spreading, dark blue, later brown, fertile flowers below. Fruits borne in long clusters (15–30 cm) on spreading stalks. Apr.–July. *Lily family*

See also: SAND BITTER-CRESS *pl. 35*; SEA ROCKET *pl. 37*; ORPINE, LIVELONG *pl. 40*; COMMON VETCH *pl. 55*; SHAGGY VETCH *pl. 55*; BLACK PEA *pl. 56*; CROWN VETCH *pl. 62*; PALE BUGLOSS *pl. 105*; MOURNFUL WIDOW, SWEET SCABIOUS *pl. 138*; WOOD SCABIOUS *pl. 138*; SPIKED RAMPION *pl. 141*; KEELED GARLIC *pl. 165*; ROSE GARLIC *pl. 166.*

Flowers small · Plant small

Spring Rock-Cress *pl. 35.* Tiny, with a flat basal rosette of oval-heart-shaped, hairy leaves. Flowering stems slender, bearing tiny violet flowers (petals 5–8 mm), with a yellowsih centre (or flowers white). Fruit long and slender. Apr.–May. *Cress family*

Blue Stonecrop *pl. 40.* An unusual stonecrop with blue flowers with white centres, found in Corsica, Sicily, and Sardinia. The leaves are very fleshy, oblong (1 cm) and often turning reddish. Apr.–May. *Stonecrop family*

Alpine Milk-Vetch *(not illustrated)* A spreading plant with loose clusters of variegated white, blue and violet flowers (1 cm). Standard often bluish, wings white, keel tipped with violet. Leaves of 4–8 pairs of elliptic leaflets. July–Aug. *Pea family*

Common Milkwort *pl. 68.* A slender erect plant with blue, pink or white flowers. Milkworts are distinguished by 2 large, brightly coloured outer sepals encircling the small. er similar-coloured, inner petals, one of which is fringed. Leaves narrow lance-shaped-May–July. *Milkwort family*

Bog Violet *pl. 76.* The pale milky-lilac flowers of this bog-loving violet are quite distinctive. Leaves more rounded and kidney-shaped than most, weakly toothed, often slightly bloomed. Apr.–June. *Violet family*

Dwarf Snowbell *pl. 91.* One of the most delicate and charming of all high alpine plants, flowering as the snow melts. The flower bells are fringed for only about a quarter of their length (in Alpine Snowbell (not illustrated) they are much more deeply fringed). Leaves tiny (1 cm), rounded kidney-shaped, leathery and dotted with glands beneath. May–Aug. *Primrose family*

Bladder Gentian *pl. 96.* Distinguished from other small-flowered annual alpine gentians by the calyx which becomes oval and swollen after flowering and has 5 broad wings. Flowers (1–1½ cm across) arising from a basal rosette. May–Aug. *Gentian family*

Blue-Eyed Mary *pl. 101.* A lowly creeping plant of woods, forming patches, with shining heart-shaped, pointed leaves. Flowers (1 cm), forget-me-not-like, but distinguished by the throat which is almost closed by 5 blunt lobes. Mar.–May. *Borage family*

Dyer's Alkanet *pl. 103.* A woody-based, spreading, densely silvery, bristly plant of the Mediterranean. Flowers usually bright blue (½ cm) with a long tube and spreading lobes, grouped into leafy clusters. Apr.–June. *Borage family*

Alpine Forget-me-Not *pl. 103.* This low-growing forget-me-not has softly downy leaves, and dense clusters of striking blue flowers (4–10 mm). Calyx covered with silvery hairs and divided to more than half its length into 5 teeth. Apr.–Sept. *Borage family*

King of the Alps   *pl. 104.* Its brilliant sky blue flowers are amongst the most striking of all alpines as they nestle in a cushion of silky, silvery leaves. It grows in mountain rock crevices and is distinguished from the forget-me-nots by its cushion-like growth and different fruit. July–Aug. *Borage family*

Common Bugle   *pl. 106.* A creeping plant with erect cylindrical or pyramidal spikes of blue flowers. Flower spikes leafy; lower leaves longer than flowers, the upper shorter and often purple-flushed. Leaves forming a rosette below; the square stem is hairy on 2 sides only. Apr.–July. *Mint family*

Pyramidal Bugle   *pl. 106.* Often very striking, with squat pyramidal spikes of bright blue or violet bracts almost hiding the small paler blue-violet flowers. Very hairy plant not forming runners; stem densely hairy all round. Apr.–Aug. *Mint family*

Dragonmouth   *pl. 114.* Not very typical of this family, with its long tubular two-lipped flowers much longer than the calyx. Flowers dark blue-violet, drooping, in many whorls forming a long spike. Leaves mostly in a neat flattened rosette with oval, conspicuously toothed, wrinkled blades. June–Aug. *Mint family*

Ivy-Leaved Toadflax   *pl. 122.* A delicate trailing plant often growing on old walls. The two-lipped flowers (1 cm) are shortly spurred; the pale throat-boss is conspicuous. Leaves small, shining, ivy-like. May–Oct. *Figwort family*

Rock Speedwell   *pl. 124.* A creeping, woody-based plant of alpine rocks with comparatively large (1 cm) brilliant blue flowers with a purple throat. Leaves opposite, somewhat fleshy, oval and shining. July–Aug. *Figwort family*

Buxbaum's Speedwell   *pl. 124.* One of several species that are common weeds. Distinguished by solitary flowers (8–12 mm) borne from the leaf axils on stalks longer than the leaves. Fruiting stalks down-curved, lobes of fruit diverging. Mar.–Oct. *Figwort family*

Creeping Speedwell   *pl. 124.* Recently introduced from Asia Minor to much of Europe. Flowers solitary, borne on very slender leaf-stalks, much longer than the leaves. Lower petal usually much paler. A creeping and rooting plant often forming mats. Apr.–May. *Figwort family*

Alpine Bartsia   *pl. 126.* Unmistakable with dark violet-purple tubular, two-lipped flowers surrounded by similar-coloured leafy bracts. Upper lip of flower forms a hood over the 3-lobed lower lip; tips of the lip usually white. A creeping plant with paired oval, wrinkled leaves. June–Aug. *Figwort family*

Common Globularia   *pl. 129.* Globularias are distinguished by blue globular heads of many small flowers. Flowers with a narrow tube and 2 inconspicuous lips. Leaves mostly in a rosette, oval and notched or three-lobed; stem leaves lance-shaped, stalkless. Apr.–June. *Globularia family*

Sheep's Bit   *pl. 141.* It could quite easily be confused with the Round-headed Rampion but distinguished by the petals which are free and do not remain attached above. A bristly plant; leaves often with undulate margins. June–Sept. *Bellflower family*

Autumn Squill   *pl. 168.* A small bulbous plant with dull lilac flowers in flat-topped clusters which later elongate. Inflorescence without bracts or leaves; petals 4-6 mm; anthers lilac. Leaves narrow, slightly grooved, appearing after flowering. Aug.–Oct. *Lily family*

Dark Grape-Hyacinth   *pl. 169.* Has conspicuously 'pinched-in' flowers which are dark blue all over (without white teeth). Flowers sweet-scented, usually with a few smaller, paler, sterile flowers at the top of the cluster. Mar.–Apr. *Lily family*

Southern Grape-Hyacinth *pl. 170*. Differs from the previous species in the more open tubular flowers with white tips to the teeth. Flowers 6–8 mm, and leaves 3–5 mm broad. (The similar more widespread Grape-Hyacinth (not illustrated) has smaller flowers and narrower leaves.) Mar.–May. *Lily family*

 Small Grape-Hyacinth *pl. 170*. Distinguished from all other species by its very tiny (3–4 mm) globular flowers with whitish teeth. Leaves narrow, grooved, becoming broader towards the apex. Mar.–May. *Lily family*

See also: BURNT CANDYTUFT *pl. 36*; ROUND-LEAVED PENNYCRESS *pl. 36*; HAIRY STONECROP *pl. 40*; VARIABLE MILKWORT *pl 68*; BIRD'S-EYE PRIMROSE *pl. 91*; FIELD GENTIAN *pl. 96*; CUT-LEAVED SELF-HEAL *pl. 110*; ALPINE CALAMINT *pl. 114*; RED-TOPPED SAGE *pl. 115*; DWARF EYEBRIGHT *pl. 127*; LESSER BROOMRAPE *pl. 131*; SHINING SCABIOUS *pl. 138*; DEVIL'S CLAW *pl. 140*.

Flowers minute · Plant medium

 Blue Eryngo *pl. 83*. As the season advances the whole plant becomes bright bluish-violet and stands out strikingly in the parched ground. It forms a rounded, much-branched bushy clump, and the thistle-like leaves are twice-cut into spiny toothed lobes. July–Aug. *Umbellifer family*

See also: FIELD ERYNGO *pl. 83*.

Flowers minute · Plant small

 Water Purslane *pl. 81*. A creeping rooting plant of damp places with tiny stalkless flowers with minute lilac petals (petals often absent, flowers appearing greenish). Stems four-angled. Plant often turns reddish as the mud dries out. May–Oct. *Loosestrife family*

 Hoary Plantain *pl. 133*. Readily distinguished in flower by its pale pinkish-purple cylindrical spikes, due to the long, coloured filaments of the stamens. Leaves oval, finely hairy, strongly five- to nine-veined, in a neat rosette, pressed flat against the ground. May–Aug. *Plantain family*

 Lamb's Lettuce, Corn Salad *pl. 136*. A small, branched annual with rounded or flat-topped clusters of minute pale lilac flowers (2 mm). Leaves spoon-shaped. Many similar-looking species are largely distinguished by their fruits. Apr.–June. *Valerian family*

BROWN

Flowers large · Plant medium

 Dragon Arum *pl. 183*. A sinister, brown-spotted plant with an unpleasant smell when in flower. The chocolate-purple spathe encircles the minute flowers at the base of the fleshy spadix, where pollination by trapped flies takes place. Leaves divided into lance-shaped leaflets. Apr.–June. *Arum family*

Flowers large · Plant small

 Snake's Tongue *pl. 183*. An unusual plant related to the previous species. The 'flower' consists of a strap-shaped tongue (8–12 cm) and an erect spadix; both attract flies. Minute florets are enclosed by the base of the spathe below ground. Later, glaucous, lance-shaped leaves appear. Apr.–July, Sept.–Oct. *Arum family*

 Friar's Cowl *pl. 183*. A weird little plant with a striped flask-shaped spathe curved over at the top, from which a short brown club-like spadix appears. Florets minute and enclosed in the spathe. Leaves arrow-shaped, small. Mar.–May, Oct.–Nov. *Arum family*

Flowers medium · Plant medium

Round-Leaved Birthwort   *pl. 8.* A strange-looking plant with erect tubular, axillary flowers with a brown flap-like hood. From a globular underground tuber arise erect stems, embraced by stalkless, almost rounded leaves. Apr.–June. *Birthwort family*

See also: WALLFLOWER *pl. 32*; HONEYWORT *pl. 105*; JUPITER'S DISTAFF *pl. 113*; LIZARD ORCHID *pl. 190.*

Flowers medium · Plant small

Asarabacca   *pl. 7.* An unmistakable, rather unattractive plant with solitary dingy-brown, bell-shaped flowers (1½ cm), and dark, glossy, kidney-shaped leaves. A low creeping plant of woodlands. Mar.–May. *Birthwort family*

Brown Bee Orchid   *pl. 188.* Usually a rather drab orchid with a deep chocolate brown, velvety, bluntly three-lobed lip. Reflective patches on lip often dull but sometimes bright blue; petals greenish. A widespread Mediterranean orchid. Feb.–May. *Orchid family*

Woodcock Orchid   *pl. 188.* A striking orchid with a rounded brownish lip variously marked with circles or lines of white and yellow, and with a yellow apical knob. There are often 2 basal swellings which may be elongated into long side-horns. Petals usually pink. Apr.–May. *Orchid family*

Fly Orchid   *pl. 188.* Perhaps the least spectacular of all European *Ophrys* species, with small dark brown flowers (1½ cm) with a blue reflective patch on the four-lobed lip. The almost thread-like inner petals are distinctive. May–June. *Orchid family*

Bee Orchid   *pl. 188.* The pink petals and fat, velvety, reddish-brown lip with yellow patterns enclosing a red patch and 2 yellow spots towards the tip, are characteristic. But the markings can be variable and more reliable characters are the curved pointed beak and the curved-under yellow apex of the lip. May–July. *Orchid family*

Bumble Bee Orchid   *pl. 188.* A small orchid easily recognized by its squat dull brown rounded lip without distinctive reflective patches. Side lobes of the lip squat and hairy; sepals green, broadly oval. Mar.–Apr. *Orchid family*

Bertoloni's Orchid   *pl. 188.* Distinguished by its long, rather rectangular, almost black velvety lip, with a brilliant shining blue, indented reflective patch, and a forward-projecting knob at the tip. Sepals and petals pinkish-purple. Apr.–June. *Orchid family*

Sawfly Orchid   *pl. 188.* Usually distinguished by its squarish or wedge-shaped lip with a broad or narrow yellow hairy margin. The reddish-brown basal patch is surrounded by blue lines and the apex of the lip is two-lobed with a yellowish knob between. Sepals broadly oval, bright pink to white with green veins; petals triangular, smaller. Mar.–May. *Orchid family*

See also: SAD STOCK *pl. 33*; MAN ORCHID *pl. 189.*

Flowers small · Plant medium

Balm-Leaved Figwort   *pl. 123.* An erect, downy, greyish plant of shady places by the sea. Flowers (8–11 mm) dull brownish-purple in lax leafy branched clusters; calyx with papery margins. Leaves nettle-like, wrinkled, toothed. May–Sept. *Figwort family*

Alpine Figwort   *pl. 123.* A mountain plant of central Europe with dark blackish-purple flowers (6–8 mm long) with white side lobes and long upper lip. Flower stalks short, sticky-haired. Leaves once or twice cut into narrow lobes. June–Aug. *Figwort family*

Black False Helleborine   *pl. 162.* A stout plant of the mountains with large, elliptic overlapping, conspicuously veined leaves in whorls of 3. The branched clusters of small blackish-purple flowers (1 cm) distinguish it from much commoner white-, green- or yellowish-flowered species. June–Aug. *Lily family*

Bird's-Nest Orchid *pl. 192.* A dull yellowish-brown saprophytic orchid living on rotting leaves, particularly in beechwoods. Flowers brownish-yellow, without a spur and with a long two-lobed lip. Green leaves absent; roots forming a bird's-nest-like tangle. May–July. *Orchid family*

See also: LESSER HONEYWORT *pl. 105.*

Flowers small · Plant small

Sea Plantain *pl. 132.* A tufted, often grey-green somewhat fleshy-leaved plant. The dense, narrowly cylindrical flowering spikes (2–12 cm) have numerous tiny brownish flowers (3 mm). Leaves linear, all basal; stems smooth. May–Sept. *Plantain family*

Branched Plantain *pl. 133.* Differs from most other plantains in its much-branched leafy stems with many rounded flower clusters (1 cm). Flowers tiny (4 mm), brownish-white. Leaves not forming a rosette, narrow, entire, or obscurely toothed. May–Sept. *Plantain family*

See also: BUCK'S-HORN PLANTAIN *pl. 133*; MARSH CUDWEED *pl. 144*; BUG ORCHID *pl. 187*.

YELLOW

Flowers large · Plant large

Large-Flowered Mullein *pl. 120.* Flowering spike long, slender and usually unbranched, with large stalkless yellow flowers (3–5 cm). Stamens white-haired. Leaves covered with yellow woolly hairs, coarsely toothed, blade decurrent. May–Aug. *Figwort family*

Large Yellow Ox-Eye *pl. 145.* A tall stout plant with large flower heads (6 cm across), recalling Elecampane. Distinguished by ribbed fruits with a short crown-like pappus, and a receptacle with many scales. Lower leaves stalked, broadly triangular heart-shaped, the upper clasping. June–Aug. *Daisy family*

Cone Flower *pl. 146.* A native of America, sometimes naturalized. Flower heads (7–12 cm), with a central cone of darker disk florets and large, down-spreading ray florets. A tall hairless plant; lower leaves often deeply lobed, the upper entire. June–Oct. *Daisy family*

Flowers large · Plant medium

Globe Flower *pl. 19.* Recognized by its bright yellow globular flowers (2½–5 cm) with rounded, overlapping incurved petals. Leaves dark green, deeply three- to five-lobed. Usually in damp mountain pastures. May–Aug. *Buttercup family*

Welsh Poppy *pl. 28.* A mountain poppy of shady places, with sulphur yellow flowers with 4 petals. Leaves with a yellow juice, grey-green below, cut into oval segments. Fruit cylindrical with a knob-like stigma. June–Aug. *Poppy family*

Prickly Poppy *pl. 29.* A native of America which is sometimes naturalized. The poppy-like flowers are pale yellow or orange (5–6 cm); calyx conspicuously spiny. Leaves spiny, thistle-like, bluish-green. Fruits elliptic, also conspicuously spiny. Summer. *Poppy family*

Yellow Horned-Poppy *pl. 29.* A glaucous leafy plant of shingle by the sea, with large pale yellow or golden-yellow flowers (6–9 cm), and conspicuous, very long curved pods (to 30 cm). Leaves deeply irregularly lobed, bristly, the upper clasping the stem. June–Aug. *Poppy family*

Californian Poppy   *pl. 29.* A popular garden plant; native of North America often escaping. Flowers orange or yellow (to 10 cm) petals shining; calyx forming a sheath like a gnome's cap, shed when the flowers open. Leaves feathery, glaucous. July–Sept. *Poppy family*

 Levant Cotton   *pl. 73.* Grown for cotton, sometimes escaping from cultivation. Flowers (7½ cm) solitary, pale yellow, often purple-centred; epicalyx deeply toothed or cut. Leaves are deeply 3- to 7-lobed. Sept. *Mallow family*

 Bladder Ketmia   *pl. 73.* An annual weed of south-east Europe, spreading to central Europe. Flowers solitary (2–4 cm) with greater or lesser amounts of dark brown at the centre. Calyx inflated in fruit, prominently veined, with 12 narrow bristly epicalyx teeth. June–Sept. *Mallow family*

 Evening Primrose   *pl. 81.* One of several North American species widely established in Europe. A tall, leafy plant with a slender spike of large primrose yellow flowers (petals 4–6 cm). Distinguished from other species by the red-spotted or -striped sepals. Rosette leaves lance-shaped, long-stalked, the upper stalkless. June-Sept. *Willow Herb - family*

 Large Yellow Loosestrife   *pl. 93.* Differs from the commoner Yellow Loosestrife (not illustrated) in its large flowers (3½ cm) and glandular-hairy petals and calyx. The calyx is not bordered with orange. Leaves all shortly stalked, in whorls of 3 or 4. July–Oct. *Primrose family*

 Great Yellow Gentian   *pl. 95.* A stout, erect plant with large, oval conspicuously ribbed and fluted leaves, clasping the stem above. Flowers yellow (2½ cm long) with 5–9 narrow petals spreading in a star, clustered in a leafy spike of several whorls. June–Aug. *Gentian family*

 Spotted Gentian   *pl. 97.* A rather sturdy plant of grasslands and thickets with a cluster of large pale yellow, broad bell-shaped flowers (4 cm long), spotted purple. Leaves grey-green, strongly 5- to 7-veined. The upper clasping. July–Sept. *Gentian family*

 Celsia   *pl. 120.* A handsome mullein with very long slender spikes of large flowers (4½ cm) with unequal petals, the 2 upper spotted with brown. Stamens only 4, violet-haired. Upper leaves grey-haired, regularly toothed, clasping the stem, the lower stalked and deeply lobed. Apr.–June. *Figwort family*

 Large Snapdragon   *pl. 121.* Closely related to the purple and varicoloured Common Snapdragon *(pl, 121)* but more robust, with oval leaves, and glandular-hairy stems. Flowers large (3½–4½ cm), usually yellow with a pale throat-boss. Apr.–Nov. *Figwort family*

 Monkey-Flower   *pl. 123.* A distinctive plant of watersides with large yellow tubular, two-lipped flowers (2½–4½ cm) with a much longer lower lip and a red spotted throat-boss. Calyx flask-like, enlarged in fruit. Leaves opposite, oval and irregularly toothed. A native of North America, now widely naturalized. June–Sept. *Figwort family*

 Elecampane   *pl. 144.* A robust plant with large flower heads (6–8 cm) and very large leaves (to 80 cm), wrinkled above, downy below, the upper clasping. Bracts of involucre green and leaf-like. The hairless, four-ribbed fruit has a long reddish pappus of hairs. May–Sept. *Daisy family*

 Yellow Chamomile   *pl. 147.* A handsome bushy plant, with deeply cut leaves and long-stalked flower heads (2½–4 cm). The spreading ray florets tend to droop at night. Ray florets sometimes absent. Leaves cut into narrow toothed segments, white-woolly below. June–Aug. *Daisy family*

 Southern Corn Marigold   *pl. 148.* Very like the Corn Marigold (not illustrated), but all leaves oblong, with fine teeth (not coarsely toothed or lobed). Flower heads 2–4 cm; involucral bracts almost entirely papery. Fruit with a crown. Apr.–June. *Daisy family*

Crown Daisy *pl. 148.* A robust, much-branched annual, often growing in abundance, producing a sheet of golden yellow in the spring. Flower heads (3–6 cm) pale yellow, often paler cream-coloured at the centre. Leaves twice-cut into narrow fine-pointed lobes. Apr.– Sept. *Daisy family*

 Arnica *pl. 151.* Large solitary orange-yellow flower heads (4–8 cm) are borne on hairy stems above a flat rosette of leaves. Rosette leaves broadly lance-shaped, downy, glandular hairy, aromatic; stem leaves opposite, smaller. May–July. *Daisy family*

  Great Leopard's-Bane *pl. 151.* An erect woodland perennial with creeping underground stems, often occurring in large patches with several yellow flower heads (4–6 cm). Rosette leaves oval-heart-shaped, long-stalked; middle stem leaves narrowed below, broadened at the base into 2 rounded lobes; the upper oval, clasping. May–July. *Daisy family*

 Chamois Ragwort *pl. 151.* An erect greyish plant of mountain pastures, with thick leathery lance-shaped leaves and one or few golden-yellow flower heads (3½–4½ cm). Ray florets 15–22; involucre with additional row of long outer bracts. June–Aug. *Daisy family*

 Flat-Topped Carline Thistle *pl. 152.* A stiff, spiny plant (10–50 cm) with thistle-like leaves and several short-stalked flower heads (2½–4 cm) in a flat-topped cluster. Ray florets absent; inner involucral bracts bright golden-yellow, outspread, giving an 'everlasting' fruit head. Stems white-felted. June–Aug. *Daisy family*

 Rough Hawkbit *pl. 158.* The large golden-yellow flower heads (2½–4 cm) are solitary. Involucral bracts dark green or blackish with rough bristly hairs (or nearly hairless). Leaves toothed or shallowly lobed, hairy or hairless in a lax rosette. May–Sept. *Daisy family*

 Field Sow-Thistle *pl. 159.* A tall handsome plant, the upper parts covered with yellowish glandular hairs. Flower heads (4–5 cm) in a loose somewhat flat-topped cluster. Leaves glaucous, oblong with deep triangular bristly lobes, the upper clasping with rounded lobes. June–Sept. *Daisy family*

 Pale Day-Lily *pl. 164.* A sturdy plant with large (6–8 cm), sweet-scented, tubular lily flowers in a cluster of 3–9. The grass-like, keeled leaves are ½–1 cm broad. June–Aug. *Lily family*

 Orange Lily *pl. 166.* A beautiful lily with erect tubular flowers with bright orange spreading petals with black spots within. Leaves in whorls of 3–5, narrowly lance-shaped, with or without small bulbils in their axils. June–July. *Lily family*

 Yellow Turk's-Cap Lily *pl. 167.* A beautiful lily of the Pyrenees, with an unpleasant smell. The drooping bright yellow flowers have curved-back petals with black dots within. Leaves numerous, overlapping, lance-shaped, with rough margins. June–July. *Lily family*

 Yellow Flag *pl. 174.* A robust waterside iris with green spear-shaped leaves (1½–2½ cm wide). Flowers large, yellow (8–10 cm) with or without orange-brown veining, borne on branched stems from green papery-margined sheaths. June–July. *Iris family*

See also: RED HORNED-POPPY *pl. 29*; JUPITER'S DISTAFF *pl. 113*; LARGE YELLOW FOXGLOVE *pl. 125*; HERB PARIS *pl. 170*; SNAKE'S HEAD IRIS, WIDOW IRIS *pl.174*.

Flowers large · *Plant small*

  Alpine Anemone *pl. 23.* A beautiful plant with large solitary white or yellow flowers (4–6 cm). Stem leaves very short-stalked, deeply cut and toothed, at first densely silky-haired, later hairless. Basal leaves similar. Fruits with long feathery plumes. May–July. *Buttercup family*

Yellow Adonis *pl. 24.* The large yellow flowers (4–8 cm), with numerous shining pointed petals, borne above fern-like leaves are unmistakable. A plant of dry hill pastures and rocks of central Europe. Apr.–May. *Buttercup family*

 Large-Flowered Leopard's-Bane *pl. 150.* An alpine plant usually with solitary flower heads (5–8 cm) borne on glandular-hairy stems. Lowest leaves oval; middle leaves with winged stalk and auricled base; uppermost broadly lance-shaped, clasping the stem; all glandular-hairy. June–Sept. *Daisy family*

 Giant Catsear *pl. 158.* A short plant with stout stems swollen below the large (3½–7 cm) solitary flower heads. Involucral bracts oval, blackish, shaggy-haired, fringed. Leaves mostly in a basal rosette. July–Sept. *Daisy family*

 Dandelion *pl. 159.* A very familiar, variable plant. Flower heads (3–6 cm) on a hollow smooth stem; lower involucral bracts down-curved. Leaves usually with deep triangular backward-pointing lobes; sometimes lobeless. Mar.–Nov. *Daisy family*

 Common Sternbergia *pl. 172.* A most beautiful autumn-flowering plant, looking like a crocus, with flowers appearing with the leaves from the bare ground. Distinguished from crocuses by the 6 stamens and papery bracts subtending the flowers. Leaves strap-shaped (½–1 cm broad) without a central white line. Sept.–Oct. *Daffodil family*

 Italian Arum *pl. 183.* Distinguished from the common Lords-and-Ladies (not illustrated) by its yellowish spathe and butter-yellow, club-like spadix, also by its leaves which appear in the autumn. A plant of southern Europe. Apr.–May. *Arum family*

See also: LONG-SPURRED PANSY *pl. 76*; DWARF IRIS *p. 175*; PYGMY IRIS *pl. 176*.

Flowers medium · Plant medium

 Birthwort *pl. 7.* An unpleasant-smelling, erect leafy plant with clusters of dull yellow trumpet-shaped flowers (2–3 cm) in the axils of the upper leaves. Leaves heart-shaped, finely toothed, and stalked. Fruit pendulous, pear-shaped. May–July. *Birthwort family*

 Wolfsbane *pl. 19.* A tall, erect, leafy, poisonous plant, usually with branched spikes of hooded flowers. Elongated conical hood, about three times as long as broad; within are the honey-bearing petals. Leaves hairy, deeply three-lobed, further cut into narrow, toothed lobes. June–Aug. *Buttercup family*

 Common Meadow Rue *pl. 26.* A tall leafy plant of damp places with dense clusters of fluffy yellow flowers, owing to the numerous long stamens. Leaves dark green, 2 to 3 times cut into wedge-shaped leaflets, each with 3–4 conspicuous terminal teeth. May–Aug. *Buttercup family*

 Wallflower *pl. 32.* A well known widely cultivated plant with delicious fragrance. The wild plants have yellow flowers, less commonly brownish. A woody-based plant with numerous lance-shaped leaves covered with forked hairs. Mar.–June. *Cress family*

 Nine-Leaved Coral-Wort *pl. 33.* A plant of mountain woods of east central Europe. Distinguished by pale yellow, or white, somewhat bell-shaped drooping flowers. Also by the leaves of the flowering stem with usually 9 toothed leaflets. Apr.–June. *Cress family*

 Fibigia *pl. 35.* An erect, densely grey-felted biennial with terminal clusters of small yellow flowers (petals 8–13 mm). Fruits distinctive: flattened and disk-shaped, oval in circumference (1½–3 cm long) with a conspicuous style. Apr.–June. *Cress family*

 White Mustard *pl. 37.* A weed of cultivation, also planted as a fodder or green manure crop, or for its seeds. Distinguished by fruits which have a long flattened, sabre-like projection at the end of the seed-bearing pod. Flowers yellow, 1–1½ cm. Leaves deeply cut. June–Aug. *Cress family*

Yellow Lupin   *pl. 53.* A native of Iberia, introduced elsewhere as a fodder crop. An erect hairy plant with whorled spikes of golden-yellow flowers (to 1½ cm). Leaves fan-shaped with 6–8 narrow to obovate leaflets. Pods hairy (to 2 cm broad); seeds mottled. Mar.–July. *Pea family*

 Large Yellow Restharrow   *pl. 57.* A shrubby, woody-based plant with leafy herbaceous branches, and leafy clusters of handsome yellow pea-flowers (1½ cm) with dark red streaking. Leaves sticky, mostly with 3 leaflets, but some with only 1 leaflet. Fruit pendulous, hairy. May–Aug. *Pea family*

 Touch-me-Not   *pl. 70.* So-called because of its explosive fruits. A hairless plant with translucent stems, swollen nodes and delicate pendulous yellow, brown-spotted flowers. The lowest yellow sepal is conical and contracts gradually into a long curved spur; the lower lip is much longer and broader than the upper. June–Aug. *Balsam family*

 Orange Balsam   *pl. 70.* A native of North America naturalized by streamsides in south Britain and north France. Flowers (2–3 cm) broadly funnel-shaped, two-lipped, with a narrow, abruptly curved spur. Leaves glaucous. June–Aug. *Balsam family*

 Hairy St John's Wort   *pl. 75.* A pale green, upright, downy plant, with rounded stems, paired oval leaves with translucent glands, and loose clusters of yellow flowers. Flowers (1½–2 cm), petals twice as long as the sepals which have black short-stalked marginal glands. June–Aug. *St John's Wort family*

 Common St John's Wort   *pl. 75.* A hairless plant, distinguished from similar species by 2 raised lines on the stem; narrowly oblong leaves with translucent glandular dots; yellow petals with minute black dots; and sepals not fringed with black glands. Flowers 2–3½ cm. May–Aug. *St John's Wort family*

 Yellow-Wort   *pl. 94.* A neat, grey-green erect plant with broad paired upper leaves which encircle the stem (perfoliate). Flowers bright yellow (1–1½ cm) with 6–8 wide-spreading petals and narrow sepals. Basal leaves in a rosette. May–Sept. *Gentian family*

 Honeywort   *pl. 105.* A handsome grey-green annual with clasping, overlapping upper leaves and drooping clusters of tubular flowers. Flowers (1–1½ cm) yellow, with a band of dark chocolate towards the base. Leaves with bristly margins, often white-spotted. Feb.–June. *Borage family*

 Large-Flowered Hemp-Nettle   *pl. 111.* A very distinctive hemp-nettle with yellow flowers (2–4½ cm), usually with a dark reddish-lilac blotch on the broad lower lip. Calyx less than half as long as corolla tube. July–Sept. *Mint family*

 Yellow Archangel   *pl. 112.* A creeping woodland dead-nettle with erect stems bearing whorls of bright yellow, two-lipped flowers (2 cm). Lower lip with brownish markings, and 3 narrow lobes. Leaves wrinkled, and conspicuously toothed. Apr.–June. *Mint family*

 Perennial Yellow Woundwort   *pl. 113.* A sweet-smelling, bushy plant with many erect stems, bearing slender, leafless whorled spikes of pale yellow flowers. Calyx with spiny-pointed lobes and spreading hairs; bracts spiny-tipped. Leaves hairy or hairless, the lower stalked, the upper narrow, stalkless. June–Sept. *Mint family*

 Jupiter's Distaff   *pl. 113.* A tall, branched, sticky glandular plant of shady places, with large, usually pale yellow, sage-like flowers (3–4 cm). Flowers less commonly brownish or streaked brown. Calyx two-lipped sticky; bracts very small. Leaves large, oval-triangular and long-pointed, coarsely toothed. June–Sept. *Mint family*

 Henbane   *pl. 117.* A very poisonous plant unpleasant to eye, nose and touch. Flowers (2–3 cm) dull yellow with a conspicuous network of purplish veins often running together at the base. Fruits conspicuous: the dry calyx forms a flask enclosing the fruit and is narrowed at the mouth to 5 triangular spine-tipped teeth. May–Sept. *Nightshade family*

White Henbane *pl. 117.* Like the preceding plant but distinguished by pale yellow flowers with a greenish or violet throat, without conspicuous veins. Upper leaves are all stalked and coarsely lobed (clasping in Henbane). Apr.–Sept. *Nightshade family*

Golden Henbane *pl. 117.* A beautiful plant found on old walls in Crete and Rhodes. Flowers bright golden yellow with a deep violet-purple throat; stamens protruding. Leaves all stalked, oval-heart-shaped, coarsely lobed, densely hairy. Mar.–July. *Nightshade family*

Dark Mullein *pl. 120.* Distinguished from many mulleins by purple stamen hairs and kidney-shaped anthers. Flowers (12–22 mm) in clusters of 5–10 in a long, usually unbranched spike. Leaves dark green, conspicuously covered with star-shaped hairs beneath; the lower are stalked. July–Sept. *Figwort family*

Moth Mullein *pl. 120.* Has solitary flowers on long stalks, longer than the calyx, in a loose slender unbranched spike. Flowers (2–3 cm) rarely white; stamens unequal, with violet hairs. Leaves hairless, glossy, coarsely and irregularly toothed. June–Aug. *Figwort family*

Wavy-Leaved Mullein *pl. 120.* A distinctive mullein with handsome white-woolly rosettes of leaves, deeply lobed with very wavy margins. Flowers (2–5½ cm) stalkless, yellow, borne in long interrupted spikes. Anthers kidney-shaped, hairs on stamens pale yellow. June–July. *Figwort family*

Dalmatian Toadflax *pl. 121.* A yellow toadflax differing from the Common Toadflax (not illustrated) in the oval or broadly lance-shaped leaves, which clasp the stem with a shallow heart-shaped base. Flowers large, yellow with an orange-brown throat-boss; flower stalks longer than bracts. June–July. *Figwort family*

Musk *pl. 123.* A glandular sticky plant of North America, naturalized in damp places in central Europe, once cultivated for its musky smell (now absent). Flowers tubular (1–2 cm across) yellow, without red spots. June–Sept. *Figwort family*

Gratiole *pl. 124.* A waterside or damp meadow plant with solitary tubular, pale yellowish, weakly two-lipped flowers (1½–2 cm), flushed with pink or purple. Leaves lance-shaped and toothed, opposite and stalkless. May–Oct. *Figwort family*

Rusty Foxglove *pl. 125.* Almost globular flowers, reddish-yellow, veined with brown, with lower lip protruding and as long again as the rest of the corolla. Leaves lance-shaped, hairless, except on the veins and undersides of the margins. July–Sept. *Figwort family*

Large Yellow Foxglove *pl. 125.* A poisonous plant of shady places in mountains with relatively large thimble-shaped flowers (3–4 cm long) in a slender spike. Flowers hairy, weakly netted with brown within. Leaves lance-shaped, finely toothed, shining, hairless above. June–Sept. *Figwort family*

Small Yellow Foxglove *pl. 125.* Readily identified by its small yellow flowers (1½–2 cm) which are hairless outside. Leaves narrow lance-shaped, glossy and quite hairless. A poisonous plant of woods and stony hills. June–Aug. *Figwort family*

Spanish Rusty Foxglove *pl. 125.* A shrubby-based plant, with dark rusty-brown flowers, dull yellow and spotted with brown without, and with white marginal hairs. Lower lip half as long as corolla tube. Leaves leathery, hairless, narrow, either entire or toothed. May–July. *Figwort family*

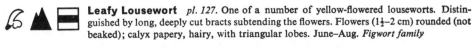 **Leafy Lousewort** *pl. 127.* One of a number of yellow-flowered louseworts. Distinguished by long, deeply cut bracts subtending the flowers. Flowers (1½–2 cm) rounded (not beaked); calyx papery, hairy, with triangular lobes. June–Aug. *Figwort family*

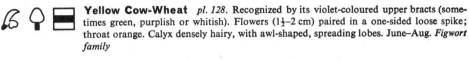 **Yellow Cow-Wheat** *pl. 128.* Recognized by its violet-coloured upper bracts (sometimes green, purplish or whitish). Flowers (1½–2 cm) paired in a one-sided loose spike; throat orange. Calyx densely hairy, with awl-shaped, spreading lobes. June–Aug. *Figwort family*

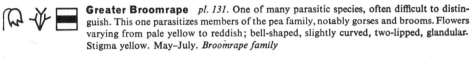 **Greater Broomrape** *pl. 131.* One of many parasitic species, often difficult to distinguish. This one parasitizes members of the pea family, notably gorses and brooms. Flowers varying from pale yellow to reddish; bell-shaped, slightly curved, two-lipped, glandular. Stigma yellow. May–July. *Broomrape family*

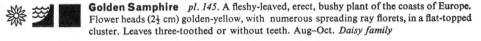 **Clove-Scented Broomrape** *pl. 131.* Parasitic on the bedstraw family. Flowers from pale yellow to pink, variously tinged with dull purple; said to smell of cloves. Flowers (2–3 cm) regularly arched in profile, densely glandular-hairy, June–July. *Broomrape family*

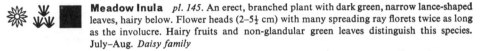 **Golden Samphire** *pl. 145.* A fleshy-leaved, erect, bushy plant of the coasts of Europe. Flower heads (2½ cm) golden-yellow, with numerous spreading ray florets, in a flat-topped cluster. Leaves three-toothed or without teeth. Aug–Oct. *Daisy family*

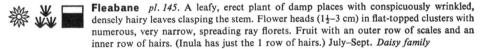 **Meadow Inula** *pl. 145.* An erect, branched plant with dark green, narrow lance-shaped leaves, hairy below. Flower heads (2–5½ cm) with many spreading ray florets twice as long as the involucre. Hairy fruits and non-glandular green leaves distinguish this species. July–Aug. *Daisy family*

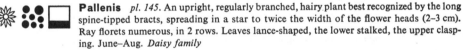 **Fleabane** *pl. 145.* A leafy, erect plant of damp places with conspicuously wrinkled, densely hairy leaves clasping the stem. Flower heads (1½–3 cm) in flat-topped clusters with numerous, very narrow, spreading ray florets. Fruit with an outer row of scales and an inner row of hairs. (Inula has just the 1 row of hairs.) July–Sept. *Daisy family*

Pallenis *pl. 145.* An upright, regularly branched, hairy plant best recognized by the long spine-tipped bracts, spreading in a star to twice the width of the flower heads (2–3 cm). Ray florets numerous, in 2 rows. Leaves lance-shaped, the lower stalked, the upper clasping. June–Aug. *Daisy family*

Nodding Bur-Marigold *pl. 146.* The plant illustrated is the variety with conspicuous spreading ray florets; these are usually absent. Flower heads (1½–2½ cm) globular, somewhat nodding. Leaves lance-shaped, simple, coarsely toothed (deeply lobed in Tripartite Bur-Marigold (not illustrated)). Fruit usually with 4 barbed bristles. July–Oct. *Daisy family*

Wood Ragwort *pl. 150.* A robust leafy plant of mountain woods, distinguished by its few involucral bracts (8–10), by having less than 8 ray florets and by its undivided leaves. Middle stem leaves half-clasping. July–Aug. *Daisy family*

Cabbage Thistle *pl. 154.* Has a dense cluster of yellowish-white flower heads surrounded by much longer broad, yellowish-green, bristly bracts. Leaves lance-shaped, deeply lobed, bristly, not spiny, the upper clasping. July–Aug. *Daisy family*

Yellow Knapweed *pl. 156.* A handsome knapweed with large pale yellow flower heads (3–5 cm), and distinctive oval involucral bracts with a horse-shoe-shaped, fringed, papery border with or without a long yellow terminal spine. Leaves rough, pinnately cut into lance-shaped lobes. July–Aug. *Daisy family*

Yellow Carthamus *pl. 157.* A branched, unpleasant-smelling, greyish, thistle-like plant with cottony, rounded stems with reddish juice. Flower heads golden-yellow (2–3 cm), encircled by spiny involucral bracts as long as the florets. May–Aug. *Daisy family*

Spotted Spanish Oyster Plant *pl. 157.* A very spiny plant sometimes confused with the preceding species, but stems winged and flower heads with ray florets only. Like the Spanish Oyster Plant (not illustrated), but distinguished by broad stem wings (2–5 mm wide at the minimum) and strong white cartilaginous borders to the leaves and stem-wings. Ray florets with minute black hairs on the outside. June–Aug. *Daisy family*

Soft Urospermum *pl. 157.* A softly hairy plant with solitary pale yellow flower heads (2–2½ cm) with a single row of neat green involucral bracts. Lower leaves deeply pinnately cut, the terminal segment largest. Fruits with a long beak with a russet-coloured 'para-chute' of hairs. May–June. *Daisy family*

Common Andryala *pl. 159.* Distinguished by its densely woolly yellowish hairs which cover the whole plant including the calyx. Flower heads (1½ cm), numerous in flat-topped clusters; spreading ray florets numerous. Apr.–July. *Daisy family*

Prickly Sow-Thistle *pl. 159.* A hairless, glossy, bristly plant with upper leaves clasping the stem with rounded lobes (lobes pointed in Common Sow-Thistle (not illustrated)). Flower heads (2–2½ cm) in an irregular umbel; ray florets only present. Pappus of fruit silvery. May–Sept. *Daisy family*

Beaked Hawksbeard *pl. 160.* An erect perennial, branched above, forming a more or less flat-topped cluster. Flower heads small (1½–2½ cm). Leaves mostly basal, deeply cut into broad, toothed lobes. Fruit with a long beak and a white pappus. May–Aug. *Daisy family*

King's Spear, Yellow Asphodel *pl. 162.* A lily-like plant with a long, rather ragged spike of yellow flowers, and narrow triangular-sectioned leaves. Flowers yellow (2–3 cm); each petal has a green midvein. Fruit globular (1–1½ cm). Apr.–May. *Lily family*

See also: SALAD MUSTARD *pl. 37*; WILD PANSY *pl. 75*; BITTER APPLE *pl. 78*; WHITE BRYONY *pl. 79*; SMALL TOBACCO *pl. 119*; CANDELABRA THISTLE *pl. 153*; BATH ASPARAGUS *pl. 169*.

Flowers medium · Plant small

Yellow Cytinus *pl. 8.* This extraordinary parasitic plant is to be looked for under *Cistus* and *Halimium* bushes. The globular head of flowers pushes through the soil from hidden roots of the host plant; there are no green leaves. The bright carmine fleshy scales contrast with the yellow petals. May–June. *Rafflesiaceae*

Winter Aconite *pl. 18.* One of the first plants to come into flower and quite unlike any other with its solitary buttercup-like flower above a frill of bright green, deeply cut leaves. Flowers glossy (2–3 cm). Feb.–Mar. *Buttercup family*

Palmate Anemone *pl. 21.* A distinctive anemone, with solitary long-stemmed pale yellow flowers (2½–3½ cm) often red-flushed beneath. Petals 10–15, narrow. Basal leaves almost circular, shallowly cut into 2–5 rounded, toothed lobes, the stem leaves with bract-like lobes. Feb.–June. *Buttercup family*

Lesser Celandine, Pilewort *pl. 25.* A plant of shady places distinguished from other buttercups by its glossy dark green, heart-shaped leaves. Flowers (2–3 cm) shining yellow, with 8–12 narrow petals (larger in southern Europe). Mar.–May. *Buttercup family*

Thora Buttercup *pl. 25.* An uncommon slender buttercup of the mountains; very poisonous (formerly used as arrow poison). Recognized by its large grey-green, kidney-shaped lower leaves and its upper, much smaller leaves. June–July. *Buttercup family*

Mountain Buttercup *pl. 25.* A variable mountain buttercup. Often a low plant with few large flowers (2–4 cm). Upper leaves cut into narrow linear lobes, contrasting with the lower rounded leaves with 3–5 round lobes. Fruit with curved beak. May–Aug. *Buttercup family*

Alpine Poppy *pl. 28.* Has a basal rosette of glaucous leaves and leafless stems bearing solitary golden-yellow (rarely red or white) flowers. The plant photographed is probably a closely related Asiatic species *(P. nudicaule)* which sometimes escapes from cultivation. July–Aug. *Poppy family*

Yellow Sundew *pl. 38.* A rare and unusual insect-catching plant of south-western Iberia and Morocco. The sticky leaves are long and narrow (10–20 cm), coiled at the tip like watch-springs. Flowers yellow (2½ cm). Apr.–Oct. *Sundew family*

Bermuda Buttercup *pl. 63.* Handsome but a serious weed of cultivated ground in the Mediterranean, often producing sheets of yellow in springtime. The umbels of yellow flowers (2–2½ cm) are long-stalked. Leaves clover-like, trifoliate, pale green, all basal. Produces numerous small bulbs by which it spreads rapidly. Dec.–May. *Wood-Sorrel family*

Yellow Wood Violet *pl. 76.* A low creeping plant of shady places recognized by its usually paired yellow flowers (1½ cm) streaked with brown. Leaves conspicuously rounded, broader than long. June–Aug. *Violet family*

Mountain Pansy *pl. 76.* An attractive pansy with conspicuous yellow, violet, or bi-coloured flowers (1½–3 cm across vertically). Spur rather short (3–6 mm), thin. Leaves variable, oval to lance-shaped, toothed; stipules cut into 3–5 lobes. July–Aug. *Violet family*

Squirting Cucumber *pl. 79.* A shaggy, sprawling plant with thick stems, coarse, rather fleshy leaves, and quite unmistakable small gherkin-like fruits which explode violently when touched. Flowers tubular (2½ cm) yellow, rather inconspicuous. Seeds poisonous; guard eyes against the exploding fruits. Apr.–Sept. *Cucumber family*

Hacquetia *pl. 83.* A small golden-yellow plant with its central cluster of tiny yellow flowers surrounded by a frill of yellow, toothed bracts, giving the appearance of a flower (2½–4 cm). Leaves all basal, divided into 3 oval leaflets. Apr. *Umbellifer family*

Oxlip, Paigle *pl. 90.* Like the Cowslip (not illustrated) with its one-sided cluster of yellow flowers, but flowers larger (1½–2 cm), pale primrose-yellow, unscented. The calyx has dark green veins (not uniformly pale green) and the corolla has no folds in the throat. Mar.–May. *Primrose family*

Auricula, Bear's-Ear *pl. 90.* An enchanting plant of limestone mountains, with clusters of fragrant white-throated, yellow flowers (1½–3 cm). Leaves fleshy in a loose rosette, toothed or entire, with a white margin, powdery when young. May–July. *Primrose family*

Primrose *pl. 90.* A well known plant with solitary, long-stalked flowers and a rosette of wrinkled leaves, all arising from a stout scaly rootstock. Flowers (2–3 cm) fragrant, usually primrose yellow, sometimes almost white, and in south-eastern Europe often pink. Mar.–May. *Primrose family*

Creeping Jenny *pl. 93.* A creeping, rooting plant, often forming mats in damp places, with pairs of rounded, shining leaves. Flowers dark yellow, somewhat bell-shaped (1½–2½ cm) solitary, short-stalked, from the axil of each leaf. May–Aug. *Primrose family*

Eastern Alpine Skullcap *pl. 108.* An uncommon, spreading plant of stony places in the hills, differing from the Alpine Skullcap in its yellow flowers, arising from green bracts. Leaves oval, stalked, deeply pinnately cut, with silvery hairs below, often hairless above. June–Aug. *Mint family*

Creeping Snapdragon *pl. 121.* A creeping plant of the Pyrenees, distinguished by stout, pale yellow, snapdragon flowers (3–4 cm), often streaked pink. Leaves unusual, being in opposite pairs, kidney-shaped, and palmately veined. Apr.–Sept. *Figwort family*

Three-Leaved Toadflax *pl. 122.* Easily recognized by its compact head of conspicuous three-coloured flowers (2 cm) with large pointed violet spurs. And by its oval glaucous leaves which are in whorls of 3. Apr.–June. *Figwort family*

 Yellow Bartsia *pl. 126.* A pale stickily-hairy, usually unbranched plant with a dense leafy spike of bright yellow flowers (1½–2 cm). Flowers with the three-lobed lower lip much longer than the upper lip; the calyx sticky. Leaves lance-shaped, toothed, stalkless. May–Sept. *Figwort family*

 Yellow Bellflower *pl. 139.* Unmistakable with its terminal cluster of densely packed tubular pale yellow flowers (1½–2½ cm). Stem thick and hollow, bearing numerous rather bristly, narrow leaves, and a basal rosette. July–Sept. *Bellflower family*

 Evax *pl. 143.* A distinctive plant with tiny woolly-white rosettes pressed to the ground. At the centre of the rosette of narrow leaves is a tight cluster of tiny, stalkless yellowish flower heads. Found in bare stony places near the Mediterranean. Apr.–May. *Daisy family*

 Edelweiss *pl. 144.* Known by all who travel in the mountains of Europe, not uncommon but not so often encountered along well beaten tracks. It forms mats of white-woolly rosettes in dry places, and erect, short and leafy flowering stems. July–Sept. *Daisy family*

 Coltsfoot *pl. 149.* An attractive plant when its stubby, scaly flowering stems push up through the soil early in the year. Flower heads solitary (1½–3½ cm) with numerous thread-like ray florets. Leaves appearing later, stout, rounded, white-felted beneath. Feb.–Apr. *Daisy family*

 Spring Groundsel *pl. 151.* Flower heads (2–3 cm) conspicuous with about 13 spreading ray florets. Involucral bracts in 2 rows. Leaves at first covered with cobweb-hairs but later becoming hairless. It has spread from south-east Europe. Apr. *Daisy family*

 Marigold *pl. 151.* A rough-haired, leafy, spreading annual weed of the south. Flower heads orange-yellow, smaller (1–2 cm), otherwise like the Pot-Marigold (not illustrated). Fruits unusual of 3 kinds: sickle-shaped, boat-shaped and curved into a ring. Apr.–Oct. *Daisy family*

 Tolpis *pl. 157.* Distinguished from other similar dandelion-flowered plants by the long thread-like involucral bracts which spread beyond the ray florets. The flower heads often have dark brown or reddish centres. May–July. *Daisy family*

 Blessed Thistle *pl. 160.* A weakly spiny thistle-like annual, a famous medicinal plant in the past. Flower heads solitary and surrounded by a circlet of oval, spiny leaves. Bracts of involucre with a long terminal spine and comb-like lateral spines. Apr.–July. *Daisy family*

 Golden Hawksbeard *pl. 160.* A slender dandelion-like plant of alpine pastures, easily distinguished by its rather dark orange or orange-red solitary flower heads borne on leafless stalks. Leaves in a rosette, shiny and shallowly lobed. June–Sept. *Daisy family*

 Mouse-Ear Hawkweed *pl. 160.* The hawkweeds are amongst the most difficult of all plants to separate. This species is distinctive with neat rosettes of leaves, creeping above-ground stolons, and solitary usually reddish-flushed flower heads (1½–2 cm). Leaves white-woolly beneath, green above, with few stiff white hairs. May–Sept. *Daisy family*

 Southern Tulip *pl. 168.* A slender tulip distinguished by its yellow flowers conspicuously flushed with reddish outside. Petals (2–3½ cm) narrow, pointed and spreading widely in the sun. Leaves usually 2, narrow, grooved and glaucous. Apr.–July. *Lily family*

 Slender Sternbergia *pl. 172.* A native of the Balkans with pale lemon-yellow flowers appearing quite naked from the soil. Leaves strap-shaped, twisted, appearing in autumn or spring after flowering. Autumn or spring. *Daffodil family*

Hoop Petticoat Daffodil *pl. 173.* A charming, widespread daffodil of Iberia ranging from grassy mountain tops to lowlands. It has solitary trumpet-like flowers with small spreading petals. Leaves few, semi-cylindrical, grooved. Feb.–Apr. *Daffodil family*

 Rush-Leaved Narcissus *pl. 173.* A slender narcissus of rocks in the mountains of Iberia. The jonquil-like flowers have a shallow trumpet and long flower tube (1½–2 cm). The flower stalk remains within the papery bract even after flowering. Leaves very slender, rush-like. Mar.–May. *Daffodil family*

 Yellow Bee Orchid *pl. 188.* One of the commonest Mediterranean bee orchids, easily distinguished by the conspicuous yellow border to the lip. Lip with a greater or lesser amount of brown, and with 2 dull bluish reflective patches. Sepals green. Mar.–May. *Orchid family*

 Elder-Flowered Orchid *pl. 189.* An orchid of mountain meadows, with a dense round cluster of pale yellow flowers (sometimes purple). Flowers with a stout conical downward-pointing spur, and shallowly three-lobed lip, indistinctly spotted. Apr.–July. *Orchid family*

 Man Orchid *pl. 189.* A slender orchid with a long narrow spike of distinctly man-like flowers. The lip has 'arms' and 'legs' and the upper petals form a helmet, 'the head'. The flowers (1½ cm) are spurless. Apr.–June. *Orchid family*

See also: PURPLE GENTIAN *pl. 97*; BELLARDIA *pl. 126*; TOOTHED ORCHID *pl. 187*.

Flowers small · Plant large

 Giant Fennel *pl. 85.* A spectacular plant of the Mediterranean, often to 3 m tall, with umbels (½ m across) of tiny yellow flowers. Leaves feathery, dark green, many times divided into thread-like segments; large swollen sheaths enclose the young flower heads. June–Aug. *Umbellifer family*

 Century Plant *pl. 171.* A native of Mexico, now a landmark of the Mediterranean coast. Colossal rosettes (to 4 m) are formed of massive spiny leaves up to 1 m. Its huge branched flower spike (to 10 m) is formed after 10–15 years and the plant then dies. June–Aug. *Agave family*

See also: ANGELICA *pl. 85*.

Flowers small · Plant medium

 Eastern Rocket *pl. 32.* An undistinguished Mediterranean weed naturalized elsewhere, with simple or 2-lobed upper leaves and long straight seed pods (4–10 cm) on thick stalks. Flowers pale yellow (10–12 mm). May–July. *Cress family*

 Woad *pl. 32.* A robust erect plant with glaucous, clasping leaves and dense terminal branched clusters of tiny bright yellow flowers. Flowers (4 mm) with petals twice as long as sepals. Fruit distinctive, flattened, paddle-shaped, pendulous (1–2½ cm). May–June. *Cress family*

 Crested Bunias *pl. 32.* A weed of the south, with curious fruits (1 cm), quadrangular with 4 crested wings on the angles and a long style (½ cm). Flowers yellow (1 cm), with heart-shaped petals. Lower leaves deeply cut, the upper entire. May–June. *Cress family*

 Great Yellow-Cress *pl. 33.* A tall, hollow-stemmed fleshy plant of watersides, with lance-shaped stem leaves, regularly toothed (not lobed). Flowers small (6 mm) in branched leafless spikes. Fruits egg-shaped (1½ cm). June–Sept. *Cress family*

 Wild Mignonette *pl. 38.* Distinguished by its dense, slender, almost scentless spikes of small greenish-yellow flowers, with tiny, much-cut petals and numerous protruding stamens. Leaves deeply cut into numerous narrow wavy-edged lobes. Fruit oblong, three-lobed. June–Sept. *Mignonette family*

Wild Lentil *pl. 54*. A spreading, softly hairy plant with dense, long-stemmed clusters of pale yellow flowers (1½ cm), as long as the leaves. Leaves with 10–15 pairs of hairy leaflets. Pods oval, inflated (1–1½ cm), densely hairy. June–July. *Pea family*

 Yellow Vetchling *pl. 55*. Well known as a botanical oddity with leaves replaced by a tendril and stipules (1–3 cm) much enlarged and leafy. Flowers (1 cm), pale yellow, usually solitary. A rather weak pale scrambling annual. Apr.–June. *Pea family*

 Winged Vetchling *pl. 55*. A blue-grey annual, grown for fodder in the south, with winged stems and leaf stalks. Upper leaves with 1–2 pairs of oval leaflets and a branched tendril; lower leaves with only tendrils. Flowers (1½–2 cm), solitary, pale yellow. Mar.–June. *Pea family*

 Tall Melilot *pl. 57*. There are about 16 species of melilot in Europe, mostly similar. This one has flowers (5–7 mm) with petals all the same length, and hairy, netted fruits, which turn black when ripe. May–Sept. *Pea family*

 Sickle Medick *pl. 58*. Closely related to Lucerne but with yellow flowers and sickle-shaped ring-like (sometimes straight) pods. Flowers (5–8 mm) in dense rounded clusters (to 1½ cm). Leaves with 3 narrow oblong or wedge-shaped leaflets. May–Aug. *Pea family*

 Large Birdsfoot-Trefoil *pl. 61*. An erect rather weak, hairy plant with stolons, and with dense flat-topped clusters of 5–15 deep yellow flowers (10–15 mm). Distinguished from the Birdsfoot-Trefoil (not illustrated) by calyx teeth which spread in bud, and larger leaflets (1½–2 cm). May–Aug. *Pea family*

 Small Balsam *pl. 70*. The smallest-flowered balsam, introduced from Asia and naturalized. Flowers pale yellow (only ½–1½ cm); spur straight, conical, varying in length. An erect hairless leafy annual with translucent stems and exploding fruits. Apr.–Oct. *Balsam family*

 Mountain St John's Wort *pl. 75*. Has dense globular clusters of fragrant, pale yellow flowers (1–1½ cm), on long almost leafless stems. Leaves stalkless half-clasping with a row of black glands on the lower margin. Sepals with conspicuous glandular teeth. June–July. *St John's Wort family*

 Tuberous Comfrey *pl. 102*. A rough, bristly-haired plant, forming patches in shady places, with terminal clusters of tubular, pale yellow flowers (1–1½ cm). Lowest leaves oval, stalked; middle leaves large, broadly lance-shaped, stalked; uppermost stalkless. Roots tuberous. Mar.–June. *Borage family*

 Lesser Honeywort *pl. 105*. A glaucous, hairless plant, with alternate clasping upper leaves, sometimes white-spotted and warty. Flowers in a one-sided drooping cluster, yellow with greater or lesser amounts of brownish-purple; corolla (1–1½ cm) divided to the middle into narrow lobes. May–Aug. *Borage family*

 Yellow Scabious *pl. 137*. One of many yellow-flowered scabiouses. It has flattened yellow flower heads (2 cm), the outermost florets nearly twice as large as the inner. Upper leaves once- or twice-cut into very narrow lobes; the lower uncut or deeply lobed. Calyx teeth brown. July–Aug. *Scabious family*

 Spiked Rampion *pl. 141*. The only rampion with a long cylindrical spike of yellow flowers (3–8 cm) (sometimes blue). Flowers (1 cm) with the narrow petals fused at their tips, separated below. Lowest leaves heart-shaped, long-stalked; middle and upper leaves progressively narrower, eventually stalkless. May–July. *Bellflower family*

 Canadian Golden-Rod *pl. 142*. A robust perennial (1–2 m) with a dense pyramidal cluster of numerous tiny golden-yellow flower heads (½ cm long). Ray florets inconspicuous. Leaves lance-shaped (10–15 cm), toothed. From North America. Aug.–Sept. *Daisy family*

Golden-Rod   *pl. 143.* Usually rather lowly, little-branched, with an oblong, leafy cluster of small flower heads (7–10 mm), each with 6–12 spreading ray florets. Involucre of several rows of greenish-yellow bracts with papery margins. Lower leaves stalked, broader, the upper stalkless, lance-shaped. July–Sept. *Daisy family*

 Ploughman's Spikenard   *pl. 144.* An erect, downy plant with a dense flat-topped cluster of small yellow flower heads (1 cm). Bracts of involucre greenish, hairy, with outcurving tips. Leaves thickly downy beneath, the upper stalkless, all finely toothed. July–Sept. *Daisy family*

 Tansy   *pl. 147.* An aromatic plant, with flat-topped clusters of hard, small, yellow, button-like flower heads (7–12 mm), without ray florets. Leaves pinnately cut into about 12 pairs of leaflets which are further pinnately lobed or toothed. June–Oct. *Daisy family*

 Wormwood   *pl. 149.* A bushy, silvery plant with long spikes of tiny drooping yellowish ovoid flower heads (3–4 mm) borne on silky, grooved stems. Leaves pinnately lobed, silky on both sides, strongly aromatic. July–Sept. *Daisy family*

 St Barnaby's Thistle   *pl. 155.* Unlike any other plant, with white-cottony, wavy-winged stems, and pale yellow flower heads (12 mm) with long stiff spreading yellow spines. Lower leaves pinnately lobed; upper narrow, uncut; all whitish and cottony-haired. July–Sept. *Daisy family*

See also: SPANISH CATCHFLY *pl. 15*; LARGE MEDITERRANEAN SPURGE *pl. 66*; SEA SPURGE *pl. 66*; WOOD SPURGE *pl. 66*; CAPER SPURGE *pl. 67*; SUN SPURGE *pl. 67*; WINGED SEA LAVENDER *pl. 94*; WILD MADDER *pl. 98*; COMMON VINCETOXICUM *pl. 99*.

Flowers small · Plant small

 Purslane   *pl. 11.* A quite hairless spreading plant, with fleshy leaves and stems and solitary yellow flowers (8–12 mm). Petals 5–6, opening in the sun, soon falling. Leaves (1–2 cm) oval, stalkless. May–Oct. *Purslane family*

 Spiny-Fruited Buttercup   *pl. 26.* A pale green, shining annual of damp places, with rounded, lobed leaves, and inconspicuous glossy flowers (3–6 mm). Distinguished by its rather large fruits (7–8 mm), with a broad margin and spines on the sides. Apr.–June. *Buttercup family*

 Erect Hypecoum   *pl. 30.* A delicate, grey-green plant, with feathery leaves and small orange-yellow flowers (1–1½ cm). Petals distinctive, conspicuously three-lobed and unequal. Fruit long, slender, curved and jointed. May–June. *Poppy family*

 Yellow Corydalis   *pl. 30.* An attractive fern-like plant with a cluster of golden-yellow, tubular two-lipped flowers (1½–2 cm). Petals 4: the upper hooded, the lower boat-shaped and 2 narrow side petals; spur short, down-curved. Apr.–Sept. *Poppy family*

 Yellow Whitlow-Grass   *pl. 34.* A tiny alpine of rocks and stony pastures with neat rosettes of stiff, bristly-haired leaves. Flowering stems short, bearing a dense cluster of bright yellow flowers (8–9 mm). Fruit paddle-shaped. Apr.–June. *Cress family*

 Rock Stonecrop   *pl. 40.* One of many yellow-flowered stonecrops. Distinguished by drooping globular flower clusters in bud, which become flat-topped in flower, concave in fruit. Flowers usually with 7 petals (6–7 mm). The fat, cylindrical-pointed leaves are evenly arranged along the non-flowering stems. June–Aug. *Stonecrop family*

 Stonecrop, Wall-Pepper   *pl. 40.* A cheerful little plant forming mats with fleshy, globular leaves (3–5 mm) and bright yellow starry flowers. Flowers 12 mm; petals 5, with pointed tips. The leaves are hot and peppery to the taste. June–July. *Stonecrop family*

Roseroot, Midsummer-Men *pl. 40.* An arctic or mountain rock plant, forming clumps of short stout stems bearing numerous glaucous fleshy overlapping leaves. The plants are one-sexed; male flowers with yellowish-green petals and purple anthers; female flowers smaller with greenish carpels which become bright red in fruit. May–Aug. *Stonecrop family*

 Yellow Mountain Saxifrage *pl. 41.* A rather weak, mat-forming plant. Flowers (1 cm) yellow and red-spotted, with widely spaced narrow petals and red anthers. Leaves fleshy, narrow, pointed, often with hairy margins. June–Aug. *Saxifrage family*

 Opposite-Leaved Golden Saxifrage *pl. 42.* A glossy, weak, bright green plant with tiny flowers in flat clusters, sometimes in abundance in damp shady places forming a golden-green carpet. Flowers without petals (3–4 mm). Leaves rounded and shallowly-toothed, in opposite pairs. Mar.–June. *Saxifrage family*

 Spring Cinquefoil *pl. 46.* A small, variable creeping plant forming mats and bearing a cluster of a few bright yellow flowers (1–1½ cm). Basal leaves with 5 toothed leaflets; stipules with the green part linear. Mar.–June. *Rose family*

 Hairy Medick *pl. 58.* Distinguished largely by its fruits, as is the case with the other 37 species in Europe. Fruit of this species somewhat disk-shaped (4–9 mm), with 1½ to 4 close spirals and 2 rows of spines on the outer margin of each spiral, and a strongly netted surface. Flowers (3–4 mm) in close heads of 3–8. May–June. *Pea family*

 Sea Medick *pl. 58.* A low spreading, densely woolly-white plant of sands by the Mediterranean, with distinctive spirally-coiled woolly fruits, with or without spines. Flowers (6–8 mm) in short-stalked clusters. Apr.–June. *Pea family*

 Brown Trefoil *pl. 60.* Readily distinguished by its neat globular heads (8–20 mm) of yellow flowers which turn leather-brown with age. Flowers 7–9 mm. A low, erect, or spreading annual of rocky mountain pastures. July–Aug. *Pea family*

 Kidney-Vetch *pl. 61.* An extremely variable plant, with yellow, pink, crimson-purple or white flowers. Flower clusters dense, often in pairs, half-encircled by 2 deeply divided bracts pressed against the cluster. Flowers (1–1½ cm) with shaggy, inflated calyx. Leaves with 1–6 pairs of leaflets, the terminal leaflet often much larger. May–Aug. *Pea family*

 Bladder Vetch *pl. 61.* A creeping, greyish annual, with dense stalkless heads of pale yellow flowers tipped with orange or red, later replaced by an enlarged and inflated silky calyx enclosing the fruit. Leaves with 1–2 pairs of leaflets, the terminal one much larger and broader. Mar.–July. *Pea family*

 Maltese Cross, Small Caltrops *pl. 64.* So named because of its fruit, with 5 long spines and 5 short tough spines; whichever way it falls some spines stick upwards. Small yellow flowers (7–10 mm) axillary. Leaves with 5–8 neat pairs of silvery-haired leaflets. Apr.–Sept. *Caltrop family*

 Marsh St John's Wort *pl. 75.* A weak, creeping or half-floating, mat-forming plant of acid bogs, with silvery-green, hairy clasping leaves. Flowers (1½ cm) pale yellow, few in a cluster towards the ends of the short erect leafy stems. June–Sept. *St John's Wort family*

 Spotted Rockrose *pl. 78.* A variable, hairy annual with a loose cluster of yellow flowers (8–12 mm), blotched with purple-brown. Basal leaves in a rosette, much broader than the narrow upper leaves. Apr.–June. *Rockrose family*

 Yellow Bird's Nest *pl. 86.* A yellowish or whitish, waxy-looking plant, sometimes found pushing up through leaf litter in shady woods. The drooping, one-sided cluster of pale tubular flowers (1–1½ cm) is distinctive. A saprophyte, without green leaves. June–Spet. *Wintergreen family*

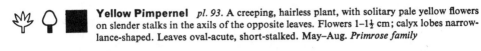

Yellow Pimpernel *pl. 93.* A creeping, hairless plant, with solitary pale yellow flowers on slender stalks in the axils of the opposite leaves. Flowers 1–1½ cm; calyx lobes narrow-lance-shaped. Leaves oval-acute, short-stalked. May–Aug. *Primrose family*

Golden Drop *pl. 105.* An extremely bristly, stiff erect, pale yellowish-green plant, with one-sided drooping clusters of yellow tubular flowers (2 cm). Distinguished from Honey-wort by absence of brown on flowers and by the calyx, deeply lobed nearly to the base. May–June. *Borage family*

Ground-Pine *pl. 106.* A low, grey-green, hairy plant which smells strongly of pine when crushed. The small bright yellow flowers (5–12 mm) are two-lipped; lower lip often red-spotted. Leaves deeply divided into 3 strap-shaped, glandular lobes. May–Aug. *Mint family*

Mountain Germander, Alpine Penny Royal *pl. 107.* A low spreading, woody-based plant of the mountains. Small whitish-yellow flowers (1–1½ cm) are borne in flattened terminal clusters. Leaves numerous, narrow-lance-shaped, green above, white-felted beneath, with inrolled margins. May–Aug. *Mint family*

Cut-Leaved Self-Heal *pl. 110.* Flowers (1½ cm) usually yellowish-white (sometimes purple-flushed, as in the photograph). Distinguished from the Common Self-Heal (not illustrated) by upper leaves, which are often deeply cut into narrow lobes, with whitish hairs beneath, and by stems which are densely white-haired on the angles. June–Oct. *Mint family*

Dwarf Eyebright *pl. 127.* A tiny plant with flowers (5–6 mm) from yellow, white, bluish to violet, or a combination of these. Leaves oval (½–1 cm), the upper with 2–4 blunt or sharp teeth on each side, with stiff hairs on the margin and veins. July–Sept. *Figwort family*

Yellow-Rattle *pl. 127.* Has a swollen calyx and smaller 'pinched' two-lipped corolla, the upper lip usually purple-tipped. Leaves in opposite pairs, lance-shaped, strongly tooth-ed. A semi-parasitic plant of grasslands. The fruits rattle when dry. May–Sept. *Figwort family*

Tuberous Lousewort *pl. 127.* A low-growing plant of alpine meadows with a rosette of much-divided leaves and a leafless cluster of pale yellow flowers, which have long straight conspicuous beaks on their upper lips; also a bell-shaped calyx with leafy, toothed lobes. June–Aug. *Figwort family*

Tozzia *pl. 129.* A charming plant of damp places with loose clusters of small yellow bell-shaped flowers (6–10 mm long), spotted red. Leaves oval, with a few coarse teeth; stem fleshy, quadrangular with 2 lines of hairs. June–Aug. *Figwort family*

Lesser Broomrape *pl. 131.* A parasite, commonly on members of the pea family, particularly the clovers. Flowers (10–18 mm) pale yellow, usually tinged with dull violet; stigma purple or rarely yellow. June–Sept. *Broomrape family*

Cudweed *pl. 143.* A dull plant, covered with greyish or yellowish woolly hairs, with small globular clusters (12 mm) of numerous tiny yellowish flower heads. Flower clusters terminal or axillary. Leaves narrow, numerous, overlapping. June–Sept. *Daisy family*

Marsh Cudweed *pl. 144.* A low, weak, spreading white-woolly annual, with rounded clusters of tiny flower heads (3–4 mm), each consisting of several minute florets. Involucral bracts papery, hairy below. Leaves oblong, pointed or blunt. June–Oct. *Daisy family*

Stinking Everlasting *pl. 144.* A silvery-grey, woody-based shrubby plant with many erect leafy stems with a strong curry-like smell when crushed. Flower heads small, globular (4–6 mm), with shining silvery 'everlasting' bracts, in flat-topped clusters. Leaves narrow, inrolled. Apr.–July. *Daisy family*

Annual Asteriscus *pl. 146.* A hairy annual, with small pale yellow flower heads. Ray florets numerous, erect, surrounded by the narrow upper leaves and bracts which spread in a star. Upper leaves clasping, the lower stalked. June–Aug. *Daisy family*

Yellow Milfoil *pl. 147.* Has golden-yellow, flat-topped clusters of tiny flower heads. Individual flower heads (3 mm) with 4–6 rounded ray florets, and woolly involucral bracts with brown margins. Stems woolly-haired. May–July. *Daisy family*

Brass Buttons *pl. 149.* Introduced from South Africa, now naturalized. Flower heads tight, globular (6–10 mm) with a neat involucre of 2 rows of papery-margined bracts. Leaves strongly aromatic, irregularly cut into narrow lobes, and with white sheathing bases. July–Aug. *Daisy family*

Grey Alpine Groundsel *pl. 150.* A small silvery-leaved plant of rocky mountain pastures. Flower heads (1½ cm) with 3–5 orange-yellow rays, in a dense cluster. Leaves at first white-felted, later hairless. July–Aug. *Daisy family*

Hedypnois *pl. 158.* A Mediterranean annual, distinguished in fruit by its swollen fruit stalks with a crown of stiff, woody, incurved involucral bracts. Flower heads solitary (1½ cm) with numerous ray florets. May–June. *Daisy family*

Hollow-Stemmed Gagea *pl. 164.* All gageas look very similar. This mountain species has somewhat fleshy, hollow, linear basal leaves, circular in cross-section. Flowers (1–1½ cm) with spreading petals. Leafy bracts 2, unequal, much broader than the leaves. May–July. *Lily family*

Yellow Onion *pl. 165.* A slender onion with an umbel of small yellow flowers (4–5 mm) with projecting stamens. Two long, pointed, papery bracts, spread beyond the umbel. Leaves (1–2 mm broad) thick, smooth and channelled. June–Aug. *Lily family*

See also: MOUNTAIN HOUSELEEK *pl. 39*; PINEAPPLE WEED, RAYLESS MAYWEED *pl. 148*.

Flowers minute · Plant medium

Large Disk Medick *pl. 58.* Unmistakable in fruit, with a flattened spiral of 3–5 smooth turns, closed at the centre, and with conspicuous radiating veins when dry. Flowers (3 mm) in clusters on a short stem, ending in a fine point. Apr.–July. *Pea family*

Perfoliate Alexanders *pl. 84.* A distinctive pale green umbellifer with quite circular upper leaves clasping the stem and subtending the umbels. Lower leaves with swollen sheaths, 2 to 3 times divided into oval, toothed lobes. Fruits black, 3 mm. Apr.–June. *Umbellifer family*

Wild Parsnip *pl. 86.* A strong-smelling, erect, rough-haired plant, with flattened umbels (3–10 cm) of minute (2 mm) yellow flowers, without bracts below. Leaves large with 5–9 oval, stalked leaflets. Fruit ovoid, broadly winged. June–Sept. *Umbellifer family*

Crosswort *pl. 99.* A distinctive pale greenish-yellow plant with weak square stems with elliptic leaves in whorls of 4. Flowers (2–3 mm) whorled, in a terminal elongated cluster. Fruit blackish, smooth. Apr.–June. *Bedstraw family*

Flowers minute · Plant small

Turn-Sole *pl. 65.* A silvery erect weed of cultivated ground. The clusters of yellowish flowers are one-sexed; male clusters erect; female drooping, with rounded three-lobed fruits covered with swellings. A well-known dye plant. June–Oct. *Spurge family*

Rock Samphire *pl. 84.* A greyish, fleshy, bushy plant of rock crevices on coasts in the 'splash zone'. Umbels pale yellowish (3–6 cm across); flowers 2 mm. Leaves compound, with plump, narrow, pointed leaflets. July–Oct. *Umbellifer family*

Starry Hare's-Ear *pl. 84*. This grey-green mountain plant is easily identified by the shallow, often yellowish 'cup' of fused bracts below each umbel. Petals yellow. Leaves mostly basal, numerous, linear to lance-shaped. July–Aug. *Umbellifer family*

 Rough Valantia *pl. 98*. A tiny softly hairy plant of stony places. Plant pale yellowish-green, leaves in whorls of 4, and minute yellowish flowers in whorls. Fruit distinctive, hard, ivory-coloured, three-horned, covered with spines. Apr.–June. *Bedstraw family*

 Buck's-Horn Plantain *pl. 133*. One of the few plantains to have deeply cut or lobed leaves (sometimes twice-cut into linear lobes), in a typically flattened rosette. The often numerous erect stems bear slender cylindrical flower spikes 3–5 cm long. Apr.–Oct. *Plantain family*

See also: PROCUMBENT PEARLWORT *pl. 13*; ALPINE ASPHODEL *pl. 162*.

2 Aquatic Plants

WHITE

 White Water-Lily *pl. 18.* A familiar sight in summer when the large (10–20 cm) fragrant floating flowers open. The flat, shining, rounded leaves (10–30 cm) have a deep slit to the point of attachment to the leaf stalk. June–Sept. *Water-Lily family*

 Pond Crowfoot *pl. 26.* One of several aquatic crowfoots; it has rounded to kidney-shaped floating leaves with 3–7 shallow rounded lobes. Submerged leaves much-divided into thread-like segments. Flowers comparatively large (1½–3 cm), above water. May–July. *Buttercup family*

 Large River Water Crowfoot *pl. 26.* Like the previous plant but with no floating leaves, only tassel-like submerged leaves which collapse together out of water. A plant of fast, usually clear streams. May–Aug. *Buttercup family*

 Water Chestnut *pl. 79.* A unique plant with a floating rosette of distinctive, coarsely toothed, diamond-shaped leaves, with stout stalks with spindle-shaped buoyancy swellings. Flowers white (1–2 cm) with 4 spreading petals. Fruits top-shaped with 2–4 very stout horn-like spikes; edible. June–July. *Water Chestnut family*

 Water Soldier *pl. 161.* The submerged rosette of quill-like, toothed leaves rise to the surface at flowering time and submerge in late summer. Flowers from the axils of a sheath-like bract, on a short stem. Petals 3, rounded, crumpled; sepals 3. June–Aug. *Frog-bit family*

 Frog-Bit *pl. 161.* The small, rounded, bright green, shining, kidney-shaped leaves (3 cm) are characteristic. Flowers (2 cm), few, with 3 rounded, crumpled petals. Underwater stems slender, bearing much-branched roots; submerged leaves absent. June–Aug. *Frog-bit family*

 Bog Arum *pl. 183.* The 'flowers' comprise a broad white flat spathe loosely encircling a club-shaped spadix covered all over with tiny greenish flowers. Creeping stems below water; leaves thick-stalked, shining, heart-shaped, pointed, above water. Fruit coral-red. June–Aug. *Arum family*

See also: BOGBEAN *pl. 98.*

GREEN

 Common Starwort *pl. 105.* A pale green water weed sometimes growing on damp mud. The floating rosettes of broadly oval, overlapping leaves distinguish it from others. The submerged leaves are much narrower. Flowers and fruit are minute. Apr.–Oct. *Starwort family*

 Broad-Leaved Pondweed *pl. 161.* The largest of pondweeds, with large, oval, shining, leathery floating leaves (2½–12½ cm long). The greenish flower spike is borne on a stout stem. Floating leaves appear jointed where blade joins stalk; submerged leaves slender. June–Aug. *Pondweed family*

Posidonia *pl. 161.* A 'sea-grass' forming extensive pastures in shallow Mediterranean waters. Strap-shaped blades usually bright grass-green. Fibrous balls, often washed up on the coast, are the decaying leaf bases. Oct.–Jan. *Pondweed family*

 Sweet Flag *pl. 183.* This tall waterside plant has iris-like, sword-shaped leaves and creeping rhizomes below water. Flowers minute, borne on a club-like axis (to 8 cm long) halfway up the leaf-like stem. May–July. *Arum family*

 Great Duckweed *pl. 184.* The 'leaves' are only ½–1 cm in diameter and always float. Distinguished by the several roots hanging from the lower surface, and the rather thick leaf blades, usually purplish beneath. Flowers minute, rare. May–June. *Duckweed family*

 Duckweed *pl. 184.* Like the previous plant but blades smaller (2–5 mm) and there is only 1 root. A plant of still waters and wet mud. Apr.–June. *Duckweed family*

 Bur-Reed *pl. 184.* A tall sturdy plant growing in shallow water with stiff sword-shaped, triangular-sectioned leaves. Flowers tiny, in globular clusters on the branches; male clusters more numerous towards the end, the female larger (1–2 cm) below. Fruit a bur-like ball. June–Aug. *Bur-Reed family*

RED, PINK, PINKISH-PURPLE

 Spiked Water-Milfoil *pl. 82.* A completely submerged plant of still waters with whorls (usually 4) of feathery-dissected leaves. Flower spikes reddish, held just above water. Bracts tiny, uncut except the lowest. June–July. *Water-Milfoil family*

 Bogbean, Buckbean *pl. 98.* The trifoliate leaves held above water, with large shining, oval blades are distinctive when the plant is not in flower. Flowers (1½ cm), pale pink to whitish, with unusual conspicuously fringed petals. Apr.–June. *Bogbean family*

 Flowering Rush *pl. 161.* A beautiful water plant with its long-stemmed umbel of coral-pink flowers (2½–3 cm) borne well above water. Leaves rush-like, triangular in section, in a cluster from an underwater creeping stem. June–Aug. *Flowering Rush family*

BLUE, VIOLET, BLUISH-PURPLE

 Water Violet *pl. 92.* Has a pyramidal spike of whorls of pale lilac, yellow-eyed, primrose-like flowers (2–2½ cm) with notched petals. Leaves submerged or forming floating rosettes, pale green, deeply lacerated into narrow comb-like segments. May–July. *Primrose family*

YELLOW

 Yellow Water-Lily *pl. 18.* Yellow globular flowers, smelling of alcohol, are borne above water. Both petals and sepals yellow. Floating leaves elliptic, notched (12–40 cm long), differing from the lettuce-like, bright green, translucent submerged leaves. June–Aug. *Water-Lily family*

 Great Spearwort *pl. 25.* A slender, hollow-stemmed plant of watersides and ditches with long spear-shaped leaves, and the largest buttercup-yellow flowers (2–5 cm) of any of the genus. June–Aug. *Buttercup family*

 Fringed Water-Lily *pl. 97.* The rounded, notched, floating leaves are like those of the water-lily but much smaller (3–10 cm) and often purple-blotched. The bright yellow flowers have 5 spreading, conspicuously fringed, petal lobes. June–Sept. *Bogbean family*

Greater Bladderwort   *pl. 132.* Interesting with its feathery, much-divided submerged leaves bearing small 'trap-door' bladders (3 mm) which catch small animals. Flowers (1½–2½ cm) 2-lipped; lips more or less closed by a throat-boss; spur conical. Stem rootless, plant free-floating. June–Aug. *Butterwort family*

Great Reedmace, Cat's-Tail   *pl. 184.* A stout plant growing to 2½ m in shallow water. Flowering spikes with a slender cluster of yellow male flowers, continuous with a broader darker zone of female flowers below. In fruit the females are brown, topped by the bare axis. Leaves flat (1–2 cm wide). June–Aug. *Reedmace family*

See also: BUR-REED *pl. 184.*

3 Shrubs

Plant tall

 Snowy Mespilus *pl. 47.* The young twigs and leaves are densely covered with snowy white hairs, but later become hairless. White flowers (1½–2 cm) in clusters, petals narrow and widely spaced. Fruit blue-black, fleshy, sweet. Apr.–May. *Rose family*

 Cherry-Laurel *pl. 47.* Often wrongly called Laurel because of its large, dark, glossy green leaves (5–18 cm). Distinguished by the long erect spike of white flowers (*cf.* Laurel (not illustrated) and Spotted Laurel). Fruits oval, shining black-purple (8 mm) in long clusters. Apr.–May. *Rose family*

 Portugal Laurel *pl. 48.* A handsome shrub of Portugal, often planted as an ornamental. Distinguished from the previous species by the toothed leaves with reddish (not green) leaf stalks. Flowers in long drooping clusters longer than the leaves. May–July. *Rose family*

 Blackthorn, Sloe *pl. 49.* The white flowers (1–1½ cm) appear before the leaves in early spring on blackish, very spiny twigs. Leaves oval, toothed, hairy, and dull-coloured. The globular, blue-black, bloomed fruits (1–1¼ cm) are very astringent. Mar.–May. *Rose family*

 White Broom *pl. 52.* A switch-like shrub of coastal Iberia and North Africa, with long flexible, ribbed branches covered with silky hairs. Striking in flower with numerous white pea flowers (1–1¼ cm) clustered along slender branches. Feb.–May. *Pea family*

 Gum Cistus *pl. 77.* A dark green, sticky, aromatic evergreen of south-west Europe, with large solitary white flowers (5–8 cm), usually with brownish-purple blotches. Leaves (4–10 cm) narrowly lance-shaped, stalkless, grey-haired beneath. May–June. *Rockrose family*

 Laurel-Leaved Cistus *pl. 77.* Like the previous shrub but leaves broader, oval to lance-shaped, and stalked. The flowers are in clusters of 3–8 (not solitary) and long-stalked, and the petals are yellow-blotched. June–July. *Rockrose family*

 Myrtle *pl. 81.* A rather low, dark green, aromatic shrub, usually more than 1 m, with numerous shining, leathery, oval-pointed leaves (2–3 cm). Flowers sweet-scented (2–3 cm), long-stalked, in axils of upper leaves, with numerous projecting stamens. Fruit a blue-black berry. May–July. *Myrtle family*

 Dogwood *pl. 82.* A densely branched deciduous shrub with smooth reddish twigs, and oval, prominently veined, opposite leaves. Flowers in dense flat-topped clusters (5 cm across), followed by almost black fleshy fruit. May–June. *Dogwood family*

 Tree Heath *pl. 89.* A tall, branched, feathery-looking shrub (1–4 m), with hairy twigs covered with very numerous tiny needle-like leaves and with tiny whitish or pinkish flowers. Flowers bell-shaped (3 mm); anthers not projecting. Leaves (½ cm), grooved, dark green. Mar.–May. *Heath family*

 Lusitanian Heath *pl. 89.* Like the preceding shrub but more restricted, from south Portugal to south-west France. Distinguished by larger more cylindrical flowers (4–5 mm long), white tinged with pink, especially in bud. Leaves light green. Dec.–July. *Heath family*

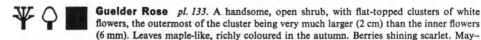

Guelder Rose *pl. 133.* A handsome, open shrub, with flat-topped clusters of white flowers, the outermost of the cluster being very much larger (2 cm) than the inner flowers (6 mm). Leaves maple-like, richly coloured in the autumn. Berries shining scarlet. May–June. *Honeysuckle family*

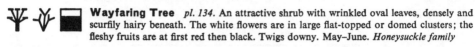

Wayfaring Tree *pl. 134.* An attractive shrub with wrinkled oval leaves, densely and scurfily hairy beneath. The white flowers are in large flat-topped or domed clusters; the fleshy fruits are at first red then black. Twigs downy. May–June. *Honeysuckle family*

Laurustinus *pl. 134.* An evergreen shrub of the Mediterranean, with leathery, dark green, shining leaves and reddish twigs. The flat or domed flower clusters are about 6 cm across; the tubular flowers 6 mm. Fruits metallic blue-black. Feb.–May. *Honeysuckle family*

Fly Honeysuckle *pl. 135.* A shrubby, non-climbing honeysuckle with paired, tubular, unscented flowers (1–1½ cm) at first white, then yellowish. Leaves grey-green, softly hairy, oval-acute. Fruit of 2 unfused red berries. May–June. *Honeysuckle family*

See also: CHERRY-PLUM *pl. 48*; QUINCE *pl. 47*; ST LUCIE'S CHERRY *pl. 49*; STRAWBERRY TREE *pl. 90.*

Plant low

Caper *pl. 31.* A low, straggling, spiny shrub with oval, fleshy glaucous leaves. The beautiful white flowers (5–7 cm) with violet stamens are short-lived. The large fruits burst to reveal crimson flesh and glossy purple seeds. The flower buds are the 'capers'. June–Sept. *Caper family*

Dewberry *pl. 44.* A blackberry-like shrub with spreading, rather weak, greyish-bloomed prickly stems. Flowers (2 cm), sometimes pinkish. The blackberry fruits have only a few large globular, bloomed berries. May–Sept. *Rose family*

Field Rose *pl. 45.* A trailing, rather weak-stemmed rose usually less than 1 m, with often purplish stems and rather few hooked prickles. Flowers pure white (3–5 cm), distinguished by the styles which are joined in a column. June–July. *Rose family*

Burnet Rose *pl. 45.* A beautiful compact rose, with small pinnate leaves with 9–11 leaflets and stems covered with small straight prickles and bristles. Flowers fragrant, solitary, cream-coloured. Hips globular, purple-black, hairless, with persisting sepals. May–June. *Rose family*

Mountain Avens *pl. 45.* An attractive creeping undershrub of the mountains, often forming extensive mats. White flowers (2½–4 cm) solitary, with 8 petals. Leaves neatly toothed, shiny above, white-woolly beneath. Fruit feathery. May–Aug. *Rose family*

Wild Cotoneaster *pl. 48.* A deciduous, twisted, often creeping shrub, with oval leaves conspicuously grey-woolly beneath. Flowers small, petals pinkish or white (3 mm). Fruit a shining red, pendulous, globular berry. Apr.–June. *Rose family*

White Flax *pl. 65.* A beautiful white-flowered, bushy flax of south-west Europe, with slender stems and narrow awl-shaped leaves. Flower buds yellow; petals often flushed with purple or violet at the base, or pink-veined. May–July. *Flax family*

Sage-Leaved Cistus *pl. 77.* The most widespread species with soft, wrinkled, sage-like leaves, and long-stalked clusters of white flowers. Flowers (2–4 cm) usually orange-centred; outer sepals broadly heart-shaped. Apr.–June. *Rockrose family*

Narrow-Leaved Cistus *pl. 77.* Distinguished by its narrow lance-shaped, sticky, dark green, wrinkled leaves with inrolled margins, and grey-haired undersides. Flowers rather small (2–3 cm), pure white, clustered. Apr.–June. *Rockrose family*

White Rockrose   *pl. 78.* A low-growing, variable, weak-stemmed shrublet, with white flowers (2 cm) with yellow centres (flowers sometimes pink). Stipules thread-like. Leaves varying from greyish-woolly to green and hairless. May–July. *Rockrose family*

Diapensia   *pl. 87.* A tiny evergreen undershrub of arctic and northern regions, forming prostrate cushions of leathery leaves. Flowers (1–1½ cm) solitary, short-stalked. May–June. *Diapensia family*

Black Bearberry   *pl. 88.* A spreading, intricately branched, deciduous shrublet with bright green, wrinkled leaves. Flowers (4 mm) white with a green throat; fruit at first red, then blue-black. May–Aug. *Heath family*

Cowberry   *pl. 89.* A creeping evergreen shrublet with glossy dark green leaves in two ranks. White flowers often tinged with pink, open bell-shaped (6 mm), borne in drooping clusters. Edible berry red. May–July. *Heath family*

Prasium   *pl. 107.* A low, twiggy shrub of the Mediterranean, with small shining nettle-like leaves, and whorls of paired white 'dead nettle' flowers. Flowers two-lipped, the upper hooded, the lower three-lobed. Calyx tubular, with spiny-tipped lobes. Apr.–June. *Mint family*

See also: BOX-LEAVED or SHRUBBY MILKWORT *pl. 68*; COMMON ROCKROSE *pl. 78*; TWIN-FLOWER *pl. 135*.

GREEN

Plant tall

Red Currant   *pl. 43.* A small bushy shrub with inclined or drooping clusters of small greenish flowers (5–7 mm) followed by acid, shining red berries. Leaves more or less heart-shaped, with 3–5 toothed lobes. Apr.–May. *Gooseberry family*

Mountain Currant   *pl. 43.* Similar to the previous species but flowers in short, more erect clusters, either of fewer, smaller female flowers or of more numerous male flowers. Leaves (2–6 cm) deeply three-lobed. Apr.–May. *Gooseberry family*

Gooseberry   *pl. 43.* Unmistakable with its formidable spines, usually grouped in threes. Flowers (1 cm) bell-shaped, drooping, with tiny turned-back sepals and tiny whitish or greenish-purple petals. Leaves deeply three- to five-lobed. Mar.–Apr. *Gooseberry family*

Tree Spurge   *pl. 66.* Stout-stemmed, much-branched above, forming a domed profile (2 m), later quite leafless during the Mediterranean summer. Leaves lance-shaped, thick, somewhat glaucous. Flower clusters with rounded bracts, and oval or half-moon-shaped shining glands. Apr.–June. *Spurge family*

Mediterranean Coriaria   *pl. 68.* Flowers greenish, in short clusters. Petals becoming fleshy and enclosing fruits at first reddish-purple then shining black. Leaves leathery, myrtle-like, three-veined; twigs quadrangular. Mar.–July. *Coriaria family*

Spindle-Tree   *pl. 71.* A slender shrub or small tree with green stems and clusters of tiny greenish flowers (8–20 mm), and narrow oval leaves. In autumn its beautiful deep pink, three-lobed fruits split to expose bright orange coverings to the seeds. Apr.–June. *Spindle-Tree family*

Buckthorn   *pl. 71.* A dense, leafy, spiny shrub or small tree, with neat oval leaves (3–6 cm) with 2–3 pairs of conspicuous side veins. Flowers green (4 mm) solitary or clustered. Fruits fleshy ((¼–1 cm), at length black, poisonous, used in dyeing. May–June. *Buckthorn family*

Sea Buckthorn *pl. 74.* A freely suckering, silvery-leaved shrub forming dense thickets on sands and also on river gravel inland. The plant is covered with distinctive silvery or brown scales. Flowers greenish, very small, appearing before the leaves. Fruit fleshy. Mar.–May. *Oleaster family*

 Alpine or **Red Elder** *pl. 134.* An attractive shrub in fruit, with drooping clusters of scarlet berries. Flowers greenish-white in dense rounded clusters. Leaves with 5–7 leaflets; pith of stems cinnamon-coloured. Apr.–May. *Honeysuckle family*

Plant low

 Reticulate Willow *pl. 3.* A low creeping rooting mat-forming shrublet of the mountains and the north with dark green wrinkled leaves, pale beneath, silky-haired when young. Catkins erect (1–3 cm), long-stalked, appearing after the leaves. May–July. *Willow family*

 Blunt-Leaved Willow *pl. 3.* The glossy hairless yellowish-green leaves distinguish this creeping shrublet. Catkins appearing at the same time as the leaves. A high mountain or arctic plant. June–July. *Willow family*

 Hastate Willow *pl. 3 .* A compact, shiny-branched shrub to 1½ m, with variable elliptic to obovate wrinkled and toothed leaves, paler and bloomed beneath, soon hairless. Catkins (6 cm) appearing with the leaves. Fruit hairless. June–July. *Willow family*

 Bog Myrtle, Sweet Gale *pl. 4.* A low, pleasantly aromatic shrub, growing in damp acid places in the north and west. Leaves (2–6 cm) greyish-green, lance-shaped and appearing after catkins. Fruit a dry waxy-coated berry. Apr.–May. *Bog Myrtle family*

 Dwarf Birch *pl. 4.* A knee-high undershrub of moors and bogs of the arctic and in mountains in central Europe, with spreading branches and rounded, deeply toothed, rather thick-textured leaves (½–1½ cm), first hairy, then hairless. Fruiting catkins (½–1 cm) erect. May. *Birch family*

 Shrubby Glasswort *pl. 10.* A fleshy, upright, shrubby plant of salt-marshes, with grey-green pointed stems appearing leafless and without flowers. Flowers insignificant, in threes in the axils of the upper fleshy bracts. Leaves fleshy, encircling the stems. Sept.–Nov. *Goosefoot family*

 Spurge Laurel *pl. 74.* A small shrub with thick flexible unbranched stems and a rosette of glossy leathery leaves at the top. Flower clusters small; calyx (8–12 mm) tubular, fleshy, greenish or dull yellow. Berries black. Feb.–Apr. *Daphne family*

 Hardy Asparagus *pl. 168.* A much-branched, wiry, scrambling shrub with stiff clusters of 4–12 angular, sharp-pointed 'needles' and often stout recurved spines below. Flowers yellowish-green (3 mm), bell-shaped. Fruit black. Mar.–June. *Lily family*

 Dwarf Fan Palm *pl. 176.* The only native European palm, usually stemless, forming dense low patches. Distinguished by large, stiff, fan-like leaves with 12–15 narrow segments and spiny leaf stalks. Flowers in dense yellowish clusters. Mar.–June. *Palm family*

RED, PINK, PINKISH-PURPLE

Plant tall

 Willow Spiraea *pl. 44.* A suckering shrub with many erect yellowish-brown stems with deciduous willow-like leaves. Its bright pink flowers are in terminal conical or cylindrical clusters. Flowers 8 mm; stamens long, projecting. June–July. *Rose family*

 Alpine Rose *pl. 45.* A low shrub (½–2 m) of mountain rocks and shady places, with sometimes reddish stems without prickles. Flowers (3½–5 cm), solitary. Fruit usually pendulous, bottle-shaped (2–2½ cm), with persistent leafy sepals. June–July. *Rose family*

Castor Oil Plant *pl. 65.* Distinctive with its very large palmately lobed leaves (to 80 cm). Either a robust annual or, more commonly in the south, a tall shrub or small tree. The reddish female flowers are borne above the male flowers in a stout spike. The large mottled seeds give the oil. Feb.–Dec. *Spurge family*

 Mastic Tree, Lentisc *pl. 68.* A dense, much-branched evergreen shrub with very aromatic, dark green, pinnate leaves with 3–6 pairs of leathery leaflets. Shrubs one-sexed: male flower clusters red at first; female clusters brownish. Fruit globular, red then black. Apr.–June. *Cashew family*

 Turpentine Tree, Terebinth *pl. 69.* A strongly resinous grey-stemmed deciduous shrub with pinnate leaves with 2–5 pairs of leaflets and a terminal one. Flowers in branched clusters, reddish-purple, appearing with the young leaves. Fruit at first coral-red, then brownish. Apr.–July. *Cashew family*

 African Tamarisk *pl. 78.* A graceful feathery shrub growing near the sea. The delicate appearance is due to the numerous slender branches with very tiny needle-like leaves (about 3 mm). Flowers tiny (3 mm), massed in cylindrical clusters. Mar.–June. *Tamarisk family*

 Pomegranate *pl. 80.* A spiny shrub with oblong-lance-shaped, shiny, deciduous leaves and striking scarlet flowers (4 cm), crumpled petals and fleshy red calyx. The fruits (9 cm) have brownish-yellow rind and sweetly-acid flesh. May–Sept. *Pomegranate family*

 Spotted Laurel *pl. 83.* A laurel-like Japanese evergreen shrub, sometimes grown for ornament. The shining leaves (8–20 cm) are often spotted with yellow. Fruiting berries scarlet (1½–2 cm). Mar.–Apr. *Dogwood family*

 Rhododendron *pl. 88.* The only large rhododendron of Europe, often planted and naturalized. Large tubular flowers (5 cm) in rounded clusters; purple and brown-spotted within. Leaves dull dark green, leathery, evergreen, paler beneath. May–June. *Heath family*

 Oleander *pl. 98.* A handsome evergreen shrub with stiff, lance-shaped leaves, often in threes, growing by dried river beds and ravines near the Mediterranean. Flowers sweet-smelling (3–5 cm), with conspicuous jagged scales on the petals. June–Sept. *Dogbane family*

 Snowberry *pl. 135.* A slender, much-branched, deciduous shrub, often forming thickets, unmistakable with its soft, snow-white, mothball-sized fruits. Flowers pink (½ cm). Leaves oval, glaucous, those on the sucker shoots deeply lobed. A native of North America, often naturalized. June–Sept. *Honeysuckle family*

See also: JUDAS TREE *pl. 50*; TREE HEATH *pl. 89*; LUSITANIAN HEATH *pl. 89*; CHASTE TREE *pl. 106.*

Plant low

 Thorny Burnet *pl. 46.* A low, rounded, spiny shrub, with numerous greyish, interlacing branches, of the eastern Mediterranean region. Flower clusters globular (½ cm). Leaves pinnate, tiny, soon falling; fruit fleshy, often bright red. Mar.–Apr. *Rose family*

 Purple Broom *pl. 51.* A spreading, almost hairless shrublet of the south-east Alps with obovate leaves. Flowers (1½–2½ cm), lilac-pink to purplish, in a leafy cluster. Apr.–May. *Pea family*

 Shrubby Restharrow *pl. 57.* A slender branched shrub with small leathery trifoliate saw-toothed leaves, of Spain and France. Flowers (1½–2 cm) pale pink veined with darker purple, in leafless branched clusters. May–July. *Pea family*

73

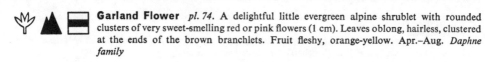

Garland Flower *pl. 74.* A delightful little evergreen alpine shrublet with rounded clusters of very sweet-smelling red or pink flowers (1 cm). Leaves oblong, hairless, clustered at the ends of the brown branchlets. Fruit fleshy, orange-yellow. Apr.–Aug. *Daphne family*

Mezereon *pl. 74.* Very sweet-scented and attractive when it comes into flower on the bare stems. A low, little-branched shrub, with pale green, thin-textured, lance-shaped leaves. Fruit a cluster of scarlet berries. Feb.–May. *Daphne family*

Large Pink Cistus *pl. 77.* A beautiful pink-flowered cistus, with short-stalked hairy, wrinkled leaves with wavy margins, greyish or greenish, with 1 main vein. Flowers (4–6 cm) loosely clustered at the ends of the stems. Apr.–June. *Rockrose family*

Grey-Leaved Cistus *pl. 77.* Perhaps the most beautiful of the pink-flowered cistuses with greyish-white, velvety, stalkless leaves covered with star-shaped hairs. Flowers (2–6 cm) in leafy clusters. An upright shrub occurring from Portugal to Italy, usually less than 1 m. Apr.–June. *Rockrose family*

Alpenrose *pl. 87.* A low shrub of mountain pastures with azalea-like evergreen leaves, rusty-brown beneath and with inrolled margins. The funnel-shaped flowers (2 cm) are in clusters of 3–8. June–Aug. *Heath family*

Hairy Alpenrose *pl. 87.* Very like the previous shrub, but the leaves are shiny on both sides, toothed and spotted with russet glands beneath. The twigs, flower stalks and calyx are all covered in rough hairs. Restricted to the Alps. June–Aug. *Heath family*

Creeping Azalea *pl. 87.* A low creeping, densely branched evergreen shrublet of the arctic and limestone mountains in the south. Flowers small ($\frac{1}{4}$ cm), in short-stalked clusters. Leaves leathery ($\frac{1}{4}$ cm), margins inrolled. June–July. *Heath family*

St Dabeoc's Heath *pl. 88.* A straggling undershrub with narrow evergreen leaves, shiny above, white-haired beneath and with inrolled margins. The distinctive nodding flask-shaped flowers (8–12 mm) have glandular hairy calyx and flower stalks. June–Oct. *Heath family*

Blue Mountain Heath *pl. 88.* A low heath-like shrublet of the north, with numerous narrow evergreen leaves, shiny above, white-hairy and inrolled beneath. Flowers (1 cm) in terminal clusters of 2–6. July–Sept. *Heath family*

Marsh Andromeda *pl. 88.* A creeping, hairless, evergreen undershrub, with slender, erect stems. Leaves ($1\frac{1}{2}$–$3\frac{1}{2}$ cm) narrow, dark green above, grey-green with inrolled margins below. Flowers ($\frac{1}{4}$ cm) long-stalked, in umbels of 2–8. May–June. *Heath family*

Bearberry *pl. 88.* An evergreen undershrub forming dense spreading mats. The oval leaves are conspicuously net-veined, dark shiny green above, paler beneath. Flowers ($\frac{1}{4}$ cm) globular-flask-shaped, as broad as long. Fruit a shining red berry. May–July. *Heath family*

Dorset Heath *pl. 90.* A straggling undershrub with hairy twigs and tiny narrow oval glandular leaves in whorls of 3, white-hairy beneath. Urn-shaped flowers (1 cm) with a one-sided contracted mouth. Apr.–Oct. *Heath family*

Spring Heath *pl. 89.* A low shrublet, more central European than most heaths. Distinguished by dark purple anthers projecting completely from the tubular corolla. Leaves mostly in whorls of 4. Often found in mountains. Dec.–June. *Heath family*

Western Mediterranean Heath *pl. 89.* Distinguished by dense rounded clusters of numerous flowers, each borne on reddish stalks 2–3 times as long as the flowers. Dark anthers project completely from the cylindrical corolla ($\frac{1}{4}$ cm). July–Dec. *Heath family*

Bilberry, Blaeberry, Whortleberry *pl. 89.* A low dense undershrub; green stems angular; leaves deciduous. Flowers drooping, broader than long, with constricted mouth and recurved teeth. Leaves toothed (1–3 cm), bright green. Fruit bloomed bluish-black, fleshy, edible. May–July. *Heath family*

 Cranberry *pl. 88.* A slender shrublet with thread-like stems and tiny evergreen leaves, usually creeping over sphagnum bogs. The small pink flowers have 4 conspicuously curved-back petals (5–6 mm), revealing the stamens. Leaves whitish beneath. Fruit fleshy, red, edible. May–July. *Heath family*

 Putoria *pl. 98.* A small, mat-forming, unpleasant-smelling shrublet of southern Europe. Flowers with long slender tube (1½ cm) and 4 spreading, often recurved lobes; stamens projecting. Leaves opposite, shining above, usually hairless, inrolled beneath. May–July. *Madder family*

 Thyme *pl. 115.* A low, densely branched, erect, greyish and very aromatic shrublet of the south-west: the well-known garden thyme. Twigs velvety; leaves (½–1 cm) gland-dotted, velvety and inrolled beneath. Flowers pink or whitish (4–6 mm), hairy outside. Apr.–July. *Mint family*

 Wild Thyme *pl. 115.* A creeping, mat-forming shrublet, only slightly aromatic. Flowers (3–6 mm) in rounded or sometimes spike-like clusters of many whorls. Distinguished by its 4-angled stems, densely hairy on 2 sides, hairless or nearly so on 2 opposite sides; leaves (4–6 mm) opposite, ciliate. Apr.–Sept. *Mint family*

 Twinflower *pl. 135.* An attractive, low, creeping shrublet with slender downy stems and tiny paired oval leaves. Flowers pinkish-white, paired, on slender stems, sweet-scented; corolla (8 mm) tubular. Usually in mountain coniferous forests. July–Aug. *Honeysuckle family*

See also: DEWBERRY *pl. 44*; WILD COTONEASTER *pl. 48*; WHITE FLAX *pl. 65*; BOX-LEAVED or SHRUBBY MILKWORT *pl. 68*; WHITE ROCKROSE *pl. 78*; COMMON ROCKROSE *pl. 78*.

BLUE, VIOLET, BLUISH-PURPLE

Plant tall

 Chaste Tree *pl. 106.* An attractive, slender shrub with white-felted branches and leaves with 5–7 narrow leaflets. Flowers (6–9 mm) tubular, densely clustered, pale lilac, sometimes pink. Berries reddish-brown. June–Sept. *Verbena family*

 Tree Germander *pl. 107.* A slender shrub with small, shining evergreen leaves, conspicuously white-felted beneath, and white-felted twigs. Flowers blue to violet, with a very large, three-lobed lower lip (1½ cm) and no upper lip. Feb.–June. *Mint family*

 Rosemary *pl. 107.* A well-known aromatic shrub with lavender-like leaves. Flowers two-lipped, with much longer curved stamens and style. Leaves (2–3½ cm) glossy, dark green above, white-haired beneath, margins inrolled. Jan.–Dec. *Mint family*

 Buddleia *pl. 121.* A tall deciduous ornamental shrub, native of China, often naturalized. The sweet-scented flowers are tubular (1 cm long) and frequented by butterflies. Calyx and flower stalks densely white-felted. July–Aug. *Buddleia family*

Plant low

 Hedgehog Broom *pl. 52.* A spiny, low-domed, dense cushion-forming shrub of dry mountain slopes in the south-west. Flowers (1½–2 cm) clustered amongst the rigid spike-tipped branches. Young branches and leaves silvery-haired. May–June. *Pea family*

Lesser Periwinkle *pl. 97.* A trailing, slender-stemmed woody plant, with paired ever-green leaves. Flowers (2½–3 cm across) on short erect herbaceous stems; the spreading petals are curiously asymmetrical, as though given a rotatory twist. Feb.–May. *Dogbane family*

 Scrambling Gromwell *pl. 104.* A scrambling, spreading or bushy undershrub. Flowers tubular (1 cm across) with spreading triangular lobes, silky-haired outside, the throat closed within with hairs. Leaves (1 cm) with bristly adpressed hairs. May–June. *Borage family*

 French Lavender *pl. 108.* A branched, bushy, aromatic undershrub with white or grey-felted leaves and dense clusters of mauve flowers topped by large violet-purple bracts. Bracts of flower cluster oval, papery, veined and usually violet-purple-flushed. Apr.–June. *Mint family*

 Three-Lobed Sage *pl. 113.* An aromatic undershrub with greyish, wrinkled, sage-like leaves, usually with 2 distinctive small lobes at the base. Flowers pale violet (2 cm), in whorls on sticky hairy stems. Native of Greece and Italy. Feb.–Sept. *Mint family*

 Hyssop *pl. 115.* A small aromatic erect undershrub with numerous, clustered, narrow leaves. Flowers (1 cm) blue or violet, in stalkless whorls forming a leafy spike. Flowers two-lipped, the upper conspicuously notched. Sometimes grown as a pot-herb. June–Sept. *Mint family*

 False Sodom Apple *pl. 118.* A prickly undershrub with interlacing branches cover-ed, like the leaves, with stiff yellow spines. Flowers (2½ cm) shortly tubular with spreading lobes. Leaves deeply lobed. Fruit 2–3 cm. May–Aug. *Nightshade family*

 Shrubby Globularia *pl. 129.* A lax branched, rather spindly undershrub with stiff bristle-tipped glaucous evergreen leaves, and brittle woody twigs. Flower heads (1½–2 cm), sweet-scented; individual flowers tubular with a single three-lobed lip. Oct.–Mar. *Globularia family*

 Matted Globularia *pl. 129.* A spreading, woody, mat-forming shrublet, often spread-ing over rocks and screes in mountains, with rosettes of fleshy, spoon-shaped leaves. Flower heads (1 cm) borne on short, nearly leafless stems; flowers tubular, 3-lobed. May–July. *Globularia family*

See also: white flax *pl. 65.*

YELLOW

Plant tall

 Barberry *pl. 27.* A deciduous shrub, with needle-like spines in threes, and bristly-margined oval leaves. Flowers (6–8 mm) yellow, fragrant, in pendulous clusters; stamens sensitive, springing inwards when agitated. Fleshy berries edible. May–June. *Barberry family*

 Black Broom *pl. 51.* A medium-sized shrub 1–2 m, with trifoliate leaves and slender leafless spikes of numerous yellow pea-flowers (7–10 mm). Flowers with wings shorter than keel; petals turning black when dried. June–July. *Pea family*

 Stalkless-Leaved Broom *pl. 51.* A rather slender shrub from Spain to Italy, with stalkless trifoliate upper leaves, with broadly oval fine-pointed leaflets (1–2 cm). Flowers (1–1½ cm) in few-flowered clusters. Pods hairless, brown. Apr.–June. *Pea family*

 Broom *pl. 51.* A magnificent sight in full bloom, and easily recognized by its many erect five-angled, switch-like, often leafless green branches. Flowers golden-yellow (2 cm) with coiled styles and curved stamens, which 'explode' from the keel. Pods later black, hairy. Apr.–June. *Pea family*

 Spanish Broom *pl. 52.* Even more striking than the previous species; easily distinguished by the smooth, rounded, rush-like, glaucous branches. Flowers larger (2–2½ cm) very sweet-scented; standard rounded, and keel pointed. Leaves usually absent. Pod black becoming hairless. May–Aug. *Pea family*

 Bladder Senna *pl. 53.* Unlike any other shrub with its large, bladder-like, parchment-textured pods (4–7 cm). Flowers yellow (2 cm), in drooping clusters of 2–8. The leaves have 7–15 pairs of oval leaflets. Apr.–July. *Pea family*

 Southern Adenocarpus *pl. 55.* A straggly, weak-stemmed shrub with pods covered by warty swellings. Flowers (1–1½ cm) in terminal clusters. Leaves trifoliate; stems silvery-haired, angular, without spines. May–Sept. *Pea family*

 Scorpion Senna *pl. 62.* An erect, green-twigged shrub, with long slender fruits (5–10 cm), jointed into 7–10 cylindrical sections. Flowers (2 cm) in long-stalked clusters. Leaves with 2–4 pairs of oval, often notched leaflets, and a larger terminal leaflet. Apr.–June. *Pea family*

 Wig Tree, Smoke-Tree *pl. 69.* From a distance the feathery fruit stalks appear like puffs of smoke or a wig. The rounded leaves are very aromatic, pale beneath, and turn a rich red in autumn. Flowers tiny, yellowish, in branched clusters. May–July. *Cashew family*

 Mediterranean Buckthorn *pl. 71.* A dense, stiff and leafy shrub with numerous small shining leathery leaves (2–5 cm) and axillary clusters of small yellowish flowers. Fruit a fleshy berry, red then black. Common in the maquis. Mar.–Apr. *Buckthorn family*

 Prickly Pear, Barbary Fig *pl. 79.* A massive and unforgettable cactus. Large racquet-like joints are placed one above the other and have stout spines. Flowers bright yellow (6–7 cm) with numerous petals. Fruits red, yellow, purple; edible, but beware of the spines. June–July. *Cactus family*

 Cornelian Cherry *pl. 82.* An attractive shrub or small tree when it breaks into flower before the leaves in spring. Leaves oval, long-pointed with conspicuous veins. Fruit shiny red, ovoid (1–1½ cm long), acid. Mar. *Dogwood family*

 Jerusalem Sage *pl. 110.* A handsome, branched, grey-leaved shrub usually 1 m or more, Flowers borne in 1–3 tight whorls from the upper pairs of leaves. Upper lip broad, arching over the 3-lobed lower lip. Calyx teeth spiny-tipped. May–June. *Mint family*

 Shrub Tobacco *pl. 119.* A slender, branched, poisonous shrub of South America; often planted for ornament. Flowers (3–4 cm) in dense drooping clusters, corolla hairy outside. Leaves glaucous, entire, oval-elliptic. Apr.–Oct. *Nightshade family*

See also: FLY HONEYSUCKLE *pl. 135.*

Plant low

 Osyris *pl. 7.* A small switch-like undershrub, recalling broom, with angled green stems and narrow leaves. Flowers tiny (8 mm) with 3 spreading triangular petals. Fruit globular (½ cm) fleshy, later bright red. Apr.–June. *Sandalwood family*

 Mistletoe *pl. 7.* A parasitic shrub growing on the branches of many trees, particularly apples and their allies. Flowers yellowish, clustered, tiny, but the white, waxy, fleshy fruits (1 cm) are well known. Leaves evergreen, yellowish-green. The red-fruited plant *V. cruciatum* is found in south-west Spain. Feb.–Apr. *Mistletoe family*

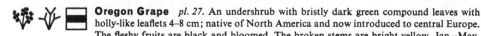

 Oregon Grape *pl. 27.* An undershrub with bristly dark green compound leaves with holly-like leaflets 4–8 cm; native of North America and now introduced to central Europe. The fleshy fruits are black and bloomed. The broken stems are bright yellow. Jan.–May. *Barberry family*

 Shrubby Aeonium *pl. 39.* A succulent North African plant with straight, light brown, rather woody stems, ending in flat rosettes (10 cm across) of numerous, overlapping, bristly-toothed leaves. Flowers (2 cm across) with numerous, narrow, spreading petals. Dec.–Mar. *Stonecrop family*

 Shrubby Cinquefoil *pl. 46.* A much-branched, rather compact erect or creeping undershrub, its compound leaves with 5 lance-shaped leaflets, grey-green and inrolled beneath. Flowers (2–2½ cm) with rounded petals; calyx with 5 large teeth alternating with 5 smaller teeth (epicalyx). June–Aug. *Rose family*

 Spiny Broom *pl. 51.* A very spiny gorse-like, intricately branched shrub or undershrub, with green, ribbed stems. Flowers (1–2 cm) in clusters of 5–15. Leaves with 3 leaflets, blackening when dry. Pods densely woolly. Mar.–June. *Pea family*

 Hairy Broom *pl. 51.* A very hairy, but spineless undershrub, usually spreading erect. Flowers (2–2½ cm) yellow with darker blotches, calyx densely hairy. Leaves with 3 leaflets, densely hairy below. Pod (2½–4 cm) hairy. Apr.–June. *Pea family*

 Spanish Gorse *pl. 52.* A dense, much-branched, spiny undershrub of Spain and France forming domed bushes. Flowers (1 cm) in globular clusters at ends of leafy branches, the upper petal (standard) hairless, the lowest (keel) hairy. Pods mostly hairless. May–Sept. *Pea family*

 Winged Broom *pl. 52.* A low creeping shrublet with unusual conspicuously and broadly winged stems, only narrowed at the joints. Flowers (1–1½ cm) in dense clusters. The leaves are few, undivided and softly hairy. Pods hairy. May–Sept. *Pea family*

 Dwarf Furze *pl. 53.* An extremely spiny gorse-like spreading undershrub, but spines (1 cm) flexible and more bristle-like than in related members. Flowers (8–10 mm) densely clustered along the stem; calyx almost as long as petals. Pod short (7 mm), persisting. July–Oct. *Pea family*

 Greek Spiny Spurge *pl. 66.* In a dry summer looking like a hemisphere of wire-netting. In spring covered with small apple-green leaves and bright yellow, flattened flower clusters. In Europe found only in Greece, Crete and the islands. Mar.–May. *Spurge family*

 Common Rue *pl. 67.* A grey-green bushy undershrub with very strong-smelling leaves. The flowers (1½–2 cm) have wide-spreading, usually toothed petals. Leaves much dissected into oval segments. Poisonous; introduced to central Europe from the south. May–July. *Rue family*

 Box-Leaved or **Shrubby Milkwort** *pl. 68.* A creeping shrublet of open woods and rocky places, mainly in mountains, with leathery evergreen leaves (1½–3 cm). Flowers (1½–2 cm) yellow, flushed purple, or less commonly pink, white or red; lower lip 3-lobed. Apr.–Sept. *Milkwort family*

 Fleshy-Leaved Thymelaea *pl. 73.* A much-branched, rather dense undershrub with small fleshy, overlapping scale-like leaves, cottony above, dark green beneath, on white-woolly branches. Flowers yellowish (¼ cm) in short clusters. Oct.–May. *Daphne family*

Silvery-Leaved Thymelaea *pl. 73.* A small undershrub or shrublet with numerous silky-haired (not fleshy) leaves ranged up the branched stems. Flowers (¼ cm) with 4 spreading 'petals', densely silky-haired outside. Apr.–May. *Daphne family*

Tutsan *pl. 74.* A low bushy half-evergreen undershrub with oval-heart-shaped, opposite, stalkless leaves (5–10 cm). Flowers (2 cm) in rather flat-topped clusters. Fruit a fleshy berry, green, red and finally black, the calyx persisting. June–July. *St John's Wort family*

 Rose of Sharon *pl. 75.* A low evergreen undershrub, often covering large patches, easily recognized by its very large (7–8 cm) yellow flowers with numerous stamens. The stems are quadrangular in section and the oval leaves 5–10 cm. July–Sept. *St John's Wort family*

 Rosemary-Leaved Halimium *pl. 78.* An upright bushy undershrub of Iberia, with very narrow shining rosemary-like leaves (1–3½ cm), grey-haired and inrolled beneath. Flowers pale yellow (2½ cm); calyx hairless. Fruit covered with star-shaped hairs. Feb.–May. *Rockrose family*

 Common Rockrose *pl. 78.* A straggling, scarcely woody shrublet with green or grey-green leaves each with a pair of tiny stipules about twice as long as the leaf stalk. Flowers (2 cm) in one-sided clusters, usually yellow but rarely pink, orange or white. Calyx conspicuously veined. May–Aug. *Rockrose family*

 Wild Jasmine *pl. 95.* An undershrub with green twigs, semi- or fully evergreen shining leaves with 3 thick oval leaflets. The yellow tubular flowers (1½ cm across) have 5 spreading lobes. The fruit is a small black berry. May–June. *Olive family*

 Hyssop-Leaved Sideritis *pl. 109.* A bushy, leafy shrublet with numerous narrow pointed leaves. The two-lipped flowers (1 cm) are borne in dense cylindrical clusters from broad spiny-toothed bracts. The calyx also has spiny teeth. July–Aug. *Mint family*

 Small Jerusalem Sage *pl. 110.* A small undershrub which is scarcely woody, with white-felted stems and grey leaves, wrinkled above, white-felted beneath. Flowering stems erect, herbaceous with 6–10 separated whorls of flowers, each whorl with clasping, long-pointed, paired bracts. Flowers 2-lipped (2–3 cm), densely felted. May–July. *Mint family*

 Blue Honeysuckle *pl. 135.* A shrubby non-climbing honeysuckle of mountain woods and marshes with paired yellowish tubular flowers (1–1½ cm) on common stalks shorter than the flowers. Leaves elliptic blunt, slightly hairy beneath. Fruit paired blue-black and bloomed, hence its name. May–June. *Honeysuckle family*

 Rock Phagnalon *pl. 145.* A small compact, scarcely woody shrublet with white-woolly stems and narrow leaves, green above with cobweb hairs, white-felted beneath with wavy margins. Flower heads (1 cm), with brown, papery involucral bracts pressed tightly to the flower heads. Apr.–June. *Daisy family*

 Sea Asteriscus *pl. 146.* A spreading, mat-forming shrublet of rocks and banks by the sea with stalked rough-haired oblong leaves. The flower heads (4 cm) are marigold-like with many broad ray florets with finely toothed tips, and similar-coloured disk florets. May–July. *Daisy family*

See also: SPURGE LAUREL, *pl. 74.*

4 Trees

WITH CONES

Leaves needle-like

Greek Fir *pl. 1.* A large broadly pyramidal tree of Greece and Macedonia, distinguished by stiff sharp-pointed leaves (1½–3 cm), with 2 whitish bands beneath, arranged all round greyish twigs. Male cones bright red; female cones erect, fragmenting, leaving a central axis. May–June. *Pine family*

Norway Spruce *pl. 1.* A tall slender pyramidal forest tree with spreading branches and pendulous twigs. Distinguished by its long rusty-brown, hanging cones (10–18 cm). Needle-leaves stiff, spiny-tipped. May–June. *Pine family*

European Larch *pl. 1.* The only deciduous conifer in Europe. A graceful conical tree with pale green leaves in clusters on the pendulous branchlets. Cones (1½–4 cm) globular, erect when ripe, only reddish when young. Apr.–June. *Pine family*

Maritime Pine *pl. 1.* This dark green pine is distinguished by its very long (10–25 cm), thick, paired needles with spiny tips. Cones (8–22 cm), large, conical, almost stalkless, bright shiny brown. Apr.–May. *Pine family*

Aleppo Pine *pl. 1.* Quite unlike the previous pine, having bright green, very slender, flexible, paired needles (6–15 cm), borne on silvery-grey twigs and branches. The conical cones (5–12 cm) are shiny brown. Forms open forests in dry rocky places near the Mediterranean. Mar.–May. *Pine family*

Black Pine *pl. 1.* A sombre tree forming forests in mountains, with dark green, usually very long leaves (more than 8 cm). Cones (3–8 cm) like those of the Scots Pine (not illustrated), almost stalkless, shiny light brown or yellowish-brown. There are several subspecies including the Austrian and Corsican Pines. May. *Pine family*

Juniper *pl. 2.* A dense grey-green shrub or small tree of the lowlands, or a low creeping shrub in high mountains. Needle-like leaves (to 2 cm) with a single whitish band on the upper surface. Female cones berry-like (6–9mm), first green, then blue-black, aromatic, used for flavouring. May–June. *Cypress family*

Prickly Juniper *pl. 2.* Very like the previous species but leaves with 2 whitish bands on upper surface and more spiny. Berry-like cones (½–1½ cm) first yellow, then reddish. Restricted to Mediterranean. May. *Cypress family*

Yew *pl. 2.* When in fruit quite unmistakable; a fleshy cup encircles the solitary seed (replacing the female cone). Distinguished by its dark green, flattened leaves, mostly in 2 ranks on the twigs. Poisonous to many animals. Apr. *Yew family*

Leaves scale-like

Funeral Cypress *pl. 2.* Usually encountered as a slender dark green columnar ornamental tree. Native of Greece and Crete, but in a form with a wide crown and horizontal spreading branches. Distinguished by tiny scale-like leaves and globular cones (2½–4 cm), which split into flat-topped, sexagonal scales. Mar.–Apr. *Cypress family*

Phoenician Juniper *pl. 2.* Like the previous species, with small overlapping scales on the twigs. But fruit quite different, 8–14 mm, first blackish, then yellowish-green and finally dark red, not separating into scales. Feb.–Apr. *Cypress family*

 Joint-Pine *pl. 2.* A scrambling, shrubby plant of the south-eastern Mediterranean, with numerous pendulous, leafless, glaucous branches. Leaves are tiny papery scales. Fruit bright red, globular, fleshy (like that of Yew). May–June. *Joint-Pine family*

WITH CATKINS

Leaves rounded, heart-shaped or oval

 Great Sallow, Goat Willow *pl. 3.* Shrub or small tree of lowlands. Leaves long (5–10 cm) rounded to oval, not more than twice as long as wide, softly grey-haired. Male (in photograph) and female catkins appear early in year before leaves. Mar.–Apr. *Willow family*

 Aspen *pl. 3.* A slender tree with delicate pale foliage, well-known for its fluttering leaves. Leaves are more or less circular; leaf stalks conspicuously flattened. Both male and female catkins stout, and appearing before the leaves. Mar.–Apr. *Willow family*

 Common Silver Birch *pl. 4.* A very graceful small tree with silvery-white branches and long pendulous warty twigs. The leaves are double-toothed (2½–7 cm). Male catkins (3–6 cm) pendulous; female catkins at first erect. Apr.–May. *Birch family*

 Alder *pl. 4.* A medium-sized tree of damp places with a dark fissured trunk and bright green, usually hairless, double-toothed leaves. Male catkins long, pendulous, clustered; female catkins small, becoming cone-like and woody, persisting into the following winter. Feb.–Apr. *Birch family*

 Grey Alder *pl. 4.* Like the previous tree but distinguished by the finely hairy leaves which have greyish undersides, and which are pointed. The bark is grey and smooth. Feb.–Mar. *Birch family*

 Hornbeam *pl. 5.* A small tree, often coppiced, easily recognized in fruit by the three-lobed cup in which the solitary seed sits. (The similar Eastern Hornbeam (not illustrated) has a toothed, not lobed cup.) Bark smooth and grey; trunk fluted. Leaves oval-pointed, double-toothed (4–10 cm), not unlike those of the Elm (not illustrated). Apr.–May. *Hazel family*

 Kermes or **Holly Oak** *pl. 5.* Usually a low-growing, spiny dense shrub, but also a small tree. Male catkins clustered, long, pendulous. Fruits ripen in the second year, and acorn-cups have spreading spine-tipped scales. Spiny leaves hairless beneath when mature. Apr.–May. *Beech family*

See also: WYCH ELM *pl. 5*; WHITE MULBERRY *pl. 6*; ORIENTAL PLANE *pl. 43*.

Leaves lance-shaped or narrow

 White Willow *pl. 3.* A rather large tree, with long slender leaves, silvery-grey with silky hairs. Trunk grey, fissured; often pollarded. Catkins (3–6 cm) appear at the same time as the young leaves. Apr.–May. *Willow family*

 Sweet or **Spanish Chestnut** *pl. 5.* A massive tree with fluted bark and large glossy leaves with bristly marginal teeth. The long yellowish male spike-like catkins appear late in the year with the leaves. The chestnuts in their spiny green casing are well known. May–July. *Beech family*

Leaves lobed or compound

 Walnut *pl. 4*. A large deciduous tree with smooth grey, later fissured bark, and large pinnate leaves with 7–9 oval leaflets (each 6–15 cm). Fruit green, globular (4–5 cm); within is the walnut. Apr.–May. *Walnut family*

 Valonia Oak *pl. 5*. A sturdy, rather small, semi-evergreen oak of south-east Europe. Leaves leathery, greyish below, with shallow bristle-tipped lobes or teeth. Fruit very large (to 4 cm), acorn-cup with stout spreading scales. Apr.–May. *Beech family*

 Common Oak *pl. 5*. A massive tree often the dominant forest tree on heavier lowland soils in central Europe. Distinguished from similar deciduous oaks by the long-stalked fruit clusters. Apr.–May. *Beech family*

WITH FLOWERS

WHITE

 Quince *pl. 47*. A beautiful small tree, often found as a hedgerow shrub, with large white cup-shaped flowers (4–5 cm). Leaves large, oblong (5–10 cm), woolly beneath. Fruit large, pear-shaped, green, woolly, remaining hard, edible when cooked. May. *Rose family*

 Whitebeam *pl. 47*. A small tree, handsome in leaf, flower and fruit. Flower clusters flat-topped, flowers 1–1½ cm. Leaves conspicuously white-felted beneath; upper surface pale green. Fruits scarlet in a flat-topped cluster. May–June. *Rose family*

 Rowan, Mountain Ash *pl. 48*. A slender graceful tree with grey trunk and handsome compound leaves with 4–9 pairs of oblong toothed leaflets. Flowers (1 cm) in flat-topped clusters. Fruit scarlet, very striking. May–June. *Rose family*

 Cherry-Plum *pl. 48*. A small tree (more often a hedgerow shrub) with solitary white flowers (2–2½ cm) appearing with the first leaves. Twigs hairless; leaves rather glossy, hairless above. Edible fruit globular, plum-like (2–2½ cm), yellowish or red; stone round, smooth-sided. Apr.–May. *Rose family*

 Wild Cherry *pl. 49*. Magnificent in flower when covered with bunches of white flowers (1½–2 cm) as the young golden-brown foliage first appears. Trunk shiny red-brown, with horizontal-peeling bark. Cherries red, sweet or bitter. Apr.–May. *Rose family*

 Bird-Cherry *pl. 49*. A small deciduous tree with long drooping or ascending clusters of numerous sweet-smelling flowers. Bark dark brown, strong-smelling. Fruits egg-shaped (6–8 mm), black and astringent. Apr.–June. *Rose family*

 St Lucie's Cherry *pl. 49*. A small deciduous tree or shrub of bushy places, with short, stalked clusters (3½–5 cm long) of few, sweet-smelling white flowers (1½ cm). Leaves oval, bright glossy green, hairy beneath. Fruits (½ cm) turning black, bitter. Apr.–May. *Rose family*

 False Acacia, Locust *pl. 53*. A small tree, often with spiny suckers, with a twisted trunk, compound leaves, and hanging clusters of sweet-smelling white pea-flowers. Flowers (1½–2½ cm) blotched with yellow, rarely pink. Leaves with 7–15 pairs of oval leaflets. Apr.–June. *Pea family*

 Sweet Orange *pl. 67*. A native of Asia, widely cultivated particularly near the Mediterranean. When not in fruit it can be distinguished by its oval-oblong pointed, dark green leaves with a narrowly winged leaf-stalk. Flowers white (1–1½ cm), with a ravishing scent. Spring. *Rue family*

Lemon *pl. 67.* The flowers (2 cm) are larger than those of the orange, flushed with red outside. Leaves often irregularly toothed, the stalks very narrowly winged. The pale yellow fruit with nipple-like tip is unmistakable. Spring. *Rue family*

 Horse-Chestnut *pl. 69.* Magnificent in May with pyramidal 'candles' of large white flowers. Notable for its sticky buds, horse-shoe leaf scars, large fan-like leaves, and in particular its glossy brown 'conkers' in their spiny green casing. May. *Horse-Chestnut family*

 Holly *pl. 71.* An unmistakable small tree or shrub with shiny leathery, usually spiny, evergreen leaves and scarlet berries. Trees one-sexed. Flower clusters small, globular, stalkless, nestling amongst the leaves. Apr.–May. *Holly family*

 Strawberry Tree *pl. 90.* A small evergreen tree or tall shrub, with globular, red fruits (1½–2 cm) recalling strawberries. Flowers (7 mm) in clusters, flask-shaped, cream-coloured. Leaves glossy, hairless and finely toothed; twigs reddish. Oct.–Jan. *Heath family*

 Manna or **Flowering Ash** *pl. 94.* Like the common Ash (not illustrated) with large compound leaves with several pairs of lance-shaped leaflets, but flower clusters conspicuous. Flowers whitish with narrow petals (to 1½ cm), sweet-scented, appearing with the leaves. Apr.–May. *Olive family*

 Olive *pl. 94.* Typical of the Mediterranean, and restricted to the Mediterranean climatic zone. The silvery-grey foliage and grey, gnarled, twisted trunks, are a feature of the southern landscape. (The wild form is a shrub with spiny stems and small oval leaves.) Fruit green, then blackish-purple, producing the valuable oil. May–June. *Olive family*

 Catalpa, Indian Bean *pl. 129.* This beautiful shapely small ornamental tree bears large green heart-shaped leaves (to 25 cm) and pyramidal clusters of large (3–4 cm) tubular white flowers. Pods slender, hanging (to 40 cm). June–July. *Bignonia family*

GREEN

 White Mulberry *pl. 6.* Native of China, widely planted in Europe. The raspberry-like fruit is white, pink or purplish. (Common Mulberry (not illustrated) has red to almost black fruit.) Flower cluster catkin-like, greenish. Leaves smooth and shiny. May. *Mulberry family*

 Oriental Plane *pl. 43.* A massive handsome tree with greyish flaking bark and deeply 5- to 7-lobed leaves. Flowers borne in slender, hanging clusters, followed by 3–6 globular, bristly balls (2 cm). (The London Plane (not illustrated) has shallowly, bluntly lobed leaves and usually 2 fruit balls.) May–June. *Plane Tree family*

 Carob, Locust Tree *pl. 49.* A small, stout evergreen tree with dark green compound leaves, giving welcome shade. Leaves with 2–5 oval glossy leathery leaflets. Pods thick, pulpy (12–20 cm), appearing direct from the branches. Aug.–Oct. *Pea family*

 Tree of Heaven *pl. 68.* A beautiful deciduous, shade-giving tree (often planted) with very large, neatly pinnate leaves, and 3-winged fruits, turning bright reddish-brown in the autumn. Leaves ½–1 m, leaflets broadly lance-shaped (to 13 cm). Flowers greenish-yellow (7–8 mm), in branched spikes. July–Aug. *Quassia family*

 Sycamore *pl. 69.* A medium to large tree with smooth grey trunk, later flaking, and dark, dull green, coarsely five-lobed leaves. The greenish-yellow flowers are in pendulous clusters. Fruit with 2 diverging aeroplane-propeller-like blades. Apr.–May. *Maple family*

 Norway Maple *pl. 69.* More attractive than the preceding tree, with paler shining leaves with 5 triangular, parallel-sided, long-pointed toothed lobes. Flowers appearing before the leaves, sweet-smelling and borne in upright clusters. Apr.–May. *Maple family*

Canary Palm *pl. 176.* Characteristic of Mediterranean boulevards and coastal roads The great upward-arched leaves may be as long as 7 m. Fruits small, date-like, dry and inedible, preceded by branched clusters of small greenish flowers. Mar.–May. *Palm family*

See also: CASTOR OIL PLANT *pl. 65*; BUCKTHORN *pl. 71*; SPINDLE-TREE *pl. 71*.

RED, PINK, PINKISH-PURPLE

 Wych Elm *pl. 5.* A tall elm with upward-sweeping branches arising low down, forming a wide canopy. Leaves (5–16 cm) very rough above, with 2 unequal basal lobes, the largest concealing the leaf stalk. Flowers in reddish clusters appearing before the leaves. Feb.– Apr. *Elm family*

 Persian Acacia, Pink Siris *pl. 50.* A small tree, from tropical Asia and Africa, planted as an ornamental. The dense globular flower clusters have numerous, long pinkish stamens. Leaves compound, twice-cut into numerous small leaflets. July–Aug. *Pea family*

 Judas Tree *pl. 50.* Beautiful when the pea-shaped flowers appear before the leaves, and in fruit, with its long reddish-brown pods. Leaves neatly kidney-shaped, untoothed, rather pale green. Native of south-east Europe, often planted elsewhere. Mar.–May. *Pea family*

 Red Horse-Chestnut *pl. 69.* Similar to the common horse-chestnut but flowers pink or red and fruit cases almost smooth or with few spikes. Sometimes grown for ornament. May–June. *Horse-Chestnut family*

YELLOW

 Loquat *pl. 48.* A small tree with large, glossy, dark green, strongly veined leaves (15–20 cm), rusty brown or greyish beneath. The sweet-scented yellowish-white flowers are densely clustered. Grown for its golden-yellow, plum-sized fruits. Nov.–Apr. *Rose family*

 White Sallow, Sydney Golden Wattle *pl. 49.* One of a number of wattles planted in the south for ornament and soil stabilization. It has long slender spikes of bright yellow flowers borne from the axils of willow-like leaves (5–15 cm). Mar.–Apr. *Pea family*

 Golden Rain, Laburnum *pl. 50.* Well-known for its glorious, abundant cascades of yellow pea-like flowers (2 cm) and soft green trifoliate leaves. Very poisonous tree; all parts are dangerous, particularly the seeds. May–June. *Pea family*

See also: MEDITERRANEAN BUCKTHORN *pl. 71*; CORNELIAN CHERRY *pl. 82*.

5 Woody Climbers

 Alpine Clematis *pl. 23.* A delicate climbing or scrambling plant of woods in the mountains, with beautiful solitary, drooping, somewhat bell-shaped flowers (4–6 cm). Pale yellow sterile stamens present. Leaves compound with lance-shaped leaflets. May–July. *Buttercup family*

 Traveller's Joy, Old Man's Beard *pl. 24.* Often climbing into the crown of a tree, with its stout, coiled stem. Flowers (2 cm) in branched clusters. Leaves with 3–9 leaflets. Fruits feathery. June–Aug. *Buttercup family*

 Fragrant Clematis *pl. 24.* Like the previous species but a plant of the Mediterranean, distinguished by twice-cut leaves with numerous leaflets. Flowers larger (1½–3 cm), very sweet-scented; petals hairless above. June–Aug. *Buttercup family*

 Ivy *pl. 82.* A well-known evergreen climber which may eventually smother large trees. Flower only formed on well illuminated shoots. Leaves glossy, three- to five-lobed, but very variable according to position. Fruit black (6–8 mm). Sept.–Nov. *Ivy family*

 Common Jasmine *pl. 95.* A native of Asia, often grown for ornament and sometimes naturalized. Flowers (2½ cm long), very fragrant, used in perfumery. Leaves deciduous, compound with 3–7 lance-shaped leaflets. May–Sept. *Olive family*

 Silk-Vine *pl. 97.* Unmistakable in flower (2¼ cm) with brownish spreading petals greenish beneath, and slender thread-like appendages. Leaves lance-shaped, glossy, later falling. Fruit large, cylindrical (12 cm). July. *Milkweed family*

 Honeysuckle *pl. 135.* The most widespread honeysuckle, distinguished by the uppermost pair of leaves below the flowers being unfused. Flowers (4–5 cm), deliciously sweet-scented. Fruit a globular cluster of shining red berries. June–Sept. *Honeysuckle family*

 Deciduous Mediterranean Honeysuckle *pl. 135.* Like the previous species but a plant of the Mediterranean with the uppermost leaves below flower clusters fused together and encircling the stem. Flowers whitish-yellow, often flushed with pink, borne on a short stalk. Leaves leathery, later falling. May–June. *Honeysuckle family*

6 Rushes, Grasses, and Sedges

RUSHES

Distinguished by their inconspicuous greenish or brownish flowers, with 6 rather scaly petals, 6 stamens, and an ovary with 3 feathery styles. Flowers variously massed together, into dense heads or into branched clusters. The leaves are rush-like, narrow, rounded, channelled, or they may be grass-like and flattened. Usually tufted plants.

 Hard Rush *pl. 177*. Distinguished by glaucous, hard tough, strongly ribbed (12–18 ridges), rounded stems, without leaves. Flowers borne in a rather loose, one-sided cluster about ¾ of the way up the stems. Sheaths at base of stem, shining, blackish-purple. June–Aug. *Rush family*

 Soft Rush *pl. 177*. Differs from the previous plant in its glossy, soft, smooth, bright yellowish-green stems, with numerous fine lines. Flowers in a loose many-branched cluster, branches erect, spreading or reflexed. Leaves absent, basal sheaths dull brown. June–Sept. *Rush family*

 Conglomerate Rush *pl. 177*. Readily distinguished by its dense globular cluster of nearly stalkless flowers pressed against the stem. Stems not glossy, with numerous fine ridges, particularly below the flower clusters. June–Sept. *Rush family*

 Black Alpine Rush *pl. 177*. A slender rush of central Europe, distinguished by its dense one-sided cluster of purplish-black flowers overtopped by the stem. A tufted plant with very slender stems and brown basal sheaths. July–Sept. *Rush family*

 Heath Rush *pl. 177*. Has a basal rosette of numerous stiff channelled out-spreading leaves pressed against the ground. Flowers in branched, rather dense clusters on leafless stems, with the lowest leafy bract less than half the length of the flower cluster. June–Sept. *Rush family*

 Sharp-Pointed Rush *pl. 177*. A robust tufted, plant to 1½ m found growing by the sea with stiff sharp-pointed leaves. Flowers in dense clusters, overtopped by the stiff sharp-pointed bract. Fruits as long as the scale-like petals. Mar.–July. *Rush family*

 Jointed Rush *pl. 177*. When the flattened leaves are pulled through the fingers the jointed partitions of the pith can be felt. Flowers very dark chestnut-brown, in branched, usually spreading clusters. Fruit dark, shining and abruptly narrowed to a fine point. June–Sept. *Rush family*

 Snowy Woodrush *pl. 177*. Distinguished from true rushes by flattened grass-like leaves, usually with long, white scattered hairs. Its rather flat-topped clusters, overtopped by the uppermost leaves, distinguish it from other similar plants. June–Aug. *Rush family*

 Field Woodrush *pl. 178*. The dense oval cluster of brown flowers, borne on stalks of different lengths, and forming an irregular umbel, distinguish it from similar plants. Leaves grass-like (2–5 mm broad) with sparse hairs. Fruit clusters drooping. Apr.–June. *Rush family*

GRASSES

Grass leaves are arranged alternately on the stem; they usually have flattened blades and a basal sheath encircling the stem. Stems hollow, swollen at the nodes. Flowers quite distinct, usually of many tiny florets grouped together in a spikelet. Each floret has a pair of chaffy boat-shaped glumes, encircling the 2–3 stamens, and a tiny ovary with 2 feathery styles. The glumes are often prolonged into fine awns.

With awns · Spikes dense

 Aegilops *pl. 178.* Readily distinguished by its tight oval head of few large spikelets, with several stiff spreading awns (2–7 cm), giving a bristly appearance. Glumes with conspicuous thick veins. A slender annual. May–July. *Grass family*

 Macaroni Wheat *pl. 178.* Not easily distinguished from several bearded (awned) wheats which are grown in south Europe in particular. Spikelets broader than long, strongly keeled (not rounded); glumes with a long fine point. Awns long and slender. May–July. *Grass family*

 Wall Barley *pl. 178.* Recalling awned wheat but easily distinguished because on each side of the fertile spikelet are long bristle-like awns. A tufted annual with broad, rather weak, pale green leaves. May–Aug. *Grass family*

 Rough Dog's-Tail *pl. 179.* A rather delicate annual grass of southern Europe. Readily distinguished by its dense, somewhat one-sided shining plume-like cluster of spikelets, with numerous very slender, spreading awns. Apr.–July. *Grass family*

 Italian Rye-Grass *pl. 180.* Rye-grasses are distinguished by alternately placed spikelets arranged edgeways on to the jointed axis. An annual plant distinguished from the Perennial Rye-Grass (not illustrated), by the presence of awns and larger spikelets which are longer than the outer glume. May–Oct. *Grass family*

 Hare's-Tail *pl. 181.* A delicate annual of the Mediterranean region, well known as a decorative grass with its densely velvety, extremely soft, oval spikes. Flower spikes very pale, covered with numerous long white hairs, and longer, very fine awns. Apr.–July. *Grass family*

 Meadow Fox-Tail *pl. 181.* A rather tall perennial grass (30–120 cm) of meadowlands, distinguished by its long slender, cylindrical spike of closely clustered spikelets arranged round the axis, each with 1 slender, rather inconspicuous, awn about as long as the spikelet. Glumes with fine hairs on the keel. Apr.–July. *Grass family*

 Timothy Grass, Cat's-Tail *pl. 181.* Not unlike the previous species but the florets are quite distinct. Each pair of glumes ends in a short stiff, spike-like awn, thus each spikelet has two awns (the previous plant 1 awn to each spikelet). A common meadow grass. May–Aug. *Grass family*

 Foxtail or **Italian Millet** *pl. 182.* Sometimes grown as a crop, also occurring as a casual in waste places. Distinguished by its very dense cylindrical, rather lobed spike made up of clusters of spikelets with conspicuous awn-like bristles. Leaves broad ($\frac{1}{2}$–$1\frac{1}{2}$ cm). May–July. *Grass family*

With awns · Spikes branched

 Upright Brome *pl. 178.* A stiff, erect, tufted grass with long-stalked spikelets arranged in whorls. Flowering cluster erect or nodding becoming narrow, bunched, and rather dense. Lower leaves with inrolled margins. May–July. *Grass family*

Hairy Brome   *pl. 178.* A tall grass (1–1½ m) with slender, drooping spikelets in a loose, arched cluster. Spikelets long (2–4 cm), spindle-shaped, with short bristly awns. A grass of wood verges and shady thickets. June–Aug. *Grass family*

 Yellow Oat   *pl. 180.* A loosely tufted delicate-looking perennial with lax or dense, erect or nodding, pale yellowish and glistening inflorescence. Spikelets tiny (½ cm), with slender awns nearly twice as long, bent at the middle when dry. May–Aug. *Grass family*

 Animated Oat   *pl. 180.* Oats can be distinguished by their long-stalked, drooping spikelets with 2 long, often joined awns, and large paired outer glumes (3–3½ cm). Awn to 7 cm, spirally twisted below. A common weed of cultivated ground in the Mediterranean region. May–July. *Grass family*

 Wavy Hair-Grass   *pl. 180.* A delicate, beautiful grass of heaths and dry sandy places with a pyramidal cluster of tiny glistening spikelets borne on thread-like flexuous branches. Awns slender, not twice as long as the spikelets. Leaves bristle-like. June–July. *Grass family*

 Feather Grass   *pl. 182.* So-called for its extremely long feathery awns up to 35 cm, which trail in the wind. A plant of dry steppe-like areas in south and central Europe. Leaves glaucous bristle-like; spikelets (1½–2 cm) few, slender. May–July. *Grass family*

 Cockspur Grass   *pl. 182.* A rather coarse, leafy, tufted annual with ragged irregular clusters of spikelets borne on spreading, or bunched branches of different lengths. Spikelets (3–4 mm), usually with stiff rough awns, but awns sometimes absent. Leaves 8–20 mm broad. July–Oct. *Grass family*

 Erianthus   *pl. 182.* A very robust grass of southern Europe forming large tufts and with long plume-like spikes, first spreading, then bunching together. Spikelets awned, covered by long silky hairs. Leaves (1–1½ cm broad) rough, sheaths hairy. Aug.–Oct. *Grass family*

 Bothriochloa   *pl. 182.* Distinguished by the 2–10 narrow finger-like spikes arising from the tip of the stem. Each spike (3–6 cm) has numerous awned spikelets arranged closely along the branches. A glaucous tufted perennial with narrow grooved leaves (2–3 mm). Apr.–Nov. *Grass family*

 Hyparrhenia   *pl. 182.* Like the previous plant but spikes paired, arising from leaf-like bracts on a branched inflorescence. Spikes (2–3 cm) with numerous spikelets with bent awns (2–3 cm). A tufted perennial grass of dry places of southern Europe. Apr.–Nov. *Grass family*

Without awns · Spikes dense

 Sand Couch   *pl. 178.* Couch grasses are distinguished by their 2 rows of alternately-placed spikelets, arranged broadside to the axis. A tough creeping, glaucous plant of sandy shores and dunes. Distinguished from others by its stout spikelets (1½–3 cm). June–Aug. *Grass family*

 Couch-Grass, Twitch   *pl. 178.* A vigorous, creeping, often noxious weed. Spikelets (1–2 cm) numerous, overlapping (sometimes awned). Leaves dull green. June–Sept. *Grass family*

 Lyme Grass   *pl. 179.* A robust, glaucous grass 1–2 m, forming large tufts on sands and dunes by the sea. Flowering spike dense, cylindrical, stiff (15–35 cm). Leaves bluish-grey, stiff, sharp-pointed, 8–20 mm broad, rough above, smooth beneath. June–Aug. *Grass family*

 Blue Moor-Grass   *pl. 179.* A rather small tufted grass of dry rocky slopes or wet meadows, with persistent basal sheaths. The dense oblong spikes (1–3 cm) are glistening, bluish-grey or purplish, and borne on nearly leafless stems. Mar.–Aug. *Grass family*

Hairy Melick   *pl. 179*. A distinctive grass with a slender cylindrical spike (8–15 cm) densely covered with silvery-white, or yellowish, silky hairs. Leaves stiff, narrow, with inrolled margins, often glaucous. May–Aug. *Grass family*

 Marram Grass   *pl. 181*. A robust, stiff, grey-green grass, often colonizing mobile dunes near the sea. The pale, almost whitish, plume-like spikes are dense, cylindrical and tapering to the tip. Leaves almost circular in section, tightly inrolled, and sharp-pointed. May–July. *Grass family*

 Canary-Grass   *pl. 181*. Readily distinguished by its very dense oval spike (1½–6 cm) of numerous broad, overlapping, flattened whitish spikelets with green veins. A robust annual with flat rough leaves (3–12 mm wide). May–July. *Grass family*

 Townsend's Cord-Grass   *pl. 181*. A stiff robust plant forming extensive patches in salt marshes, able to withstand periodic salt water flooding. Spike (12–35 cm) slender, erect, pointed. It is formed of 3–6 slender branches, mostly closely pressed together; spikelets in 2 rows. Leaves stiff, smooth, and flat or inrolled above. July–Nov. *Grass family*

Without awns · Spikes branched

 Common Reed   *pl. 179*. A tall (1½–3 m) bamboo-like grass of swamps, often growing in shallow water, with feathery, brownish or purplish, erect or nodding branched spikes (15–40 cm). Stems hollow; leaves numerous, flat (1–3 cm wide). Aug.–Sept. *Grass family*

 Ampelodesma   *pl. 182*. A very robust, densely tufted grass (1–3 cm), found in dry rocky places near the Mediterranean. Spike much-branched, somewhat one-sided, purplish-green. Leaves very tough, rigid, rush-like, closely inrolled. May–Juhe. *Grass family*

 Purple Moor-Grass   *pl. 179*. A tussock-forming grass of moors and damp heaths, with long slender interrupted purplish-greenish or brownish spikes, which are either dense or loose and open. Leaves green, flat (3–10 mm wide). July–Sept. *Grass family*

 Large Quaking-Grass   *pl. 179*. A very attractive annual grass of southern Europe. The neat, plump, shining spikelets hang from very slender branches and quake in the breeze. Leaves flat, the uppermost sheath somewhat swollen. Often cultivated and dried for winter decoration. Apr.–June. *Grass family*

 Alpine Meadow-Grass   *pl. 179*. A small tufted plant of northern or alpine regions. It has an open erect or nodding branched spike, with the spikelets often sprouting on the plant (see photograph). Leaves stiff, mostly basal; the base of the stem is covered with persistent sheaths. June–Aug. *Grass family*

 Reed Sweet-Grass   *pl. 180*. A luxuriant, erect leafy aquatic grass often forming patches at the edge of open water, also in swamps. It has a long branched spike (15–45 cm) with many slender branches, at first lax, later dense and clustered. Leaves pale green, 1–2 cm wide, sheath keeled. June–Aug. *Grass family*

 Glaucous Sweet-Grass   *pl 180*. One of several green, weak, fleshy, soft grasses which grow on muddy margins of watersides. It has a long slender curved spike of many irregular branches often pressed against the axis. Leaves at first folded, then flat; basal leaves often floating. June–Sept. *Grass family*

 Tall Fescue   *pl. 180*. A loosely tufted grass (to 1½ m or more) with a long narrow loose or open, erect or nodding spike of many branches bearing long terminal spikelets (1–2 cm). Leaves flat, stiff, rough above, 8–12 mm wide. June–July. *Grass family*

 Hard Poa   *pl. 180*. A tiny stiff annual with several stems arising from the base. The spikes are one-sided, loose or dense and slender, often branched below. Spikelets tiny (4–7 mm) arranged in 2 ranks on the branches. May–July. *Grass family*

Yorkshire Fog *pl. 181.* A softly hairy, somewhat tufted, pale greyish-green grass with a pale green, pinkish or purple spike, either open and pyramidal, or dense and cylindrical. Leaves flat, narrowed to a fine point; leaf sheaths with down-pointing hairs. May–Aug. *Grass family*

 Wood Millet *pl. 181.* A loosely tufted, tall slender grass of shady places. The flowering spike forms a loose pyramid, with spreading, or reflexed, thread-like branches bearing tiny green spikelets (3–4 mm) at their tips. Leaves hairless, flat, $\frac{1}{2}$–$1\frac{1}{2}$ cm wide. May–Aug. *Grass family*

 Common or **Broom-Corn Millet** *pl. 182.* A robust annual grass often grown for fodder in the south. Distinguished by its dense, later drooping, inflorescence of numerous long branches with numerous plump hairless spikelets. Leaves 1–2 cm wide. July–Oct. *Grass family*

SEDGES *and allies*

Sedges and their allies, all members of the sedge family, *Cyperaceae*, are grass-like or rush-like. They have tiny florets arranged in spikelets; each floret consists of 1 scaly glume, 3 stamens, and an ovary with 2 or 3 feathery styles or are one-sexed with either stamens or an ovary. They differ from members of the grass family in having a single (not paired) glume to each floret. The stems of the sedges are often three-angled, never hollow like those of the grasses. Sedges differ from the true rushes in having no petals or sepals and 3 (not 6) stamens.

Spikes solitary

 Cotton-Grass, Hare's-Tail *pl. 184.* A tussock-forming sedge of wet bogs, quite unmistakable in flower and fruit, with solitary, cotton-white, ovoid spikes borne at the ends of slender stiff stems. Basal leaves thread-like; stem leaves with strongly inflated sheaths. Apr.–July. *Sedge family*

 Common Spike-Rush *pl. 185.* A slender plant, with creeping stems often below water and erect green stems with small cylindrical spikes ($\frac{1}{2}$–2 cm). Glumes brown, overlapping, with transparent margins and green midvein. Sheath at base of stem brown. May–Aug. *Sedge family*

Spikes several · Stalkless and densely clustered

 Sea Club-Rush *pl. 185.* A tall erect plant of marshes near the sea. Stem triangular-sectioned bearing a dense reddish-brown cluster of spikes much overtopped by 1 or more leafy bracts. Spikes 1–2 cm, some may be stalked. Leaves flat, keeled, 2–10 mm wide. June–Sept. *Sedge family*

 Round-Headed Club-Rush *pl. 185.* Unlike any other in having several, quite globular, greyish-brown heads ($\frac{1}{2}$–$1\frac{1}{2}$ cm) borne laterally on a much longer stem. A tufted, rush-like plant with smooth, ribbed, cylindrical, leafless stems. July–Aug. *Sedge family*

 Bog-Rush *pl. 185.* A densely tufted, wiry, rough sedge with blackish-purple heads overtopped by the lowest leafy bract. Head (1–1$\frac{1}{2}$ cm) of many stalkless spikes with shining glumes. Leaves cylindrical, sheaths shining blackish-brown. June–July. *Sedge family*

 Saltmarsh Sedge *pl. 185.* A rather small tufted sedge of salt marshes, easily distinguished by its dense globular heads. There is a solitary brownish male spike, and 2–4 rounded overlapping green female spikes (the lowest spike may be distant). Below the heads are 2–3 long, rigid, spreading or reflexed leafy bracts. Apr.–July. *Sedge family*

Oval Sedge *pl. 186.* So-called for its usually dense oval cluster of pale brown spikes, and single, usually larger, bristle-like bract. Stems three-angled; leaves narrow (2–3 mm), rough. A tufted plant of grassy places. May–Aug. *Sedge family*

Spikes several · Stalked and usually loosely clustered

 Broad-Leaved Cotton-Grass *pl. 184.* Like the common Cotton-grass (not illustrated) with several stalked erect, then drooping cottony spikelets, but the leaves of this species are flat, wider (3–8 mm), pale green, and the stems distinctly three-angled above. A tufted, not creeping, plant of alkaline flushes. Apr.–June. *Sedge family*

 Wood Club-Rush *pl. 185.* A robust plant with a loose, much-branched spreading head (to 51 cm) of numerous spikes with leafy bracts of similar length. Broad, pale green, flat leaves (to 2 cm) and a stout, leafy bluntly three-angled stem. May–Aug. *Sedge family*

 Grey Club-Rush *pl. 185.* Like the Bulrush (not illustrated) but a shorter greyish or glaucous plant (not green), with more compact flower heads. Glumes with small dark swellings on the back; stigmas 2. Often found in marshes near the sea. May–Aug. *Sedge family*

 Hop Sedge *pl. 185.* A handsome, tufted, pale greenish-yellow waterside sedge, with neat cylindrical, bristly-looking, pendulous female spikes (3–5 cm). Stems rough, sharply three-angled, with many broad (5–12 mm), rough-edged leaves. May–July. *Sedge family*

 Drooping Sedge *pl. 186.* One of the tallest and most graceful sedges, with erect arched stems ($\frac{1}{2}$–$1\frac{1}{2}$ m) and long slender pendulous female spikes (7–16 cm). Leaves dark glossy green, rough-margined, keeled (1–2 cm wide). A tufted plant of damp shady places. May–July. *Sedge family*

 Bottle Sedge *pl. 186.* A greyish sedge of peaty pools, usually rooting under water, with glaucous, inrolled leaves. The 2–4 cylindrical female spikes (2–8 cm) more or less erect, composed of yellow-green, inflated bottle-like fruits, abruptly narrowed to a long beak. May–July. *Sedge family*

 Great Pond-Sedge *pl. 186.* A robust waterside sedge with sharply three-angled stems (1–1$\frac{1}{2}$ m), and keeled leaves ($\frac{1}{2}$–2 cm wide). Male spikes 2–5, dark brown; female spikes robust (3–9 cm), often widely spaced, the lowest drooping. Fruits large (8 mm). Apr.–June. *Sedge family*

 Glaucous Sedge *pl. 186.* A distinctly glaucous, widespread grass-like sedge of dry grasslands and marshes with 2–3 dark purple-brown male spikes, and usually 2 erect or nodding female spikes. Fruits curved, greenish-yellow to blackish, with minute swellings, almost beakless. Leaves 2–4 mm wide, rough. Apr.–June. *Sedge family*

 Hairy Sedge *pl. 186.* Unmistakable, with its downy fruits and shaggy-haired leaf sheaths. Female spikes are short-stalked in the axils of the leaves, and widely spaced. A creeping sedge of damp meadows. May–July. *Sedge family*

 Common Black Sedge *pl. 186.* A variable but often tufted sedge of watersides, with three-angled stems, narrow greyish leaves and blackish fibrous leaf bases. Male and female spikes usually clustered together but sometimes distant. Glumes of female spikes usually black with a green midvein, narrower than the green or purplish, almost beakless fruits. May–July. *Sedge family*

 Dark Sedge *pl. 186.* A mountain sedge of rocks and pastures, distinguished by its fat, almost black spikes (1–2 cm), all similar, the upper erect, the lowest later nodding. Stems often curved, smoothly three-angled; leaves somewhat glaucous, flat, keeled, 3–5 mm wide. July–Aug. *Sedge family*

Family Index to Colour Plates

(1) *Abies cephalonica* × ⅕
Greek Fir   *p.80*

2 *Picea abies* × ½
Norway Spruce   *p.80*

4 *Pinus pinaster* × ¼
Maritime Pine   *p.80*

3 *Larix decidua* × 1½
European Larch   *p.80*

1

Black Pine   *p.80*
7 *Pinus nigra* × ½ *(short-leaved form)*

Aleppo Pine   *p.80*
6 *Pinus halepensis* × ½

11 *Cupressus sempervirens* × ⅔
Funeral Cypress *p.80*

14 *Juniperus phoenicea* × ½
Phoenician Juniper *p.81*

13 *Juniperus oxycedrus* × ⅘
Prickly Juniper *p.80*

12 *Juniperus communis* × ¾
Juniper *p.80*

2

Yew *p.80*
17 *Taxus baccata* × ½

Joint-Pine *p.81*
18 *Ephedra fragilis subsp.
campylopoda* × ¼

19 *Salix reticulata* $\times \frac{3}{4}$
Reticulate Willow *p.72*

20 *Salix retusa* $\times \frac{1}{2}$
Blunt-Leaved Willow *p.72*

22 *Salix hastata* ? $\times \frac{1}{3}$
Hastate Willow *p.72*

25 *Salix alba* $\times \frac{4}{5}$
White Willow *p.81*

3

Great Sallow, Goat Willow *p.81*
29 *Salix caprea* $\times \frac{1}{2}$

Aspen *p.81*
32 *Populus tremula* $\times \frac{2}{3}$

34 *Myrica gale* $\times \frac{4}{5}$
Bog Myrtle, Sweet Gale *p.72*

35 *Juglans regia* $\times \frac{1}{3}$
Walnut *p.82*

36 *Betula pendula* $\times \frac{1}{2}$
Common Silver Birch *p.81*

38 *Betula nana* $\times \frac{2}{3}$
Dwarf Birch *p.72*

4

Grey Alder *p.81*
41 *Alnus incana* $\times \frac{1}{3}$

Alder *p.81*
40 *Alnus glutinosa* $\times \frac{4}{5}$

50 *Quercus macrolepis* × ⅓
Valonia Oak *p.82*

42 *Carpinus betulus* × ⅘
Hornbeam *p.81*

52 *Quercus robur* × ½
Common Oak *p.82*

46 *Castanea sativa* × ½
Sweet or Spanish Chestnut *p.81*

5

Wych Elm *p.84*
56 *Ulmus glabra* × ⅔

Kermes or Holly Oak *p.81*
47 *Quercus coccifera* × ½

67 *Urtica pilulifera* × $\frac{4}{5}$
Roman Nettle *p.16*

(66) *Urtica dubia* × $\frac{4}{5}$
Large-Leaved Nettle *p.16*

64 *Cannabis sativa* × 1
Hemp *p.14*

6

White Mulberry *p.83*
(61) *Morus alba* × $\frac{1}{3}$

Hop *p.14*
63 *Humulus lupulus* × $\frac{1}{3}$

Alpine Bastard Toadflax *p.15*
71 *Thesium alpinum* × $\frac{2}{3}$

74 *Asarum europaeum* × ⅓
Asarabacca *p.48*

68 *Parietaria officinalis* × ⅓
Erect Pellitory-of-the-Wall *p.16*

Osyris *p.77*
70 *Osyris alba* × ⅘

73 *Viscum album* × ⅓
Mistletoe *p.77*

Birthwort *p.52*
76 *Aristolochia clematitis* × ⅔

78 *Cytinus hypocistis* × ½
Yellow Cytinus   *p.56*

77 *Aristolochia rotunda* × ⅘
Round-Leaved Birthwort   *p.48*

83 *Polygonum amphibium* × ½
Amphibious Bistort   *p.27*

81 *Polygonum hydropiper* × ⅔
Water-Pepper   *p.14*

8

Japanese Knotweed   *p.5*
88 *Reynoutria japonica* × ⅔

Pale Persicaria   *p.27*
(82) *Polygonum lapathifolium* × ½

85 *Polygonum viviparum* × 1½
Viviparous Bistort   *p.9*

97 *Rumex crispus* × ⅔
Curled Dock   *p.14*

(98) *Rumex sanguineus* × ½
Red-Veined Dock   *p.14*

9

Buckwheat   *p.6*
89 *Fagopyrum esculentum* × ½

Great Water Dock   *p.14*
96 *Rumex hydrolapathum* × ¼

Monk's Rhubarb   *p.14*
94 *Rumex alpinus* × ¹⁄₁₀

101 *Beta vulgaris subsp. maritima* ×$\frac{1}{3}$ **Beet** *p.14*

(105) *Chenopodium album* ×$\frac{1}{2}$
Fat Hen *p.16*

103 *Chenopodium bonus-henricus* ×$\frac{4}{5}$
Good King Henry *p.14*

10

Shrubby Glasswort *p.72*
(113) *Arthrocnemum fruticosum* ×$\frac{1}{2}$

Pigweed *p.14*
117 *Amaranthus retroflexus* ? ×$\frac{1}{2}$

Strawberry Goosefoot *p.14*
104 *Chenopodium foliosum* ×1

(124) *Montia sibirica* × $\frac{2}{5}$
Pink Claytonia   *p.25*

(120) *Carpobrotus acinaciformis* × $\frac{2}{5}$
Red Hottentot Fig   *p.19*

122 *Portulaca oleracea* × $\frac{1}{2}$
Purslane   *p.61*

124 *Montia perfoliata* × 1
Perfoliate Claytonia   *p.9*

11

Virginian Poke, Pokeweed   *p.26*
(119) *Phytolacca sp.* × $\frac{1}{2}$

Sea Sandwort, Sea Purslane   *p.15*
133 *Honkenya peploides* × $\frac{2}{3}$

126 *Arenaria montana* × 1
Mountain Sandwort *p.4*

136 *Stellaria holostea* × ½
Greater Stitchwort *p.2*

138 *Stellaria graminea* × 1
Lesser Stitchwort *p.6*

142 *Cerastium alpinum* × 1
Alpine Mouse-Ear Chickweed *p.4*

12

Common Mouse-Ear Chickweed *p.6*
144 *Cerastium fontanum* × 1

Water Chickweed *p.6*
145 *Myosoton aquaticum* × ½

(148) *Scleranthus annuus* × 1
Annual Knawel *p.15*

(146) *Sagina procumbens* × 1
Procumbent Pearlwort *p.16*

149 *Paronychia argentea* × ½
Silvery Paronychia *p.12*

152 *Illecebrum verticillatum* × ⅓
Illecebrum *p.9*

13

Sand Spurrey *p.30*
57 *Spergularia rubra* × 1½

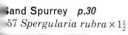

Cliff Spurrey *p.30*
156 *Spergularia rupicola* × 1

159 *Lychnis flos-jovis* × $\frac{3}{4}$
Flower of Jove *p.20*

162 *Lychnis alpina* × $\frac{1}{2}$
Red Alpine Catchfly *p.30*

161 *Lychnis viscaria* × $\frac{2}{5}$
Red German Catchfly *p.20*

14

Bladder Campion *p.2*
169 *Silene vulgaris subsp. maritima* × $\frac{1}{2}$

160 *Lychnis flos-cuculi* × ½
Ragged Robin *p.17*

167 *Silene nutans* × ⅘
Nottingham Catchfly *p.2*

(174) *Silene colorata* × 1
Pink Mediterranean Catchfly
p.30

15

Red Campion *p.20*
165 *Silene dioica* × ⅖

Spanish Catchfly *p.15*
168 *Silene otites* × ½

Berry Catchfly *p.13*
177 *Cucubalus baccifer* × ⅗

170 *Silene acaulis* ×⅔
Moss Campion *p.30*

163 *Agrostemma githago* ×⅘
Corn Cockle *p.17*

174 *Silene gallica var. quinquevulnera* ×⅔
Small-Flowered Catchfly *p.9*

181 *Saponaria officinalis* ×¼
Soapwort *p.20*

16

Rock Soapwort *p.30*
180 *Saponaria ocymoides* ×⅔

Creeping Gypsophila *p.9*
178 *Gypsophila repens* ×⅘

187 *Dianthus carthusianorum* × 1
Carthusian Pink *p.20*

190 *Dianthus monspessulanus* × ¾
Fringed Pink *p.21*

Deptford Pink *p.27*
186 *Dianthus armeria* × 1½

194 *Dianthus sylvestris* × ⅓
Wood Pink *p.21*

17

Superb Pink *p.17*
188 *Dianthus superbus* × ⅔

196 *Nymphaea alba* × ⅓
White Water-Lily   *p.66*

(203) *Nigella sativa* × 1
Garden Love-in-a-Mist   *p.2*

197 *Nuphar lutea* × 1/10
Yellow Water-Lily   *p.67*

202 *Eranthis hyemalis* × ⅔
Winter Aconite   *p.56*

18

Field Love-in-a-Mist   *p.37*
(203) *Nigella arvensis ssp. aristata* x 1¼

Greek Hellebore   *p.13*
(200) *Helleborus cyclophyllus* × ⅙

201 *Helleborus niger* × ⅓
Christmas Rose *p.2*

199 *Helleborus foetidus* × ⅘
Setterwort, Stinking Hellebore *p.13*

19

204 *Trollius europaeus* × 1/10
Globe Flower *p.49*

Common Monkshood *p.34*
210 *Aconitum napellus* × 1

Wolfsbane *p.52*
208 *Aconitum vulparia* × 1¼

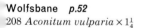

(211) *Delphinium peregrinum* × 1   *p.37*
Scaly-Seeded Larkspur

20

213 *Consolida ambigua* × 1⅕
Larkspur   *p.37*

211 *Delphinium elatum* × ⅘
Alpine Larkspur   *p.34*

Field Larkspur *p.37*
(213) *Consolida regalis* × 1⅓

Hepatica *p.40*
219 *Hepatica nobilis* × ⅘

217 *Anemone palmata* $\times \frac{2}{5}$
Palmate Anemone *p.56*

(216) *Anemone hortensis* $\times \frac{1}{2}$
Broad-Leaved Anemone *p.19*

(216) *Anemone pavonina* $\times \frac{1}{2}$
Scarlet Anemone *p.19*

(214) *Anemone blanda* $\times 1$
Eastern Blue Wood Anemone *p.40*

21

Crown Anemone *p.19*
216 *Anemone coronaria* $\times \frac{2}{3}$

Crown Anemone *p.19*
216 *Anemone coronaria* $\times \frac{1}{2}$

218 *Anemone narcissiflora* × ½
Narcissus-Flowered Anemone *p.2*

221 *Pulsatilla vernalis* x ½
Spring Anemone *p.2*

214 *Anemone nemorosa* × ⅔
Wood Anemone *p.4*

(214) *Anemone apennina* × ⅔
Blue Wood Anemone *p.40*

22

Pasque Flower *p.36*
223 *Pulsatilla vulgaris* × ½

Spring Anenome *p.2*
221 *Pulsatilla vernalis* × ½

227 *Clematis alpina* $\times \frac{4}{5}$
Alpine Clematis *p.85*

220 *Pulsatilla alpina* subsp. *apiifolia* $\times \frac{3}{4}$
Alpine Anemone *p.51*

Alpine Anemone *p.51*
220 *Pulsatilla alpina* $\times \frac{1}{2}$

225 *Clematis flammula* × 1
Fragrant Clematis *p.85*

229 *Clematis integrifolia* × ½
Blue Clematis *p.34*

230 *Adonis annua* × ⅘
Pheasant's Eye *p.21*

24

Traveller's Joy, Old Man's Beard *p.85*
224 *Clematis vitalba* × ½

Yellow Adonis *p.52*
231 *Adonis vernalis* × 1

233 *Ranunculus ficaria* × $\frac{4}{5}$
Lesser Celandine, Pilewort   *p.56*

234 *Ranunculus thora* × $\frac{1}{2}$
Thora Buttercup   *p.56*

241 *Ranunculus montanus* × $\frac{1}{2}$
Mountain Buttercup   *p.56*

244 *Ranunculus lingua* × $\frac{1}{2}$
Great Spearwort   *p.67*

25

White Buttercup   *p.6*
246 *Ranunculus aconitifolius* × $\frac{2}{3}$

Oval-Leaved Crowfoot   *p.4*
248 *Ranunculus parnassifolius* × 1

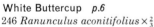

232 *Ranunculus muricatus* × 1
Spiny-Fruited Buttercup   *p.61*

257 *Thalictrum flavum* × ½
Common Meadow Rue   *p.52*

250 *Ranunculus peltatus* × ½
Pond Crowfoot   *p.66*

(251) *Ranunculus pseudofluitans* × ½
Large River Water Crowfoot   *p.66*

26

Glacier Crowfoot   *p.4*
(247) *Ranunculus glacialis* × ⅘

Mouse-Tail   *p.15*
252 *Myosurus minimus* × 1¼

258 *Paeonia officinalis* × $\frac{2}{5}$
Peony   *p.17*

259 *Paeonia mascula* × $\frac{1}{4}$
Biternate Peony   *p.17*

254 *Aquilegia alpina* × $\frac{1}{2}$
Alpine Columbine   *p.34*

253 *Aquilegia vulgaris* × $\frac{2}{3}$
Columbine   *p.34*

27

Oregon Grape   *p.78*
262 *Mahonia aquifolium* × $\frac{1}{2}$

Barberry   *p.76*
261 *Berberis vulgaris* × $\frac{4}{5}$

264 *Papaver somniferum* $\times \frac{1}{4}$
Opium Poppy *p.34*

269 *Meconopsis cambrica* $\times \frac{1}{4}$
Welsh Poppy *p.49*

271 *Roemeria hybrida* $\times \frac{1}{2}$
Violet Horned-Poppy *p.35*

28

Alpine Poppy *p.57*
(268) *Papaver nudicaule* x $\frac{1}{5}$

(267) *Papaver sendtneri* $\times \frac{1}{2}$
White Alpine Poppy   *p.2*

265 *Papaver rhoeas* $\times \frac{1}{3}$
Corn Poppy   *p.17*

272 *Glaucium flavum* $\times \frac{1}{6}$
Yellow Horned-Poppy   *p.49*

273 *Glaucium corniculatum* $\times \frac{1}{2}$
Red Horned-Poppy   *p.17*

29

Prickly Poppy   *p.49*

270 *Argemone mexicana* $\times \frac{3}{4}$

Californian Poppy   *p.50*
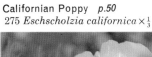
275 *Eschscholzia californica* $\times \frac{1}{3}$

(276) *Hypecoum imberbe* × ¾
Erect Hypecoum   *p.61*

277 *Corydalis claviculata* × ⅚
Climbing Corydalis   *p.6*

278 *Corydalis lutea* × ½
Yellow Corydalis,   *p.61*

30

(278) *Corydalis ochroleuca* × ⅔
Cream Corydalis   *p.9*

Ramping Fumitory   *p.6*
280 *Fumaria capreolata* × ½

Purple Corydalis   *p.30*
279   *Corydalis solida* × ½

289   *Alliaria petiolata* × 1
Garlic Mustard, Hedge Garlic   *p.6*

296 *Hesperis matronalis* × $\frac{1}{4}$
Dame's Violet   *p.37*

Caper   *p.70*
283 *Capparis spinosa* × 1

(287) *Sisymbrium orientale* × ¼
Eastern Rocket   *p.59*

292 *Isatis tinctoria* × $\frac{1}{10}$
Woad   *p.59*

299 *Cheiranthus cheiri* × $\frac{1}{10}$
Wallflower   *p.52*

293 *Bunias erucago* × $\frac{4}{5}$
Crested Bunias   *p.59*

32

Virginia Stock   *p.40*
298 *Malcolmia maritima* × 1$\frac{3}{4}$

Stock   *p.21*
300 *Matthiola incana* × $\frac{4}{5}$

(301) *Matthiola fruticulosa* × ⅓
Sad Stock   *p.25*

303 *Rorippa amphibia* × ⅘
Great Yellow-Cress   *p.59*

Nine-Leaved Coral-Wort   *p.52*
(309) *Cardamine enneaphyllos* × ½

Sea Stock   *p.21*
301 *Matthiola sinuata* × ⅔

308 *Cardamine bulbifera* × ½
Coral-Wort   *p.21*

(309) *Cardamine pentaphyllos* × 1/10
Five-Leaved Coral-Wort   *p.21*

310 *Cardamine pratensis* × 1⅓
Lady's Smock   *p.21*

(310) *Cardamine amara* × ½
Large Bitter-Cress   *p.6*

34

Yellow Whitlow-Grass   *p.61*
331 *Draba aizoides* × ⅔

Alpine Rock-Cress   *p.9*
318 *Arabis alpina* × ⅓

314 *Cardaminopsis arenosa* × ⅓
Sand Bitter-Cress *p.6*

(319) *Arabis verna* × 1
Spring Rock-Cress *p.45*

322 *Lunaria annua* × ⅓
Honesty *p.21*

35

Fibigia *p.52*
327 *Fibigia clypeata* × ⅓

Hoary Whitlow-Grass *p.10*
333 *Draba incana* × ⅔

Field Pennycress *p.6*
343 *Thlaspi arvense* × ½

337 *Cochlearia danica* × 1
Danish Scurvy-Grass *p.10*

345 *Thlaspi rotundifolium* × ¾
Round-Leaved Pennycress *p.30*

346 *Aethionema saxatile* × ½
Burnt Candytuft *p.30*

348 *Iberis amara* × 1¼
Annual Candytuft *p.10*

36

Hoary Pepperwort *p.6*
353 *Cardaria draba* × ½

Lesser Swine-Cress *p.17*
354 *Coronopus didymus* x ⅔

329 *Lobularia maritima* ×¼
Sweet Alison *p.9*

356 *Moricandia arvensis* ×¼
Violet Cabbage *p.37*

(362) *Sinapis alba* ×⅓
White Mustard *p.52*

366 *Cakile maritima* ×⅓
Sea Rocket *p.27*

37

Salad Mustard *p.3*
363 *Eruca vesicaria* ×2

Seakale *p.6*
368 *Crambe maritima* ×⅛

374 *Reseda phyteuma* × $\frac{1}{2}$
Rampion Mignonette *p.7*

372 Reseda lutea × $\frac{1}{8}$
Wild Mignonette *p.59*

373 Reseda alba × $1\frac{1}{2}$
Upright Mignonette *p.7*

38

Yellow Sundew *p.57*
(378) *Drosophyllum lusitanicum* × $\frac{3}{4}$

Great Sundew *p.10*
377 *Drosera anglica* × $\frac{3}{4}$

378 *Drosera intermedia* × 1
Long-Leaved Sundew *p.10*

382 *Sempervivum montanum* × 1
Mountain Houseleek *p.31*

381 *Sempervivum arachnoideum* × ⅓
Cobweb Houseleek *p.31*

386 *Aeonium arboreum* × ¼
Shrubby Aeonium *p.78*

39

Wall Pennywort, Navelwort *p.16*
379 *Umbilicus rupestris* × 1/10

White Stonecrop *p.10*
391 *Sedum album* × ⅓

388 *Sedum reflexum* × ¼
Rock Stonecrop *p.61*

389 *Sedum acre* × ¾
Stonecrop, Wall-Pepper *p.61*

(394) *Sedum caeruleum* × ⅘
Blue Stonecrop *p.45*

394 *Sedum villosum* × 1
Hairy Stonecrop *p.31*

40

Orpine, Livelong *p.7*
395 *Sedum telephium* subsp. *maximum* × 1

Roseroot, Midsummer-Men *p.62*
397 *Rhodiola rosea* × ½

398 *Saxifraga oppositifolia* × ⅓
Purple Saxifrage   *p.31*

(399) *Saxifraga longifolia* × ¼
Pyrenean Saxifrage   *p.7*

402 *Saxifraga aizoides* × ⅓
Yellow Mountain Saxifrage   *p.62*

(411) *Saxifraga tridactylites* × 1
Rue-Leaved Saxifrage   *p.10*

41

Androsace Saxifrage   *p.10*
409 *Saxifraga androsacea* × 1

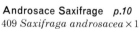

Starry Saxifrage   *p.10*
407 *Saxifraga stellaris* × ½

400 *Saxifraga paniculata* × ⅓
Livelong Saxifrage *p.10*

403 *Saxifraga rotundifolia* × ⅓
Round-Leaved Saxifrage *p.7*

411 *Saxifraga moschata* × 1
Musky Saxifrage *p.16*

(405) *Saxifraga hirsuta* × ⅓
Kidney Saxifrage *p.10*

42

Opposite-Leaved Golden Saxifrage *p.62*
(412) *Chrysosplenium oppositifolium* × ½

Grass of Parnassus *p.4*
413 *Parnassia palustris* × ½

(414) *Ribes alpinum* $\times \frac{1}{2}$
Mountain Currant *p.71*

416 *Ribes uva-crispa* $\times 1$
Gooseberry p.71

43

Oriental Plane *p.83*
418 *Platanus orientalis* $\times \frac{1}{3}$

414 *Ribes rubrum* $\times \frac{1}{2}$
Red Currant *p.71*

Arctic Bramble *p.31*
(427) *Rubus arcticus* $\times \frac{3}{4}$

426 *Rubus chamaemorus* × ½
Cloudberry *p.4*

(429) *Rubus caesius* × ⅔
Dewberry *p.70*

421 *Filipendula ulmaria* × ⅙
Meadow-Sweet *p.7*

422 *Filipendula vulgaris* × ½
Dropwort *p.7*

44

Willow Spiraea *p.72*
419 *Spiraea salicifolia* × ½

Goat's-Beard *p.12*
420 *Aruncus dioicus* × 1/10

430 *Rosa arvensis* × ½
Field Rose *p.70*

434 *Rosa pimpinellifolia* × ⅔
Burnet Rose *p.70*

435 *Rosa pendulina* × ⅓
Alpine Rose *p.72*

441 *Dryas octopetala* × ⅔
Mountain Avens *p.70*

45

Great Burnet *p.34*
438 *Sanguisorba officinalis* × ½

Water Avens *p.21*
443 *Geum rivale* × ⅓

(445) *Potentilla nitida* × ⅔
Pink Cinquefoil *p.25*

440 *Sarcopoterium spinosum* × ⅔
Thorny Burnet *p.73*

446 *Potentilla palustris* × 1¼
Marsh Cinquefoil *p.21*

448 *Potentilla rupestris* × ⅔
Rock Cinquefoil *p.3*

46

Shrubby Cinquefoil *p.78*
457 *Potentilla fruticosa* × 1

Spring Cinquefoil *p.62*
451 *Potentilla tabernaemontani* × ⅔

467 *Sorbus aria* × 1
Whitebeam *p.82*

463 *Cydonia oblonga* × $\frac{1}{2}$
Quince *p.82*

Cherry-Laurel *p.69*
483 *Prunus laurocerasus* × $\frac{4}{5}$

Snowy Mespilus *p.69*
471 *Amelanchier ovalis* × $\frac{1}{3}$

(483) *Prunus lusitanica* × ½
Portugal Laurel   *p.69*

48

Cherry-Plum   *p.82*
(477) *Prunus cerasifera* × 1

466 *Sorbus aucuparia* × ⅓
Rowan, Mountain Ash   *p.82*

470 *Eriobotrya japonica* × ¼
Loquat   *p.84*

Wild Cotoneaster   *p.70*
473 *Cotoneaster integerrimus* × ¾

482 *Prunus padus* × ⅓
Bird-Cherry *p.82*

480 *Prunus avium* × 1⅓
Wild Cherry *p.82*

476 *Prunus spinosa* × ⅘
Blackthorn, Sloe *p.69*

484 *Prunus mahaleb* × ⅘
St Lucie's Cherry *p.82*

49

Carob, Locust Tree *p.83*
486 *Ceratonia siliqua* × ⅓

White Sallow, Sydney Golden Wattle *p.84*
488 *Acacia longifolia* × ⅓

496 *Laburnum anagyroides* × 1
Golden Rain, Laburnum *p.84*

493 *Albizia julibrissin* × $\frac{1}{2}$
Persian Acacia, Pink Siris *p.84*

50

Judas Tree *p.84*
485 *Cercis siliquastrum* × $\frac{4}{5}$

498 *Calicotome villosa* × 1
Spiny Broom *p.78*

504 *Cytisus sessilifolius* × ½
Stalkless-Leaved Broom *p.76*

505 *Cytisus scoparius* × ½
Broom *p.76*

499 *Lembotropis nigricans* × ½
Black Broom *p.76*

Hairy Broom *p.78*
506 *Chamaecytisus hirsutus* × ½

Purple Broom *p.73*
(506) *Chamaecytisus purpureus* × ⅓

514 *Lygos monosperma* × ¼
White Broom *p.69*

52

Spanish Broom *p.77*
515 *Spartium junceum* × ⅕

(511) *Genista hispanica* × ¾
Spanish Gorse *p.78*

513 *Chamaespartium sagittale* × ½
Winged Broom *p.78*

Hedgehog Broom *p.75*
(515) *Erinacea anthyllis* × ½

517 *Ulex minor* × ½
Dwarf Furze   *p.78*

519 *Lupinus luteus* × ⅔
Yellow Lupin   *p.53*

525 *Colutea arborescens* × ⅓
Bladder Senna   *p.77*

53

False Acacia, Locust   *p.82*
523 *Robinia pseudacacia* × ½

Goat's Rue   *p.42*
524 *Galega officinalis* × ⅓

527 *Astragalus glycyphyllos* × ½
Milk-Vetch *p.7*

520 *Lupinus angustifolius* × ⅖
Narrow-Leaved Lupin *p.42*

627 *Coronilla varia* x ¾
Crown Vetch *p.27*

521 *Lupinus albus* × ⅓
White Lupin *p.3*

54

Pitch Trefoil *p.42*
537 *Psoralea bituminosa* × ⅖

Wild Lentil *p.60*
528 *Astragalus cicer* × ⅔

(545) *Vicia benghalensis* × 1
Reddish Tufted Vetch *p.27*

549 *Vicia sativa* × ⅔
Common Vetch *p.27*

(545) *Vicia villosa* × ⅔
Shaggy Vetch *p.27*

55

Southern Adenocarpus *p.77*
518 *Adenocarpus complicatus* × ⅘

545 *Vicia cracca* × ⅓
Tufted Vetch *p.42*

553 *Lathyrus aphaca* × ¾
Yellow Vetchling *p.60*

Winged Vetchling *p.60*
554 *Lathyrus ochrus* × ⅓

Grass Vetchling *p.27*
556 *Lathyrus nissolia* × ⅖

559 *Lathyrus tuberosus* × ⅔
Earth-Nut Pea *p.21*

565 *Lathyrus japonicus* × ½
Sea Pea *p.22*

561 *Lathyrus clymenum* × ½
Crimson Pea *p.21*

56

Black Pea *p.27*
563 *Lathyrus niger* × ⅓

(560) *Lathyrus latifolius* × ½
Everlasting Pea *p.21*

(557) *Lathyrus sativus* × ¾
Chickling Pea *p.37*

Spring Pea *p.22*
564 *Lathyrus vernus* × ⅘

Pea *p.22*
566 *Pisum sativum* × ⅓

571 *Ononis natrix* × ⅔
Large Yellow Restharrow *p.53*

(569) *Ononis fruticosa* × ⅗
Shrubby Restharrow *p.73*

570 *Ononis rotundifolia* × ⅗
Round-Leaved Restharrow *p.22*

573 *Melilotus alba* × 1/10
White Melilot *p.7*

57

Tall Melilot *p.60*
576 *Melilotus altissima* × ½

Blue Fenugreek *p.42*
577 *Trigonella caerulea* × ⅓

580 *Trigonella foenum-graecum* × ½
Fenugreek *p.10*

589 *Medicago marina* × ⅘
Sea Medick *p.62*

583 *Medicago sativa* subsp. *sativa* × ⅓
Lucerne, Alfalfa *p.43*

582 *Medicago sativa* subsp. *falcata* × ⅖
Sickle Medick *p.60*

58

Hairy Medick *p.62*
588 *Medicago polymorpha* × 1⅓

Large Disk Medick *p.64*
584 *Medicago orbicularis* × ⅘

597 *Trifolium rubens* × 1
Wood Purple Clover *p.27*

601 *Trifolium hybridum* × ½
Alsike Clover *p.7*

(601) *Trifolium montanum* × 1¼
Mountain Clover *p.7*

Crimson Clover *p.27*
595 *Trifolium incarnatum* × ⅓

Zigzag Clover *p.27*
607 *Trifolium medium* × ⅔

Mountain Sainfoin *p.22*
(636) *Onobrychis montana* × ⅘

594 *Trifolium arvense* × ⅔
Hare's-Foot Clover   *p.10*

593 *Trifolium badium* × ¾
Brown Trefoil   *p.62*

602 *Trifolium stellatum* × ¾
Star Clover   *p.31*

603 *Trifolium alpinum* × 1
Alpine Clover   *p.31*

60

Hairy Dorycnium   *p.7*
609 *Dorycnium hirsutum* × ¾

Upright Dorycnium   *p.7*
610 *Dorycnium rectum* × 1

614 *Lotus uliginosus* × ½
Large Birdsfoot-Trefoil   *p.60*

621 *Anthyllis montana* × ⅔
Mountain Kidney-Vetch   *p.31*

617 *Tetragonolobus purpureus* × 1
Asparagus Pea   *p.25*

622 *Anthyllis vulneraria* × ⅓
Kidney-Vetch   *p.62*

Alpine Sainfoin   *p.22*
635 *Hedysarum hedysaroides* × ½

Bladder Vetch   *p.62*
623 *Anthyllis tetraphylla* × 1

624 *Coronilla emerus* × ¼
Scorpion Senna   *p.77*

62

Italian Sainfoin   *p.22*
634 *Hedysarum coronarium* × ⅓

627 *Coronilla varia* × ½
Crown Vetch   *p.27*

(634) *Hedysarum glomeratum* × ⅗
Small Italian Sainfoin   *p.25*

Wood-Sorrel   *p.4*
638 *Oxalis acetosella* × ⅘

639 *Oxalis pes-caprae* × ⅓
Bermuda Buttercup   *p.57*

641 *Geranium sanguineum* × ¾
Bloody Cranesbill   *p.25*

642 *Geranium pyrenaicum* × ⅔
Mountain Cranesbill   *p.22*

(642) *Geranium nodosum* × ⅘
Broad-Leaved Cranesbill   *p.37*

63

Wood Cranesbill   *p.37*
645 *Geranium sylvaticum* × ⅔

Shining Cranesbill   *p.31*
651 *Geranium lucidum* × ½

646 *Geranium phaeum* × 1¼
Dusky Cranesbill, Mourning Widow   *p.37*

647 *Geranium macrorrhizum* × 1⅓
Rock Cranesbill   *p.22*

64

Long-Beaked Storksbill   *p.37*
(652) *Erodium gruinum* × 1¼

652 *Erodium malacoides* × ⅘
Soft Storksbill   *p.43*

Maltese Cross, Small Caltrops   *p.62*
655 *Tribulus terrestris* × ⅓

(664) *Linum suffruticosum* × $1\frac{1}{4}$
White Flax   *p.70*

659 *Linum perenne* × $\frac{2}{3}$
Perennial Flax   *p.37*

Turn-Sole   *p.64*
665 *Chrozophora tinctoria* × $\frac{1}{2}$

666 *Mercurialis perennis* × $\frac{1}{2}$
Dogs Mercury   *p.16*

65

Castor Oil Plant   *p.73*
668 *Ricinus communis* × $\frac{1}{2}$

678 *Euphorbia characias* subsp. *wulfenii* × $\frac{1}{15}$
Large Mediterranean Spurge *p.15*

678 *Euphorbia characias* × $\frac{1}{2}$
Large Mediterranean Spurge *p.15*

(670) *Euphorbia acanthothamnos* × $\frac{1}{6}$
Greek Spiny Spurge *p.78*

669 *Euphorbia dendroides* × $\frac{1}{30}$
Tree Spurge *p.71*

66

Sea Spurge *p.15*
684 *Euphorbia paralias* × $1\frac{1}{2}$

Wood Spurge *p.15*
677 *Euphorbia amygdaloides* × $\frac{1}{2}$

693 *Citrus limon* × ⅓
Lemon *p.83*

671 *Euphorbia helioscopia* × ⅔
Sun Spurge *p.15*

686 *Ruta graveolens* × ⅖
Common Rue *p.78*

690 *Citrus sinensis* × ⅓
Sweet Orange *p.82*

67

Burning Bush *p.1*
688 *Dictamnus albus* × ⅙

Caper Spurge *p.15*
676 *Euphorbia lathyris* × ½

694 *Ailanthus altissima* × ¼
Tree of Heaven *p.83*

702 *Coriaria myrtifolia* × ⅓
Mediterranean Coriaria *p.71*

696 *Polygala chamaebuxus* × ⅘
Box-Leaved or Shrubby Milkwort *p.78*

(700) *Polygala nicaeensis* × ¾
Variable Milkwort *p.31*

68

Common Milkwort *p.45*
698 *Polygala vulgaris* × 1

Mastic Tree, Lentisc *p.73*
703 *Pistacia lentiscus* × ⅘

706 *Cotinus coggygria* × ½
Wig Tree, Smoke-Tree   *p.77*

704 *Pistacia terebinthus* × ⅓
Turpentine Tree, Terebinth   *p.73*

713 *Aesculus hippocastanum* × ⅕
Horse-Chestnut   *p.83*

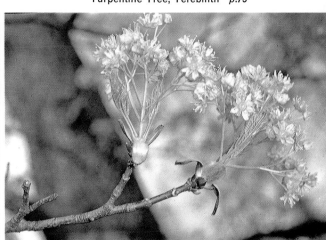

710 *Acer platanoides* × ½
Norway Maple   *p.83*

69

Red Horse-Chestnut   *p.84*
(713) *Aesculus carnea* × ⅓

Sycamore   *p.83*
708 *Acer pseudoplatanus* × ⅘

716 *Impatiens glandulifera* × ⅓
Policeman's Helmet   *p.20*

714 *Impatiens noli-tangere* × ⅘
Touch-me-Not   *p.53*

70

Small Balsam   *p.60*
715 *Impatiens parviflora* × ½

Orange Balsam   *p.53*
(714) *Impatiens capensis* × 1¼

720 *Rhamnus alaternus* $\times \frac{1}{6}$
Mediterranean Buckthorn   *p.77*

723 *Rhamnus catharticus* $\times \frac{4}{5}$
Buckthorn   *p.71*

717 *Ilex aquifolium* $\times \frac{2}{3}$
Holly   *p.83*

Spindle-Tree   *p.71*
718 *Euonymus europaeus* $\times \frac{3}{4}$

71

Spindle-Tree   *p.71*
718 *Euonymus europaeus* $\times \frac{2}{3}$

735 *Malva alcea* × ½
Large-Flowered Mallow   *p.17*

72

Tree Mallow   *p.17*
740 *Lavatera arborea* × 1

747 *Althaea officinalis* × ⅓
Marsh Mallow   *p.17*

748 *Alcea pallida* × ⅕
Eastern Hollyhock   *p.17*

Annual Mallow   *p.18*
742 *Lavatera trimestris* × ½

738 *Malva nicaeensis* $\times \frac{1}{3}$
Southern Mallow *p.43*

752 *Hibiscus trionum* $\times \frac{4}{5}$
Bladder Ketmia *p.50*

Fleshy-Leaved Thymelaea *p.78*
754 *Thymelaea tartonraira* $\times 1$

750 *Gossypium herbaceum* $\times \frac{1}{2}$
Levant Cotton *p.50*

73

Silvery-Leaved Thymelaea *p.78*
753 *Thymelaea hirsuta* $\times \frac{1}{2}$

759 *Daphne mezereum* × 1¼
Mezereon *p.74*

74

Spurge Laurel *p.72*
760 *Daphne laureola* × ½

756 *Daphne cneorum* × ¾
Garland Flower *p.74*

761 *Hippophaë rhamnoides* × ⅘
Sea Buckthorn *p.72*

Tutsan *p.79*
763 *Hypericum androsaemum* × ½

(763) *Hypericum calycinum* $\times \frac{1}{2}$
Rose of Sharon *p.79*

768 *Hypericum perforatum* $\times \frac{1}{2}$
Common St John's Wort *p.53*

765 *Hypericum hirsutum* $\times \frac{4}{5}$
Hairy St John's Wort *p.53*

764 *Hypericum montanum* $\times \frac{1}{3}$
Mountain St John's Wort *p.60*

75

Marsh St John's Wort *p.62*
766 *Hypericum elodes* $\times \frac{1}{2}$

Wild Pansy *p.40*
783 *Viola tricolor* $\times \frac{3}{5}$

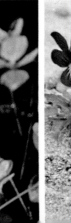

782 *Viola biflora* × ½
Yellow Wood Violet *p.57*

773 *Viola palustris* × 3
Bog Violet *p.45*

774 *Viola odorata* × ½
Sweet Violet *p.40*

777 *Viola riviniana* × 3
Common Dog Violet *p.40*

76

Long-Spurred Pansy *p.36*
786 *Viola calcarata* × ⅔

Mountain Pansy *p.57*
785 *Viola lutea* × ⅘

790 *Cistus salvifolius* × ¾
Sage-Leaved Cistus *p.70*

791 *Cistus monspeliensis* × ½
Narrow-Leaved Cistus *p.70*

787 *Cistus incanus* × ¼
Large Pink Cistus *p.74*

793 *Cistus ladanifer* × ⅔
Gum Cistus *p.69*

77

Laurel-Leaved Cistus *p.69*
794 *Cistus laurifolius* × ½

Grey-Leaved Cistus *p.74*
788 *Cistus albidus* × ⅗

798 *Tuberaria guttata* × 1
Spotted Rockrose *p.62*

803 *Helianthemum apenninum* × $\frac{4}{5}$
White Rockrose *p.71*

802 *Helianthemum nummularium* × $\frac{4}{5}$
Common Rockrose *p.79*

796 *Halimium commutatum* × 1
Rosemary-Leaved Halimium *p.79*

78

African Tamarisk *p.73*
807 *Tamarix africana* × $\frac{1}{2}$

Bitter Apple *p.13*
(812) *Citrullus colocynthis* × $\frac{1}{4}$

811 *Ecballium elaterium* × $\frac{1}{4}$
Squirting Cucumber   *p.57*

818 *Opuntia ficus-indica* × $\frac{1}{10}$
Prickly Pear, Barbary Fig   *p.77*

79

Purple Loosestrife   *p.26*
820 *Lythrum salicaria* × $\frac{1}{3}$

823 *Trapa natans* × $\frac{1}{3}$
Water Chestnut   *p.66*

White Bryony   *p.13*
815 *Bryonia cretica* × $\frac{4}{5}$

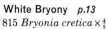

821 *Lythrum virgatum* × ½
Slender Loosestrife *p.28*

829 *Circaea lutetiana* × 1¼
Enchanter's Nightshade *p.7*

835 *Epilobium angustifolium* × ⅗
**Rosebay Willow-Herb,
Fireweed** *p.22*

Pomegranate *p.73*
827 *Punica granatum* × ½

819 *Lythrum portula* × ¼
Water Purslane   *p.47*

824 *Myrtus communis* × ⅔
Myrtle   *p.69*

(831) *Oenothera erythrosepala* x ⅛
Evening Primrose   *p.50*

834 *Oenothera rosea* × ⅔
Pink Evening Primrose   *p.22*

81

Great Hairy Willow-Herb   *p.22*
837 *Epilobium hirsutum* × ½

Broad-Leaved Willow-Herb   *p.28*
839 *Epilobium montanum* × ⅘

847 *Cornus suecica* × 1
Dwarf Cornel *p.4*

845 *Cornus mas* × ⅘
Cornelian Cherry *p.77*

82

Ivy *p.85*
848 *Hedera helix* × ¼

846 *Cornus sanguinea* × ⅖
Dogwood *p.69*

Spiked Water-Milfoil *p.67*
(843) *Myriophyllum spicatum* × ⅗

(847) *Aucuba japonica* × ½
Spotted Laurel   *p.73*

851 *Hacquetia epipactis* × ½
Hacquetia   *p.57*

852 *Astrantia major* × ½
Great Masterwort, Mountain Sanicle   *p.12*

855 *Eryngium campestre* × ⅘
Field Eryngo   *p.16*

Blue Eryngo   *p.47*
856 *Eryngium amethystinum* × ⅘

Sea Holly   *p.43*
853 *Eryngium maritimum* × 1

863 *Myrrhis odorata* × ¼
Sweet Cicely *p.8*

866 *Smyrnium perfoliatum* × ⅕
Perfoliate Alexanders *p.64*

871 *Crithmum maritimum* × ⅙
Rock Samphire *p.64*

872 *Oenanthe crocata* × ⅙
Hemlock Water Dropwort *p.12*

84

Water Dropwort *p.12*
873 *Oenanthe fistulosa* × ½

Starry Hare's-Ear *p.65*
(883) *Bupleurum stellatum* × 1

886 *Apium nodiflorum* $\times \frac{1}{2}$
Fool's Watercress   *p.12*

897 *Ferula communis* $\times \frac{1}{10}$
Giant Fennel   *p.59*

85

Angelica   *p.14*
895 *Angelica archangelica* $\times \frac{1}{12}$

379 *Conium maculatum* $\times \frac{1}{12}$
Hemlock   *p.5*

Northern Lovage   *p.12*
892 *Ligusticum scoticum* $\times \frac{1}{8}$

902 *Heracleum mantegazzianum* × 1/10
Giant Hogweed *p.5*

900 *Pastinaca sativa* × 1/10
Wild Parsnip *p.64*

904 *Tordylium apulum* × 1
Ivory-Fruited Hartwort *p.8*

917 *Monotropa hypopitys* × 2/3
Yellow Bird's Nest *p.62*

86

Nodding Wintergreen *p.11*
914 *Orthilia secunda* × 2/3

Small Wintergreen *p.31*
912 *Pyrola minor* × 2/3

910 *Daucus carota* × ½
Wild Carrot   *p.12*

(912) *Pyrola media* × ¾
Intermediate Wintergreen   *p.11*

911 *Diapensia lapponica* × 1¾
Diapensia   *p.71*

915 *Moneses uniflora* × ⅔
One-Flowered Wintergreen   *p.4*

919 *Rhododendron ferrugineum* × ⅓
Alpenrose   *p.74*

87

Hairy Alpenrose   *p.74*
(919) *Rhododendron hirsutum* × 1/10

Creeping Azalea   *p.74*
921 *Loiseleuria procumbens* × 2

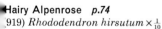

922 *Daboecia cantabrica* × ⅘
St Dabeoc's Heath   *p.74*

(922) *Phyllodoce caerulea* × ⅘
Blue Mountain Heath   *p.74*

(925) *Arctostaphylos alpina* × 2
Black Bearberry   *p.71*

920 *Rhododendron ponticum* × ⅙
Rhododendron   *p.73*

923 *Andromeda polifolia* × ⅘
Marsh Andromeda   *p.74*

88

Bearberry   *p.74*
925 *Arctostaphylos uva-ursi* × ⅘

Cranberry   *p.75*
937 *Vaccinium oxycoccos* × 1

935 *Vaccinium vitis-idaea* × ⅔
Cowberry   *p.71*

936 *Vaccinium myrtillus* × ⅘
Bilberry, Blaeberry, Wortleberry   *p.75*

(927) *Erica lusitanica* × 1
Lusitanian Heath   *p.69*

927 *Erica arborea* × 1/20
Tree Heath   *p.69*

89

Spring Heath   *p.74*
933 *Erica herbacea* × ⅗

Western Mediterranean Heath   *p.74*
934 *Erica multiflora* × ½

Sticky Alpine Primrose   *p.40*
945 *Primula viscosa* × ½

924 *Arbutus unedo* × ½
Strawberry Tree *p.83*

929 *Erica ciliaris* × ⅔
Dorset Heath *p.74*

940 *Primula elatior* × ½
Oxlip, Paigle *p.57*

942 *Primula vulgaris* × ½
Primrose *p.57*

90

Auricula, Bear's-Ear *p.57*
941 *Primula auricula* × ½

Flesh-Coloured Androsace *p.32*
953 *Androsace carnea* × ⅔

943 *Primula farinosa* × 1⅓
Bird's-Eye Primrose *p.31*

(944) *Primula minima* × ½
Least Primrose *p.25*

(945) *Primula hirsuta* × ⅔
Red Alpine Primrose *p.25*

946 *Primula integrifolia* × ⅔
Entire-Leaved Alpine Primrose *p.25*

91

Dwarf Snowbell *p.45*
(956) *Soldanella pusilla* × ¾

Alpine Androsace *p.31*
949 *Androsace alpina* × 1

Alpine Bells *p.25*
955 *Cortusa matthioli* × 1

957 *Hottonia palustris* × ⅛
Water Violet   *p.67*

960 *Cyclamen repandum* × ⅔
Repand Cyclamen   *p.26*

(959) *Cyclamen graecum* × ½
Greek Cyclamen   *p.25*

958 *Cyclamen hederifolium* × ⅔
Sowbread   *p.25*

92

Common Cyclamen   *p.25*
959 *Cyclamen purpurascens* × ⅘

Sea Milkwort   *p.32*
968 *Glaux maritima* × 1

965 *Trientalis europaea* × 1
Chickweed Wintergreen   *p.4*

(963) *Lysimachia punctata* × ⅓
Large Yellow Loosestrife   *p.50*

Shrubby Pimpernel   *p.38*
(967) *Anagallis linifolia* × 1½

962 *Lysimachia nemorum* × 1
Yellow Pimpernel   *p.63*

Creeping Jenny   *p.57*
961 *Lysimachia nummularia* × ⅓

972 *Limonium sinuatum* × ⅓
Winged Sea Lavender *p.43*

975 *Armeria maritima* × ⅛
Thrift, Sea Pink *p.32*

(976) *Armeria fasciculata* × ⅙
Spiny Thrift *p.32*

985 *Olea europaea* × ½
Olive *p.83*

94

Manna or Flowering Ash *p.83*
979 *Fraxinus ornus* × ⅓

Yellow-Wort *p.53*
988 *Blackstonia perfoliata* × 1¼

986 *Centaurium erythraea* × 4/5
Common Centaury *p.32*

984 *Jasminum officinale* × 4/5
Common Jasmine *p.85*

1002 *Swertia perennis* × 2/3
Marsh Felwort *p.38*

Great Yellow Gentian *p.50*
996 *Gentiana lutea* × 2/5

Wild Jasmine *p.79*
983 *Jasminum fruticans* × 1

(992) *Gentiana clusii* × $\frac{1}{3}$
Stemless Trumpet Gentian   *p.36*

992 *Gentiana kochiana* × $\frac{2}{3}$
Trumpet Gentian   *p.36*

991 *Gentiana verna* × 1
Spring Gentian   *p.40*

(990) *Gentiana utriculosa* × $\frac{2}{3}$
Bladder Gentian   *p.45*

989 *Gentiana cruciata* × $\frac{1}{2}$
Cross Gentian   *p.38*

Marsh Gentian   *p.36*
993 *Gentiana pneumonanthe* × $\frac{2}{3}$

German Gentian   *p.26*
(999) *Gentianella germanica* x $\frac{3}{4}$

998 *Gentiana purpurea* × ½
Purple Gentian *p.26*

1004 *Nymphoides peltata* × ⅓
Fringed Water-Lily *p.67*

997 *Gentiana punctata* × ½
Spotted Gentian *p.50*

994 *Gentiana asclepiadea* × ⅔
Willow Gentian *p.35*

1005 *Vinca minor* × ½
Lesser Periwinkle *p.76*

97

Herbaceous Periwinkle *p.41*
(1005) *Vinca herbacea* × ⅖

Silk-Vine *p.85*
1009 *Periploca graeca* × ⅔

1003 *Menyanthes trifoliata* × ½
Bogbean, Buckbean *p.67*

98

Oleander *p.73*
1007 *Nerium oleander* × ⅙

1013 *Putoria calabrica* × ⅖
Putoria *p.75*

1030 *Valantia hispida* × 1½
Rough Valantia *p.65*

Wild Madder *p.15*
1031 *Rubia peregrina* × ⅔

1011 *Asclepias syriaca* × ⅔
Silkweed   *p.20*

1010 *Vincetoxicum hirundinaria* × ½
Common Vincetoxicum   *p.8*

1014 *Sherardia arvensis* × 1
Field Madder   *p.43*

99

Sweet Woodruff   *p.11*
1027 *Galium odoratum* × ⅗

Crosswort   *p.64*
1029 *Cruciata laevipes* × 1¼

Marsh Bedstraw   *p.8*
(1022) *Galium palustre* × ½

1039 *Convolvulus althaeoides* × 1
Mallow-Leaved Bindweed   *p.18*

1032 *Polemonium caeruleum* × ½
Jacob's Ladder   *p.38*

(1039) *Convolvulus elegantissimus* × ½
Elegant Bindweed   *p.18*

1035 *Convolvulus tricolor* × ½
Dwarf Convolvulus   *p.36*

100

Sea Bindweed   *p.18*
1041 *Calystegia soldanella* × 1

Ivy-Leaved Morning Glory   *p.34*
(1033) *Ipomoea hederacea* × ½

1044 *Cuscuta epithymum* × 1¼
Common Dodder   *p.34*

1045 *Heliotropium europaeum* × ⅓
Heliotrope   *p.8*

101

Eastern Comfrey   *p.8*
(1053) *Symphytum orientale* × ⅓

1047 *Omphalodes verna* × ⅘
Blue-Eyed Mary   *p.45*

Blue Hound's-Tongue   *p.43*
(1049) *Cynoglossum creticum* × ⅔

1053 *Symphytum tuberosum* $\times \frac{2}{5}$
Tuberous Comfrey *p.60*

(1052) *Symphytum* × *uplandicum* $\times \frac{3}{5}$
Blue Comfrey *p.43*

102

Alkanet *p.43*
1058 *Pentaglottis sempervirens* $\times \frac{3}{5}$

1049 *Cynoglossum officinale* $\times \frac{1}{2}$
Hound's-Tongue *p.28*

Large Blue Alkanet *p.38*
1056 *Anchusa azurea* $\times \frac{1}{6}$

1054 *Borago officinalis* × ¼
Borage   *p.38*

1055 *Anchusa officinalis* × ½
True Alkanet   *p.43*

(1054) *Trachystemon orientalis* × ½
Eastern Borage   *p.38*

1061 *Alkanna tinctoria* × 1¼
Dyer's Alkanet   *p.45*

1067 *Myosotis alpestris* × 1
Alpine Forget-me-Not   *p.45*

103

Northern Shorewort, Oyster Plant   *p.43*
1062 *Mertensia maritima* × ⅗

Water Forget-me-Not   *p.43*
1065 *Myosotis scorpioides* × 1

1064 *Pulmonaria longifolia* × ⅘
Narrow-Leaved Lungwort *p.43*

104

Vipers Bugloss *p.38*
1082 *Echium vulgare* × ⅛

1070 *Eritrichium nanum* × 1
King of the Alps *p.46*

1074 *Lithospermum diffusum* × 1
Scrambling Gromwell *p.76*

Blue Gromwell *p.38*
1073 *Lithospermum purpurocaeruleum* × ⅔

1072 *Lithospermum officinale* $\times \frac{2}{5}$
Gromwell *p.12*

1076 *Onosma echioides* $\times \frac{3}{4}$
Golden Drop *p.63*

1081 *Echium italicum* $\times 1$
Pale Bugloss *p.28*

105

Blue Bugle *p.44*
1090 *Ajuga genevensis* $\times \frac{1}{2}$

1079 *Cerinthe major* $\times \frac{1}{3}$
Honeywort *p.53*

1078 *Cerinthe minor* $\times \frac{1}{2}$
Lesser Honeywort *p.60*

Common Starwort *p.66*
1088 *Callitriche stagnalis* $\times 1$

1083 *Echium lycopsis* × ½
Purple Vipers Bugloss   *p.38*

106

Chaste Tree   *p.75*
1087 *Vitex agnus-castus* × ⅓

1091 *Ajuga pyramidalis* × ½
Pyramidal Bugle   *p.46*

1094 *Ajuga chamaepitys* × ⅔
Ground-Pine   *p.63*

Common Bugle   *p.46*
1089 *Ajuga reptans* × 1¼

1099 *Teucrium chamaedrys* × ½
Wall Germander *p.32*

1103 *Teucrium montanum* × ⅔
Mountain Germander, Alpine Penny Royal *p.63*

1101 *Teucrium fruticans* × ⅘
Tree Germander *p.75*

1105 *Rosmarinus officinalis* × ⅓
Rosemary *p.75*

107

Ground-Pine Germander *p.8*
1096 *Teucrium*
pseudochamaepitys × ¾

Prasium *p.71*
1106 *Prasium majus* × 1⅔

1107 *Scutellaria alpina* $\times \frac{2}{3}$
Alpine Skullcap *p.41*

(1107) *Scutellaria orientalis* $\times 1$
Eastern Alpine Skullcap *p.57*

1108 *Scutellaria galericulata* $\times \frac{2}{3}$
Skullcap *p.44*

108

French Lavender *p.76*
1110 *Lavandula staechas* $\times \frac{1}{15}$

1116 *Nepeta cataria* × $\frac{1}{3}$
Catmint *p.8*

1118 *Glechoma hederacea* × $\frac{2}{3}$
Ground Ivy *p.38*

1115 *Sideritis hyssopifolia* × 1
Hyssop-Leaved Sideritis *p.79*

109

Bastard Balm *p.22*
1121 *Melittis melissophyllum* × $\frac{1}{2}$

White Horehound *p.8*
1112 *Marrubium vulgare* × $\frac{1}{3}$

1123 *Phlomis lychnitis* $\times \frac{1}{3}$
Small Jerusalem Sage *p.79*

(1122) *Phlomis tuberosa* $\times \frac{1}{2}$
Tuberous Jerusalem Sage *p.23*

1120 *Prunella laciniata* $\times \frac{2}{3}$
Cut-Leaved Self-Heal *p.63*

110

Jerusalem Sage *p.77*
1124 *Phlomis fruticosa* $\times \frac{1}{10}$

Large Self-Heal *p.41*
(1120) *Prunella grandiflora* $\times \frac{1}{2}$

1126 *Galeopsis tetrahit* × 1
Common Hemp-Nettle *p.28*

(1126) *Galeopsis speciosa* × ⅔
Large-Flowered Hemp-Nettle *p.53*

Large Red Dead-Nettle *p.23*
(1131) *Lamium orvala* × ¾

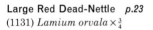

1130 *Lamium maculatum* × ⅘
Spotted Dead-Nettle *p.23*

111

Henbit *p.32*
1127 *Lamium amplexicaule* × ¾

1132 *Galeobdolon luteum* × ⅔
Yellow Archangel   *p.53*

1133 *Leonurus cardiaca* × ⅖
Motherwort   *p.28*

1138 *Stachys palustris* × 1
Marsh Woundwort   *p.28*

112

Black Horehound   *p.28*
1134 *Ballota nigra* × ⅓

Downy Woundwort   *p.23*
1140 *Stachys germanica* × ⅕

1146 *Salvia glutinosa* × 1
Jupiter's Distaff   *p.53*

Silver Sage   *p.3*
(1144) *Salvia argentea* × 1½

1136 *Stachys recta* × 1⅓
Perennial Yellow Woundwort   *p.53*

(1143) *Salvia triloba* × ⅕
Three-Lobed Sage   *p.76*

113

Clary   *p.38*
1144 *Salvia sclarea* × ½

1169 *Mentha aquatica* × ½
Water Mint   *p.44*

1171 *Mentha longifolia* × ⅓
Horsemint   *p.44*

116

Gipsy-Wort   *p.8*
1166 *Lycopus europaeus* × ⅕

1167 *Mentha pulegium* × ⅓
Penny-Royal   *p.44*

Scopolia   *p.23*
1175 *Scopolia carniolica* × ⅗

1176 *Hyoscyamus niger* × 1⅓
Henbane *p.53*

(1177) *Hyoscyamus aureus* × ½
Golden Henbane *p.54*

117

Deadly Nightshade *p.39*
1174 *Atropa bella-donna* × ⅘

1177 *Hyoscyamus albus* × ¾
White Henbane *p.54*

Deadly Nightshade *p.39*
1174 *Atropa bella-donna* × ⅗

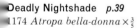

(1186) *Datura metel* × $\frac{1}{3}$
Large-Flowered Thorn-Apple *p.1*

118

Thorn-Apple *p.1*
1186 *Datura stramonium* × $\frac{4}{5}$

1185 *Mandragora officinarum* × $\frac{3}{4}$
Mandrake *p.41*

1180 *Solanum sodomeum* × $\frac{2}{5}$
False Sodom Apple *p.76*

Thorn-Apple *p.1*
1186 *Datura stramonium* × $\frac{2}{3}$

1178 *Physalis alkekengi* × ⅕
Bladder Cherry *p.3*

1187 *Nicotiana glauca* × ⅔
Shrub Tobacco *p.77*

1188 *Nicotiana rustica* × ½
Small Tobacco *p.13*

(1188) *Nicotiana tabacum* × ⅓
Large Tobacco *p.23*

Apple of Peru *p.35*
1179 *Nicandra physalodes* × ⅘

Bittersweet, Woody Nightshade *p.44*
1181 *Solanum dulcamara* × ½

1192 *Verbascum blattaria* $\times \frac{1}{2}$
Moth Mullein *p.54*

1196 *Verbascum creticum* $\times \frac{1}{4}$
Celsia *p.50*

1190 *Verbascum nigrum* $\times 1$
Dark Mullein *p.54*

120

Large-Flowered Mullein *p.49*
(1193) *Verbascum thapsiforme* $\times \frac{1}{10}$

Wavy-Leaved Mullein *p.54*
(1195) *Verbascum undulatum* $\times \frac{1}{5}$

1200 *Asarina procumbens* × 1¼
Creeping Snapdragon *p.57*

1198 *Antirrhinum latifolium* × ½
Large Snapdragon *p.50*

(1192) *Verbascum phoeniceum* × ⅗
Purple Mullein *p.39*

1189 *Buddleja davidii* × ¼
Buddleia *p.75*

121

Common Snapdragon *p.50*
1197 *Antirrhinum majus* x ½

Dalmatian Toadflax *p.54*
(1205) *Linaria dalmatica* × ⅔

1202 *Linaria repens* × 1¼
Pale Toadflax *p.44*

1199 *Antirrhinum orontium* × ⅔
Weasel's Snout *p.23*

1204 *Linaria alpina* × 1
Alpine Toadflax *p.41*

(1204) *Linaria triornithophora* × ½
Great Purple Toadflax *p.39*

122

Ivy-Leaved Toadflax *p.46*
1210 *Cymbalaria muralis* × ½

Three-Leaved Toadflax *p.58*
1208 *Linaria triphylla* × ⅔

1215 *Scrophularia scorodonia* × ⅘
Balm-Leaved Figwort *p.48*

(1216) *Scrophularia hoppii* × ¼
Alpine Figwort *p.48*

123

1211 *Anarrhinum bellidifolium* × ⅓
Blue Snapdragon *p.44*

Musk *p.54*
(1217) *Mimulus moschatus* × ⅘

Monkey-Flower *p.50*
1217 *Mimulus guttatus* × ½

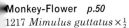

1223 *Veronica persica* × ½
Buxbaum's Speedwell *p.46*

1218 *Gratiola officinalis* × ⅘
Gratiole *p.54*

124

Rock Speedwell *p.46*
(1220) *Veronica fruticans* × 2

1224 *Veronica filiformis* × 1¼
Creeping Speedwell *p.46*

Brooklime *p.44*
1225 *Veronica beccabunga* × ⅔

1230 *Digitalis ferruginea* × ½
Rusty Foxglove   *p.54*

1232 *Digitalis grandiflora* × ⅘
Large Yellow Foxglove   *p.54*

1233 *Digitalis lutea* × ⅔
Small Yellow Foxglove   *p.54*

Spanish Rusty Foxglove   *p.54*
1233) *Digitalis obscura* × ⅔

Foxglove   *p.23*
1234 *Digitalis purpurea* × ¼

1238 *Parentucellia viscosa* × 1
Yellow Bartsia   *p.58*

1237 *Bellardia trixago* × $\frac{3}{4}$
Bellardia   *p.26*

1241 *Odontites verna* × $\frac{1}{3}$
Red Bartsia   *p.32*

126

Alpine Bartsia   *p.46*
1236 *Bartsia alpina* × 1

Southern Red Bartsia   *p.32*
1239 *Parentucellia latifolia* × $1\frac{1}{4}$

1235 *Erinus alpinus* × ½
Alpine Erinus *p.32*

1242 *Euphrasia rostkoviana* × ⅔
Common Eyebright *p.11*

(1244) *Euphrasia minima* × 1⅓
Dwarf Eyebright *p.63*

1247 *Rhinanthus minor* × 1¼
Yellow-Rattle *p.63*

127

Leafy Lousewort *p.55*
1252 *Pedicularis foliosa* × ½

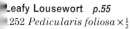

Tuberous Lousewort *p.63*
1250 *Pedicularis tuberosa* × ⅓

1254 *Pedicularis recutita* × ⅓
Truncate Lousewort   *p.28*

1258 *Melampyrum arvense* × 1
Field Cow-Wheat   *p.23*

128

Yellow Cow-Wheat   *p.55*
1259 *Melampyrum nemorosum* × ¾

1255 *Pedicularis kerneri* × ⅔
Rhaetian Lousewort   *p.32*

Common Lousewort   *p.28*
(1256) *Pedicularis sylvatica* × ⅘

1261 *Tozzia alpina* × 2
Tozzia   *p.63*

1264 *Globularia vulgaris* × $\frac{2}{3}$
Common Globularia   *p.46*

129

Catalpa, Indian Bean   *p.83*
1265 *Catalpa bignonioides* × $\frac{2}{3}$

1262 *Globularia alypum* × $\frac{1}{5}$
Shrubby Globularia   *p.76*

Matted Globularia   *p.76*
1263 *Globularia cordifolia* × $\frac{1}{2}$

1266 *Acanthus mollis* × ¼
Bear's Breech *p.1*

1267 *Acanthus spinosus* × ⅙
Spiny Bear's Breech *p.1*

130

Toothwort *p.26*
1269 *Lathraea squamaria* × ⅔

Purple Toothwort *p.41*
(1269) *Lathraea clandestina* × 1

1268 *Ramonda myconi* × 1
Ramonda *p.41*

1274 *Orobanche crenata* × ¼
Bean Broomrape *p.3*

1275 *Orobanche caryophyllacea?* × 1
Clove-Scented Broomrape *p.55*

Lesser Broomrape *p.63*
1277 *Orobanche minor* × ⅔

Greater Broomrape *p.55*
1272 *Orobanche rapum-genistae* × ⅓

1279 *Pinguicula alpina* × 1
Alpine Butterwort *p.11*

(1280) *Pinguicula grandiflora* × ½
Large-Flowered Butterwort *p.41*

132
Greater Bladderwort *p.68*
1281 *Utricularia vulgaris* × 1¼

1280 *Pinguicula vulgaris* × 1
Common Butterwort *p.41*

Sea Plantain *p.49*
1287 *Plantago maritima* × ⅙

1292 *Plantago media* × 1¼
Hoary Plantain *p.47*

1285 *Plantago coronopus* × ¼
Buck's-Horn Plantain *p.65*

1298 *Viburnum opulus* × ½
Guelder Rose *p.70*

1283 *Plantago indica* × 1
Branched Plantain *p.49*

133

Danewort *p.8*
1295 *Sambucus ebulus* × ½

Danewort *p.8*
1295 *Sambucus ebulus* × ⅓

1299 *Viburnum lantana* × ½
Wayfaring Tree   *p.70*

1299 *Viburnum lantana* × ½
Wayfaring Tree   *p.70*

134

Laurustinus   *p.70*
1300 *Viburnum tinus* × 1

1297 *Sambucus racemosa* × ⅓
Alpine or Red Elder

Alpine or Red Elder   *p.72*
1297 *Sambucus racemosa* × ⅓

1305 *Lonicera etrusca* × ⅔ **Deciduous** (1303) *Lonicera caerulea* × 1   **Blue Honeysuckle** *p.79*
Mediterranean Honeysuckle *p.85*

1302 *Lonicera xylosteum* × ½
Fly Honeysuckle *p.70*

1307 *Linnaea borealis* × 1⅓
Twinflower *p.75*

Snowberry *p.73*
1301 *Symphoricarpos rivularis* × ⅔   1304 *Lonicera periclymenum* × ⅔   **Honeysuckle** *p.85*

(1315) *Valeriana montana* × 1
Mountain Valerian *p.29*

136

Red Valerian *p.29*
1316 *Centranthus ruber* × $\frac{2}{3}$

1309 *Valerianella locusta* × $\frac{2}{5}$
Lamb's Lettuce, Corn Salad *p.47*

1315 *Valeriana tripteris* × $\frac{1}{3}$
Three-Leaved Valerian *p.29*

Valerian *p.28*
1313 *Valeriana officinalis* × $\frac{1}{2}$

(1316) *Centranthus angustifolius* × ⅘
Narrow-Leaved Red Valerian *p.29*

(1318) *Dipsacus laciniatus* × ⅔
Cut-Leaved Teasel *p.8*

137

1308 *Adoxa moschatellina* × 1⅓
Moschatel, Town Hall Clock *p.16*

Yellow Scabious *p.60*
1327 *Scabiosa ochroleuca* × ⅘

Fedia *p.33*
1312 *Fedia cornucopiae* × 1⅕

1322 *Knautia arvensis* × 1⅓
Field Scabious   *p.44*

1326 *Scabiosa atropurpurea* × 1
Mournful Widow, Sweet Scabious   *p.29*

(1325) *Scabiosa lucida* × 1
Shining Scabious   *p.33*

1323 *Knautia sylvatica* × ⅓
Wood Scabious   *p.29*

138

Clustered Bellflower   *p.39*
1333 *Campanula glomerata* × ⅔

Spiked Bellflower   *p.39*
(1332) *Campanula spicata* × ⅓

1330 *Campanula barbata* × ¾
Bearded Bellflower   *p.41*

1332 *Campanula thyrsoides* × ¼
Yellow Bellflower   *p.58*

Bats-in-the-Belfry   *p.35*
1340 *Campanula trachelium* × ⅘

Narrow-Leaved Bellflower   *p.35*
1336 *Campanula persicifolia* × ⅔

(1339) *Campanula scheuchzeri* × ⅔
Scheuchzer's Bellflower *p.41*

1338 *Campanula cochleariifolia* × ⅘
Fairy's Thimble *p.41*

1342 *Campanula rapunculoides* × ⅔
Creeping Bellflower *p.39*

1343 *Campanula bononiensis* × 1
Pale Bellflower *p.39*

140

Diamond-Leaved Bellflower *p.39*
1344 *Campanula rhomboidalis* × ⅘

Devil's Claw *p.33*
(1352) *Phyteuma comosum* × 1

(1350) *Phyteuma betonicifolium* × 1
Blue-Spiked Rampion *p.44*

1350 *Phyteuma spicatum* × $\frac{1}{10}$
Spiked Rampion *p.60*

1347 *Legousia speculum-veneris* × $\frac{4}{5}$
Venus' Looking-Glass *p.42*

1352 *Phyteuma orbiculare* × $1\frac{3}{4}$
Round-Headed Rampion *p.44*

141

Sheep's Bit *p.46*
1355 *Jasione montana* × 1

Hemp Agrimony *p.29*
1357 *Eupatorium cannabinum* × $\frac{1}{5}$

1363 *Aster alpinus* × ⅖
Alpine Aster   *p.36*

(1359) *Solidago gigantea* × ⅓
Canadian Golden-Rod   *p.60*

142

Sea Aster   *p.39*
1365 *Aster tripolium* × 1

1362 *Bellidastrum michelii* × ⅓
False Daisy   *p.2*

European Michaelmas Daisy   *p.35*
1364 *Aster amellus* × ½

1374 *Evax pygmaea* × $\frac{4}{5}$
Evax *p.58*

1358 *Solidago virgaurea* × $\frac{2}{3}$
Golden-Rod *p.61*

143

Cudweed *p.63*
1375 *Filago vulgaris* × 1

1369 *Erigeron acer* × $\frac{2}{3}$
Blue Fleabane *p.42*

Cat's-Foot *p.11*
1378 *Antennaria dioica* × $\frac{1}{2}$

1388 *Inula helenium* $\times \frac{1}{3}$
Elecampane *p.50*

144

Ploughman's Spikenard *p.61*
1387 *Inula conyza* $\times \frac{1}{3}$

1379 *Leontopodium alpinum* $\times \frac{4}{5}$
Edelweiss *p.58*

1385 *Helichrysum stoechas* $\times \frac{1}{6}$
Stinking Everlasting *p.63*

Marsh Cudweed *p.63*
1380 *Gnaphalium uliginosum* $\times \frac{2}{3}$

1390 *Inula crithmoides* × $\frac{1}{10}$
Golden Samphire   *p.55*

(1391) *Inula britannica* × $\frac{1}{3}$
Meadow Inula   *p.55*

1386 *Phagnalon rupestre* × $\frac{1}{3}$
Rock Phagnalon   *p.79*

1393 *Pulicaria dysenterica* × $\frac{1}{2}$
Fleabane   *p.55*

145

Pallenis   *p.55*
1395 *Pallenis spinosa* × $\frac{1}{2}$

Large Yellow Ox-Eye   *p.49*
1397 *Telekia speciosa* × $\frac{1}{3}$

1398 *Asteriscus maritimus* $\times \frac{2}{3}$
Sea Asteriscus *p.79*

1399 *Asteriscus aquaticus* $\times \frac{1}{2}$
Annual Asteriscus *p.64*

1402 *Xanthium spinosum* $\times \frac{2}{3}$
Spiny Cocklebur *p.15*

1401 *Xanthium strumarium* $\times \frac{1}{2}$
Cocklebur *p.15*

146

Cone Flower *p.49*
1403 *Rudbeckia laciniata* $\times \frac{1}{3}$

Nodding Bur-Marigold *p.55*
1406 *Bidens cernua var. radiata* $\times \frac{1}{2}$

1419 *Achillea nana* × 1
Dwarf Milfoil *p.11*

1413 *Chamaemelum nobile* × ½
Chamomile *p.5*

1407 *Galinsoga parviflora* × ⅘
Gallant Soldier *p.8*

Yellow Chamomile *p.50*
1409 *Anthemis tinctoria* × ⅓

Yellow Milfoil *p.64*
1421 *Achillea tomentosa* × ½

Tansy *p.61*
1426 *Chrysanthemum vulgare* × ⅕

(1424) *Chrysanthemum myconis* × ⅓
Southern Corn Marigold   p.50

1425 *Chrysanthemum coronarium* × 1/12
Crown Daisy   p.51

148

Marguerite   p.1
1427 *Chrysanthemum leucanthemum* × ¼

1429 *Chrysanthemum parthenium* × ⅙
Feverfew   p.3

Pineapple Weed, Rayless Mayweed   p.16
1432 *Matricaria matricarioides* × ½

1433 *Cotula coronopifolia* × 1
Brass Buttons *p.64*

1440 *Petasites hybridus* × ½
Butterbur *p.33*

White Butterbur *p.11*
1441 *Petasites albus* × ⅔

439 *Tussilago farfara* × ½
Coltsfoot *p.58*

Wormwood *p.61*
436 *Artemisia absinthium* × ⅓

1445 *Adenostyles alliariae* × ½
Common Adenostyles   *p.29*

150

Wood Ragwort   *p.55*
(1456) *Senecio nemorensis* × ¼

1443 *Homogyne alpina* × 1⅕
Alpine Coltsfoot   *p.33*

1448 *Doronicum grandiflorum* × ¼
Large-Flowered Leopard's-Bane   *p.52*

Grey Alpine Groundsel   *p.64*
(1452) *Senecio incanus* × ⅖

1447 *Doronicum pardalianches* × ⅓
Great Leopard's-Bane *p.51*

1460 *Calendula arvensis* × ⅓
Marigold *p.58*

1464 *Xeranthemum annuum* × ½
Pink Everlasting *p.18*

452 *Senecio vernalis* × ⅔
Spring Groundsel *p.58*

1446 *Arnica montana* × ¼
Arnica *p.51*

151

Chamois Ragwort *p.51*
455 *Senecio doronicum* × ¼

Stemless Carline Thistle *p.2*
1467 *Carlina acaulis* × ⅓

(1475) *Saussurea alpina* × 1
Alpine Saussurea   *p.39*

152
Woolly Burdock   *p.23*
1472 *Arctium tomentosum* × 2/3

1462 *Echinops ritro* × 1/3
Globe-Thistle   *p.35*

1469 *Carlina corymbosa* × 1/3
Flat-Topped Carline Thistle   *p.51*

Musk Thistle   *p.18*
1478 *Carduus nutans* × 1/2

1479 *Carduus personata* $\times \frac{1}{4}$
Great Marsh Thistle *p.20*

(1484) *Cirsium candelabrum* $\times \frac{1}{8}$
Candelabra Thistle *p.2*

153

Grey Thistle *p.24*
1488 *Cirsium acarna* $\times \frac{1}{2}$

1481 *Notobasis syriaca* $\times \frac{2}{3}$
Syrian Thistle *p.23*

Tuberous Thistle *p.24*
(1489) *Cirsium tuberosum* $\times \frac{2}{3}$

1483 *Cirsium spinosissimum* $\times \frac{1}{5}$
Spiniest Thistle *p.3*

1482 *Cirsium oleraceum* $\times \frac{1}{3}$
Cabbage Thistle *p.55*

(1491) *Cynara scolymus* $\times \frac{1}{4}$
Globe Artichoke *p.34*

1485 *Cirsium eriophorum* $\times \frac{1}{3}$
Woolly Thistle *p.18*

154

Stemless Thistle *p.19*
1490 *Cirsium acaulon* $\times \frac{1}{2}$

Galactites *p.39*
1493 *Galactites tomentosa* $\times \frac{2}{3}$

1494 *Onopordum acanthium* × ⅘
Scotch Thistle, Cotton Thistle   *p.18*

1492 *Silybum marianum* × ¾
Milk-Thistle, Holy Thistle   *p.18*

St Barnaby's Thistle   *p.61*
1499 *Centaurea solstitialis* × ⅘

1495 *Onopordum illyricum* × ⅔
Southern Scotch Thistle   *p.18*

155

Saw-Wort   *p.24*
1497 *Serratula tinctoria* × 1⅕

1501 *Centaurea cyanus* × 2
Cornflower *p.39*

1500 *Centaurea calcitrapa* × ⅔
Star Thistle *p.29*

1503 *Centaurea salonitana* × ½
Yellow Knapweed *p.55*

1506 *Centaurea rhapontica* × ⅘
Giant Knapweed *p.18*

156

Wig Knapweed *p.18*
(1504) *Centaurea phrygia* × ½

Plume Knapweed *p.19*
1504 *Centaurea nervosa* × ⅖

(1526) *Urospermum dalechampii* × ⅔
Soft Urospermum *p.56*

1507 *Centaurea conifera* × ½
Cone Knapweed *p.20*

1508 *Carthamus lanatus* × ⅖
Yellow Carthamus *p.55*

(1510) *Scolymus maculatus* × ½
Spotted Spanish Oyster Plant *p.56*

157

Cupidone *p.40*
1511 *Catananche coerulea* × ⅔

Tolpis *p.58*
1515 *Tolpis barbata* × ⅘

1519 *Hedypnois rhagadioloides* × ½
Hedypnois   *p.64*

1512 *Cichorium intybus* × ½
Chicory   *p.35*

158

Giant Catsear   *p.52*
1521 *Hypochoeris uniflora* × ⅓

1528 *Tragopogon porrifolius* × 1¼
Salsify   *p.35*

Rough Hawkbit   *p.51*
1524 *Leontodon hispidus* × 1⅓

1538 *Sonchus arvensis* × ½
Field Sow-Thistle *p.51*

1539 *Sonchus asper* × ⅓
Prickly Sow-Thistle *p.56*

159

1533 *Andryala integrifolia* × ⅘
Common Andryala *p.56*

Dandelion *p.52*
1535 *Taraxacum officinale* × ⅓

Blue Sow-Thistle *p.37*
1537 *Cicerbita alpina* × ⅙

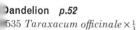

1541 *Lactuca perennis* × ⅔
Blue Lettuce *p.35*

1545 *Prenanthes purpurea* × ¼
Prenanthe *p.40*

1509 *Cnicus benedictus* × ¾
Blessed Thistle *p.58*

1549 *Crepis aurea* × ⅘
Golden Hawksbeard *p.58*

160

Mouse-Ear Hawkweed *p.58*
1550 *Hieracium pilosella* × ⅓

Beaked Hawksbeard *p.56*
1546 *Crepis vesicaria* × ⅕

1565 *Stratiotes aloides* $\times \frac{1}{4}$
Water Soldier   *p.66*

1566 *Hydrocharis morsus-ranae* $\times \frac{1}{3}$
Frog-Bit   *p.66*

1564 *Butomus umbellatus* $\times \frac{1}{3}$
Flowering Rush   *p.67*

161

Broad-Leaved Pondweed   *p.66*
1570 *Potamogeton natans* $\times \frac{4}{5}$

Posidonia   *p.67*
1580 *Posidonia oceanica* $\times \frac{1}{10}$

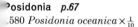

(1583) *Tofieldia calyculata* × 1
Alpine Asphodel *p.17*

1586 *Veratrum album* × ¼
White False Helleborine *p.9*

162

King's Spear, Yellow Asphodel *p.56*
1593 *Aphodeline lutea* × ⅗

1585 *Aphyllanthes monspeliensis* × ⅗
Blue Grass-Lily *p.42*

Black False Helleborine *p.48*
(1586) *Veratrum nigrum* × ⅔

1588 *Colchicum autumnale* × ⅗ **p.20** 1587 *Merendera montana* × ⅗ **Merendera p.20**
Autumn Crocus, Meadow Saffron

1595 *Paradisea liliastrum* × ⅓ St Bruno's Lily **p.1**

1591 *Asphodelus aestivus* × ¼ Asphodel **p.1**

163

Hollow-Stemmed Asphodel **p.24**
1592 *Asphodelus fistulosus* × 1/10

1589 *Bulbocodium vernum* × ⅔ Bulbocodium **p.20**

1596 *Anthericum liliago* × ½
St Bernard's Lily *p.1*

(1601) *Gagea graeca* × 1
Greek Lloydia *p.11*

164

Pale Day-Lily *p.51*
(1597) *Hemerocallis lilioasphodelus* × ⅘

1601 *Gagea fistulosa* × 1
Hollow-Stemmed Gagea *p.64*

Lloydia *p.11*
1629 *Lloydia serotina* × ⅘

1603 *Allium schoenoprasum* × ½
Chives *p.29*

(1604) *Allium sphaerocephalon* × 1⅕
Round-Headed Leek *p.29*

1606 *Allium flavum* × ⅘
Yellow Onion *p.64*

1607 *Allium carinatum* × 1
Keeled Garlic *p.29*

White Garlic *p.3*
1609 *Allium neapolitanum* × ½

Triquetrous Garlic *p.3*
1610 *Allium triquetrum* × ⅓

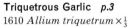

1615 *Allium ampeloprasum* $\times \frac{1}{3}$
Wild Leek   *p.9*

1616 *Allium ursinum* $\times \frac{1}{2}$
Ramsons   *p.11*

166

Red Lily   *p.19*
(1619) *Lilium pomponium* $\times \frac{1}{3}$

1611 *Allium roseum* $\times \frac{2}{3}$
Rose Garlic   *p.30*

Orange Lily   *p.51*
1620 *Lilium bulbiferum* $\times \frac{3}{4}$

1622 *Fritillaria meleagris* $\times \frac{2}{3}$
Snake's Head, Fritillary *p.19*

1619 *Lilium pyrenaicum* $\times \frac{1}{2}$
Yellow Turk's-Cap Lily *p.51*

Martagon Lily *p.19*
1618 *Lilium martagon* $\times \frac{1}{3}$

1650 *Asparagus acutifolius* × ¾
Hardy Asparagus *p.72*

1628 *Erythronium dens-canis* × ⅔
Dog's Tooth Violet *p.33*

1626 *Tulipa oculus-solis* × ⅓
Eyed Tulip *p.19*

1625 *Tulipa australis* × ⅓
Southern Tulip *p.58*

168

Peruvian Squill *p.45*
1632 *Scilla peruviana* × ⅔

Autumn Squill *p.46*
1636 *Scilla autumnalis* × 1

1630 *Urginea maritima* × $\frac{2}{5}$
Sea Squill   *p.9*

1640 *Ornithogalum pyrenaicum* × $\frac{4}{5}$
Bath Asparagus   *p.13*

(1638) *Endymion hispanicus* × $\frac{1}{4}$
Spanish Bluebell   *p.40*

169

Dark Grape-Hyacinch   *p.46*
1646 *Muscari commutatum* × 1

Tassel Hyacinth   *p.45*
1645 *Muscari comosum* × $\frac{1}{5}$

1658 *Paris quadrifolia* × ½
Herb Paris *p.13*

1648 *Muscari botryoides* × ⅘
Small Grape-Hyacinth *p.47*

1639 *Ornithogalum umbellatum* × ½
Star-of-Bethlehem *p.5*

1635 *Scilla bifolia* × ⅘
Alpine Squill *p.42*

170

Bluebell *p.42*
1638 *Endymion non-scriptus* × ⅗

Southern Grape-Hyacinth *p.47*
(1647) *Muscari neglectum* × ⅘

643 *Hyacinthus orientalis* × ½
Hyacinth *p.42*

657 *Convallaria majalis* × ½
Lily-of-the-Valley *p.11*

Sweet-Scented Solomon's Seal *p.11*
654 *Polygonatum odoratum* × ½

1660 *Agave americana* × $\frac{1}{100}$
Century Plant *p.59*

171

Solomon's Seal *p.9*
1655 *Polygonatum multiflorum* × $\frac{2}{3}$

1661 *Leucojum vernum* × 1
Spring Snowflake *p.5*

172

Three-Leaved Snowflake *p.5*
(1662) *Leucojum trichophyllum* × 1½

1662 *Leucojum aestivum* × ⅘
Summer Snowflake *p.3*

1664 *Sternbergia lutea* × ½
Common Sternbergia *p.52*

Slender Sternbergia *p.58*
(1664) *Sternbergia colchiciflora* × ⅔

668 *Narcissus requienii* × ½
Rush-Leaved Narcissus **p.59**

1663 *Galanthus nivalis* × ½
Snowdrop **p.5**

566 *Narcissus bulbocodium* × 1
oop Petticoat Daffodil **p.59**

1671 *Narcissus poeticus* × ½
Pheasant's-Eye Narcissus **p.1**

utumn Narcissus **p.5**
572 *Narcissus serotinus* × ¾

White Hoop Petticoat Daffodil **p.5**
(1666) *Narcissus cantabricus* × ⅔

1690 *Iris pseudacorus* $\times \frac{1}{2}$
Yellow Flag *p.51*

1683 *Hermodactylus tuberosus* $\times 1$
Snake's Head Iris, Widow Iris *p.13*

174

Purple Autumnal Crocus *p.36*
1676 *Crocus nudiflorus* $\times \frac{1}{2}$

1673 *Pancratium maritimum* $\times \frac{1}{5}$
Sea Daffodil *p.1*

Purple Crocus *p.5*
1678 *Crocus albiflorus* $\times \frac{2}{3}$

684 *Iris sisyrinchium* $\times \frac{2}{3}$
Barbary Nut *p.42*

(1685) *Iris xiphioides* $\times \frac{1}{10}$
Pyrenean Iris *p.35*

686 *Iris graminea* $\times 1$
Grass-Leaved Iris *p.35*

1693 *Iris germanica* $\times \frac{1}{2}$
Common Iris *p.36*

175

Spanish Iris *p.35*
685 *Iris xiphium* $\times \frac{1}{5}$

Dwarf Iris *p.36*
1692 *Iris chamaeiris* $\times \frac{1}{2}$

(1695) *Gladiolus byzantinus* × $\frac{1}{2}$
Eastern Gladiolus *p.19*

1695 *Gladiolus segetum* × $\frac{2}{3}$
Field Gladiolus *p.19*

176

Canary Palm *p.84*
1718 *Phoenix canariensis* × $\frac{1}{60}$

1691 *Iris pumila* × $\frac{2}{3}$
Pygmy Iris *p.36*

Dwarf Fan Palm *p.72*
1719 *Chamaerops humilis* × $\frac{1}{10}$

(1707) *Juncus articulatus* × ⅔
ointed Rush   *p.86*

1701 *Juncus jacquinii* × ⅓
Black Alpine Rush   *p.86*

1705 *Juncus acutus* × ⅓
Sharp-Pointed Rush   *p.86*

177

Hard Rush   *p.86*
1698 *Juncus inflexus* × 1

1700 *Juncus subuliflorus* × ⅔
onglomerate Rush   *p.86*

1699 *Juncus effusus* × ⅓
Soft Rush   *p.86*

eath Rush   *p.86*
702 *Juncus squarrosus* × ⅕

Snowy Woodrush   *p.86*
1712 *Luzula nivea* × ½

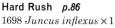

1735 *Hordeum murinum* × 1⅓
Wall Barley *p.87*

178

Sand Couch *p.88*
1727 *Agropyron junceiforme* × ⅘

1714 *Luzula campestris* × ⅓
Field Woodrush *p.86*

1720 *Bromus erectus* × ¼
Upright Brome *p.87*

Aegilops *p.87*
1730 *Aegilops ovata* × 1¼

1722 *Bromus ramosus* × ⅓
Hairy Brome *p.88*

1728 *Agropyron repens* × ¼
Couch-Grass, Twitch *p.88*

Macaroni Wheat *p.87*
(1732) *Triticum durum* × 1

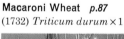

1736 *Elymus arenarius* × $\frac{1}{20}$
Lyme Grass *p.88*

1737 *Sesleria caerulea* × $\frac{1}{4}$
Blue Moor-Grass *p.88*

1740 *Phragmites communis* × $\frac{1}{15}$
Common Reed *p.89*

179

1742 *Molinia caerulea* × $\frac{1}{4}$
Purple Moor-Grass *p.89*

1746 *Briza maxima* × $\frac{1}{2}$
Large Quaking-Grass *p.89*

Hairy Melick *p.89*
1745 *Melica ciliata* × 1

Rough Dog's-Tail *p.87*
1748 *Cynosurus echinatus* × $\frac{2}{3}$

Alpine Meadow-Grass *p.89*
1751 *Poa alpina* × $\frac{2}{3}$

1765 *Avena sterilis* × ⅔
Animated Oat *p.88*

180

Italian Rye-Grass *p.87*
(1760) *Lolium multiflorum* × ½

1755 *Glyceria maxima* × ¼
Reed Sweet-Grass *p.89*

(1756) *Glyceria declinata* × ½
Glaucous Sweet-Grass *p.89*

(1757) *Festuca arundinacea* × ⅘
Tall Fescue *p.89*

1759 *Catapodium rigidum* × ⅔
Hard Poa *p.89*

Wavy Hair-Grass *p.88*
1772 *Deschampsia flexuosa* × ⅛

Yellow Oat *p.88*
1764 *Trisetum flavescens* × ½

1770 *Holcus lanatus* $\times \frac{1}{2}$
Yorkshire Fog   *p.90*

1779 *Lagurus ovatus* $\times \frac{1}{2}$
Hare's-Tail   *p.87*

1775 *Ammophila arenaria* $\times \frac{1}{4}$
Marram Grass   *p.89*

181

Townsend's Cord-Grass   *p.89*
1796 *Spartina* $\times$ *townsendii* $\times \frac{3}{5}$

1780 *Alopecurus pratensis* $\times \frac{1}{2}$
Meadow Fox-Tail   *p.87*

1784 *Phleum pratense* $\times \frac{1}{2}$
Timothy Grass, Cat's-Tail   *p.87*

Wood Millet   *p.90*
1791 *Milium effusum* $\times \frac{1}{4}$

Canary-Grass   *p.89*
1795 *Phalaris canariensis* $\times \frac{2}{3}$

1786 *Stipa pennata* $\times \frac{1}{4}$
Feather Grass   *p.88*

(1803) *Panicum miliaceum* $\times \frac{1}{3}$
Common or Broom-Corn Millet   *p.9*

1807 *Erianthus ravennae* $\times \frac{1}{15}$
Erianthus   *p.88*

182
Ampelodesma   *p.89*
1741 *Ampelodesma mauritanica* $\times \frac{1}{10}$

1804 *Echinochloa crus-galli* $\times \frac{1}{2}$
Cockspur Grass   *p.88*

(1805) *Setaria italica* $\times \frac{1}{2}$
Foxtail or Italian Millet   *p.87*

Hyparrhenia   *p.88*
1809 *Hyparrhenia hirta* $\times \frac{2}{5}$

Bothriochloa   *p.88*
1808 *Bothriochloa ischaemum* $\times \frac{2}{3}$

1816 *Acorus calamus* × ⁴⁄₅
Sweet Flag *p.67*

1817 *Calla palustris* × ¹⁄₄
Bog Arum *p.66*

1818) *Arum italicum* × ¹⁄₃
talian Arum *p.52*

1819 *Dracunculus vulgaris* × ¹⁄₅
Dragon Arum *p.47*

183

Snake's Tongue *p.47*
820 *Biarum tenuifolium* × ¹⁄₂

Friar's Cowl *p.47*
1821 *Arisarum vulgare* × 1

1834 *Eriophorum latifolium* $\times \frac{2}{3}$
Broad-Leaved Cotton-Grass *p.91*

1827 *Typha latifolia* $\times \frac{1}{5}$
Great Reedmace, Cat's-Tail *p.68*

184

Bur-Reed *p.67*
1825 *Sparganium erectum* $\times \frac{1}{3}$

1835 *Eriophorum vaginatum* $\times \frac{1}{2}$
Cotton-Grass, Hare's-Tail *p.90*

Great Duckweed and Duckweed *p.67*
1822, 1823 *Lemna polyrhiza, L. minor* $\times \frac{4}{5}$

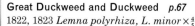

1840 *Scirpus sylvaticus* $\times \frac{1}{3}$
Wood Club-Rush *p.91*

1839 *Scirpus maritimus* $\times \frac{1}{3}$
Sea Club-Rush *p.90*

1841 *Scirpus holoschoenus* $\times 1\frac{1}{2}$
Round-Headed Club-Rush *p.90*

185

Grey Club-Rush *p.91*
(1843) *Scirpus*
tabernaemontani $\times \frac{1}{15}$

1846 *Eleocharis palustris* $\times \frac{1}{4}$
Common Spike-Rush *p.90*

1847 *Schoenus nigricans* $\times \frac{2}{3}$
Bog-Rush *p.90*

Saltmarsh Sedge *p.90*
1851 *Carex extensa* $\times \frac{1}{2}$

Hop Sedge *p.91*
1853 *Carex pseudocyperus* $\times \frac{1}{3}$

1854 *Carex pendula* $\times \frac{1}{3}$
Drooping Sedge *p.91*

1857 *Carex rostrata* $\times \frac{1}{4}$
Bottle Sedge *p.91*

1858 *Carex riparia* $\times \frac{2}{5}$
Great Pond-Sedge *p.91*

186

Common Black Sedge *p.91*
1861 *Carex nigra* $\times 1$

1859 *Carex flacca* $\times \frac{3}{4}$
Glaucous Sedge *p.91*

1860 *Carex hirta* $\times \frac{2}{5}$
Hairy Sedge *p.91*

Oval Sedge *p.91*
1867 *Carex ovalis* $\times \frac{2}{5}$

Dark Sedge *p.91*
1869 *Carex atrata* $\times 1$

1884 *Orchis papilionacea* × ½
Pink Butterfly Orchid   *p.33*

1886 *Orchis coriophora* × ¼
Bug Orchid   *p.33*

1898 *Dactylorhiza majalis* × 1¼
Broad-Leaved Marsh Orchid
p.24

187

**Dark-Winged Orchid,
Burnt Orchid**   *p.33*
1888 *Orchis ustulata* × 1

1892 *Orchis purpurea* × ½
Lady Orchid   *p.24*

1889 *Orchis tridentata* × ⅔
Toothed Orchid   *p.26*

Jersey Orchid   *p.24*
1893 *Orchis laxiflora* × ½

Wavy-Leaved Monkey Orchid   *p.24*
(1890) *Orchis italica* × 1

1873 *Ophrys fusca* × 1¾
Brown Bee Orchid *p.48*

1874 *Ophrys lutea* × ⅔
Yellow Bee Orchid *p.59*

1882 *Ophrys*
tenthredinifera × 1
Sawfly Orchid *p.48*
188

Bee Orchid *p.48*
1878 *Ophrys apifera* × 1

1877 *Ophrys insectifera* × 2
Fly Orchid *p.48*

1876 *Ophrys scolopax* × 1¼
Woodcock Orchid *p.48*

Bertoloni's Orchid *p.48*
1881 *Ophrys bertolonii* × 1¼

Bumble Bee Orchid *p.48*
1879 *Ophrys bombyliflora* × 1

1895 *Orchis quadripunctata* $\times \frac{2}{5}$
Four-Spotted Orchid *p.33*

1891 *Orchis militaris* $\times 1$
Soldier or Military Orchid *p.26*

(1900) *Dactylorhiza fuchsii* $\times 1\frac{1}{2}$
Spotted Orchid *p.26*

189

Man Orchid *p.59* $\times 1\frac{2}{3}$
1905 *Aceras anthropophorum*

899 *Dactylorhiza sambucina* $\times 1$
Ider-Flowered Orchid *p.59*

1901 *Nigritella nigra* $\times \frac{4}{5}$
Black Vanilla Orchid *p.33*

Southern Serapias *p.26*
(1903) *Serapias neglecta* $\times 1$

Long-Lipped Serapias *p.26*
1904 *Serapias vomeracea* $\times 1$

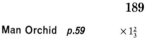

1907 *Himantoglossum hircinum* × ⅔
Lizard Orchid   *p.13*

190

Giant Orchid   *p.24*
1906 *Himantoglossum longibracteatum* × 1

1909 *Herminium monorchis* × ½
Musk Orchid   *p.16*

1908 *Anacamptis pyramidalis* × 2
Pyramidal Orchid   *p.30*

Fragrant Orchid   *p.30*
1912 *Gymnadenia conopsea* × 1¼

1914 *Platanthera bifolia* × 1⅔
Lesser Butterfly Orchid *p.5*

1915 *Platanthera chlorantha* × 1⅓
Greater Butterfly Orchid *p.3*

921 *Limodorum abortivum* × 1¼
imodore *p.36*

1920 *Cephalanthera rubra* × ⅘
Red Helleborine *p.24*

Marsh Helleborine *p.24*
916 *Epipactis palustris* × ½

Long-Leaved Helleborine *p.3*
(1919) *Cephalanthera longifolia* × ⅔

1913 *Leucorchis albida* × 2
Small White Orchid *p.13*

1925 *Goodyera repens* × 1
Creeping Lady's Tresses *p.12*

1922 *Spiranthes spiralis* × 1
Autumn Lady's Tresses *p.12*

1924 *Neottia nidus-avis* × $\frac{1}{3}$
Bird's-Nest Orchid *p.49*

192

Lesser Twayblade *p.33*
(1923) *Listera cordata* × $1\frac{1}{4}$

Coral-Root Orchid *p.16*
1926 *Corallorhiza trifida* × $\frac{3}{4}$

Index

KEY TO SYMBOLS

FLOWER FORM

Solitary or large and medium flowers

 Individual flowers with unfused petals (3 or less; 4; 5 or more)

 Individual flowers with fused petals (3 or less; 4; 5 or more)

 Tubular, funnel- or bell-shaped flowers

 Two-lipped flowers

 Pea-flowers

Small clustered flowers

 Tight rounded or semicircular heads

 Brush-like or button-like heads

 Dandelion-like heads (ray florets only)

 Daisy-like heads (ray and disk florets)

 Branched spikes or clusters

 Solitary spikes, cones or catkins

 Flat-topped or domed clusters

HABITAT

 Mountains (above tree-line), alpine meadows, rocks screes, cliffs

 Woodlands in lowlands and mountains

 Brushwood, thickets, maquis, heaths

 Grasslands (below tree-line)

 Stony and rocky ground, steppes, garigues, bare undisturbed ground

 Cultivated ground, disturbed ground, waste places, walls

 Marshes, swamps, bogs, water

 Coasts, rocks, sands, salt marshes, shingle

 Variety of lowland and hill habitats

DISTRIBUTION IN EUROPE

 North

 North and central

 Central

 West and south-west

 East and south-east

 South and Mediterranean

 South and central

Widespread and throughout